SALVAGED TREASURES

Designing & Building with Architectural Salvage

SALVAGED TREASURES

Michael Litchfield

Photographs by
Rosmarie Hausherr

Illustrations by Leonard Davis

VNR VAN NOSTRAND REINHOLD COMPANY
New York Cincinnati Toronto London Melbourne

Copyright © 1983 by Michael Litchfield
Photographs, copyright © 1983 by Rosmarie Hausherr

Library of Congress Catalog Card Number 82–17608
ISBN 0–442–25841–0

Printed in the United States of America
Designed by Ronald F. Shey
Line illustrations by Leonard Davis

Published by Van Nostrand Reinhold Company Inc.
135 West 50th Street
New York, NY 10020

Fleet Publishers
1410 Birchmount Road
Scarborough, Ontario M1P 2E7, Canada

Van Nostrand Reinhold Australia Pty. Ltd.
480 Latrobe Street
Melbourne, Victoria 3000, Australia

Van Nostrand Reinhold Company Limited
Molly Millars Lane
Wokingham, Berkshire, England RG11 2PY

16 15 14 13 12 11 10 9 8 7 6 5 4 3 2 1

Library of Congress Cataloging in Publication Data

Litchfield, Michael.
  Salvaged treasures.

  Bibliography: p. 249
  Includes index.
  1. Buildings—Repair and reconstruction.
2. Architecture—Conservation and restoration.
I. Title.
TH3401.L57 1983   690′.83′0288   82–17608
ISBN 0–442–25841–0

Contents

Acknowledgments

In our far-ranging quest for architectural salvage and its reuse, we were aided by many kind friends, most of whom are credited in these pages and all of whom are listed in the Sources of Supply in the back of the book. We would like especially to thank:

H. Weber Wilson, who is shown in the sequence on stained glass repair;
Albert DiBartolomeo of DiBartolomeo Woodworking, responsible for the excellent sequence about repairing and reconditioning doors;
John Beglin of the JO-EL Shop, who illuminated us about lamp repair and delighted us with his wit;
Keith Tartler of San Francisco Victoriana, whose mastery of his art is seen in the plaster series;
Trey Loy, who lent us his tools, his body, and his works in the heavy-timber chapter;
Steve Israel of the Great American Salvage Company
Scott Witter, whose story and photos comprise chapter 12; and
Joseph Kitchel, for sharing insights and contacts in the building world.

Hometown Treasures

Safety

Each chapter of this book opens with specific safety tips. Read them. Whether you are wrestling an object loose from its mounting on-site or cleaning up a piece in the relative calm of your own workshop, safety is of first importance. The following general suggestions apply to most tasks.

- Get a tetanus shot. Demolition sites are often messy, with unsure footing and nail-infested lumber. In short, they are dangerous.
- Use a voltage tester before cutting into or otherwise disturbing finish surfaces such as walls, ceilings, or floors (see figs. 4–1 to 4–3). When using a voltage tester, hold onto its insulated parts; never touch the exposed, bare-wire prongs of the tester. First turn off the electricity by identifying the circuit and flipping off the circuit breaker that controls it or by *removing* the controlling fuse. Leave a sign at the service panel announcing the work in progress, so no one reconnects the current. Apply the tester to all outlets, and then proceed cautiously.
- Wear goggles and gloves. Wear a hard hat around heavy work.
- Reconnoiter all work sites for sound footing. Use sturdy scaffolding for work over your head.
- Read the labels for all chemicals and the operation manuals for all tools.
- Remove all nails as you dismantle an assembly. You can never anticipate when you must descend a ladder in a hurry—that is no time to land on a nail.
- Never work when you are tired, inattentive, or intoxicated.
- Hire professional help if you have doubts about safe procedure; you can learn a lot by just observing.

Back rooms and attics contain the great finds of salvaging; wanting only tinkering and polishing, these dusty treasures will cost less than those already refurbished.

Tools

At the beginning of each chapter in this book is a list of the specialized tools needed; descriptions and illustrations of those tools are found within the text that follows. In general, you can salvage successfully without a lot of expensive equipment; *how* you use tools is all telling. Always proceed slowly and deliberately, envisioning the stresses upon the piece at hand.

- A voltage tester should be the first tool in your box; it will prevent your being shocked by electricity that you thought was turned off. Disconnect electricity and then test with the voltage tester: if its bulb does not light, you may proceed (see figs. 4-1 to 4-3).
- Goggles and gloves save your eyesight and your skin; do not work without them.
- Shims—tapered pieces of wood (usually cedar shingles)—allow you to remove even fragile objects without harm.
- Drywall screws are the universal attachers; nonpercussive, these screws are far better than nails. A magnetized screwdriver bit for your electric drill will enable you to drive screws one-handed.
- A flat bar (also called a utility bar) is the universal removal tool, flat enough to fit behind tight spaces and sturdy enough to be struck with a hammer.

Always buy good-quality tools and read operation manuals before starting work. Use tools only for the purposes intended by the manufacturer.

Architectural salvaging—saving buildings and parts of buildings—has great appeal. Salvage can be mysterious and exotic, for it often comes from faraway places, and when pieces are cleaned and shined, a magical transformation of sorts occurs, not unlike raising a genie from a lamp. This mystical aura is definitely cultivated by those who collect and sell architectural artifacts, especially those who stuff warehouses so full that you must thread your way through them, much as you would meander through an oriental bazaar.

Salvaging is especially new to America—we have been big spenders for so long that saving and recycling are novel to us—but it is obviously the wave of the future. For decades it was public policy to tear down any buildings that began to look seedy, demolition invariably occurring in those neighborhoods least able to protect themselves from urban coalitions of demolition contractors and developers. By the mid-1960s, however, with the rise of community groups committed to preservation, bulldozer development slowed appreciably. What sense was there, citizens wanted to know, in paying five thousand dollars to tear down a building that would cost one hundred thousand to replace? Where it was impossible to leave a building standing, at least it was possible to save and reuse some of the more lovely or useful parts. And, as the cost of building materials skyrocketed in the next two decades, salvaging architectural materials—including structural members—made better and better economic sense.

This first chapter is mostly about sources of supply, and the accompanying pictures of salvage and salvagers are intended to introduce you to the field. The rest of the book is largely how-to information to help you transform the pieces you buy. Accompanying the tips about assessment, removal, reconditioning, and reuse are photos of the best pieces we saw in our journey around the States. Salvage, as you will see, has wonderfully regional flavors.

Salvage is remarkably widespread: all major cities have emporiums and most towns large enough for two gas pumps have at least a scrap yard. For that matter, most families have a cache of such stuff in attics, garages, and basements. Historically, people seem to have been saving and recycling housing parts almost as long as they have been building. The facing stones of the Great Pyramids, to cite a prominent example, were pried off sometime after the fall of the last dynasties. These granite facing stones—each weighing several tons— gave the structures a slick, monolithic look when new, far different from the stepped sides that tourists now walk up. To be sure, centuries of wind and sand took their toll on the pyramids, but scavengers left their mark as well. In our own Southwest, the Indians of the Mesa Verde had to move every few hundred years when their springs dried up. As they relocated, they tore down old stone buildings and reused the blocks on new sites, because while adobe was quite common to the region, stone was not—and the tools with which to cut and shape stone were even less common.

Early European settlers in America were assiduous savers. When families moved west, they often removed and packed window glass if they were lucky enough to have any (glass was not commonly used until the nineteenth century). Likewise, houses were sometimes

1-1. **This castle in Mount Airy, Maryland, has taken eighteen years to build and is not finished yet. Constructed entirely from recycled materials, it features an oak-paneled study, stained glass galore, crenellated towers, turrets, and a great sense of fun.**
Allen Brown

burned down so that nails—incredibly dear—could be retrieved. Moreover, wars recycled building materials, notably metal: entire neighborhoods were denuded of cast-iron fences, window grilles, and whatever plumbing parts were handy. Only urban renewal was better at swallowing up materials. Though it seems unfortunate that houses be torn down at all, the truth is that buildings too have life spans; they rise and fall just as families do.

Looking at salvage, I often wonder about the lives that have been involved with it. For example, if a stone head depicts a young lady, who sculpted the head? Was there a live model for it? Was she a loved one, perhaps in a country left behind? Who bought the stone—a beer baron with a stickpin in his cravat? What happened to the family that lived in the house—are any alive? This kind of nostalgia seems mawkish some days, but all of us have reflective moments, and living with salvage has a way of revivifying the past.

SOURCES OF SUPPLY

Because architectural salvage varies from whole houses to doors to light fixtures, generalizing about sources of supply is tricky. It is fair to say, however, that buying salvage at the source—an abandoned or newly dismantled house—is an insider's game. The most common route for materials is from house owner (including government agencies) to demolition contractor to salvage dealer. Because contractors and dealers make their livings by cultivating personal contacts who know of upcoming jobs, they can strike the best deals. By familiarizing yourself with what is available through commercial sources, public auctions, and the like, you will improve your chances of buying first-hand.

1-2. Stone heads and ornamental cornice blocks.
Urban Archaeology

NEIGHBORHOOD SOURCES

You are already an insider to one of the best sources of supply—your neighborhood. "For Sale" ads in weekly shopper and daily newspapers abound, and because advertisers are anxious to sell, you are in a good bargaining position. Moreover, most sellers have only a vague idea of the worth of items. The only salient disadvantage to this source is that you may have to run around and look at many unsuitable pieces before you find what you are after. Ask as many questions as you can on the phone before visiting the seller: query size, condition, materials, style. Radio "swap and sell" programs are other good leads. In addition to responding to others' ads, place one of your own.

Flea markets and garage sales are excellent haunts for small items because you can examine them closely. For the best bargains, go early in the morning, preferably a little before the sales start: by midmorning the big wallets will have arrived. The last hour or two of such sales is also a good time, assuming that everything has not been sold.

By then, sellers will be happy not to transport the piece once more. Negotiating is a fine art: be low-key and prudent, reckoning the cost and labor of reconditioning in the price you offer. Buying several pieces at once is another good ploy, since the larger total price may give you leverage.

Take note of run-down properties in your area. Such dwellings are often owned by absentee landlords or older people who are short of money. Your town lister or real estate assessor will have tax records identifying owners of all buildings. One of the best arguments of the would-be salvager is that the old place is a tax burden and a public liability that the owner would be better off without. But most property laws preclude a salvager's buying the building only because the owner of the *property* is still liable for any accidents that may befall the salvager on-site. To avoid this problem, heavy-timber salvager Alex Grabenstein of Frederick, Maryland, hires out to the property owner as the building's dismantler—the building still belongs to the owner. After the structure is down,

Alex then buys the pieces and carries them away, but he never owns the standing property. Liability laws just do not recognize a distinction between the intact house and the land it is on. This question of liability is the stickler in whole-house dismantling. Gregory Schipa of Brookfield, Vermont, who dismantles, moves, and then reassembles post-and-beam houses, tells prospective sellers he will "... remove the building and rake the lawn," thus leaving the site free from any debris—from any evidence that an old wreck was ever there, in fact.

Finally, do not forget the dump. This outlet will not be practicable if you live in an urban area, but if you live in a rural or semirural area, tell the dump guard what you are after; a little silver in the palm will increase his interest in your wants.

Many suburban communities have "junk" days or weeks, usually in the spring—a time when home owners put out whatever oversized trash they want transported to the dump, and often a particularly rich time for salvaging pieces that are still in very good condition. If you are a city dweller, canvass the streets on pick-up days. These sources may seem unsavory, but it is astounding what people throw away—Tiffany shades have landed in the out-pile when they fell from fashion, rest assured.

BUILDING TRADESPEOPLE

Most people who build for a living—carpenters, plumbers, electricians, and the like—collect materials. Called upon to renovate, they in-

variably save the old pieces they remove because they know well the cost of replacements. Of the many salvagers I have worked with, I like this group the best. They appreciate a fellow-salvager's interest, are fair about the items they sell, will offer tips about reuse and installation (or will install pieces for you), and they usually save those small parts without which a fixture will not work.

If you want to buy only that one elusive part from a tradesperson, however, do not carp if the price seems high. Five or ten dollars for two water nuts, for example, is cheap if those are the only parts your salvaged lavatory lacks. By selling those parts, the tradesperson may be decommissioning one of his or her own fixtures. Besides, that individual had the insight and opportunity to save the missing parts in

1-3. Alex Grabenstein of Vintage Lumber and Construction Company dismantles barns—many of which are chestnut—in western Maryland.

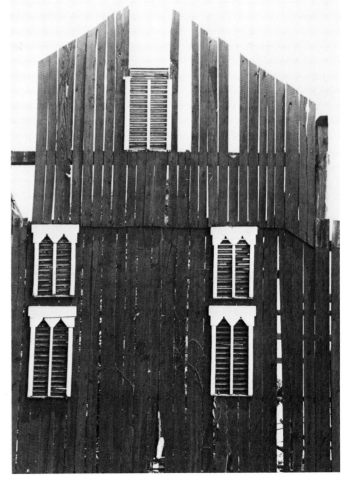

1-4. The richly figured wood from dismantled barns is re-erected in post-and-beam dwellings, as here, or milled down as flooring.

Vintage Lumber and Construction Company

the first place—so if you need them, pay up.

DEMOLITION CONTRACTORS

Most large salvage is handled by demolition contractors after a municipality accepts their bid to tear down a place. Once hired, the contractor may sell off pieces as he likes, all completely legal, unless proscribed by the contract. The best way to strike a deal for masonry sections, girders, joists, and so on, is to speak with the foreman or supervisor on the site.

Dealing with on-site bosses varies greatly. You will almost always have to wait around until that person has time to talk with you. (Making strangers wait is a builder's way of minimizing less-than-serious inquiries.) Make an offer for what you want. Some bosses will negotiate, some will not. Use building lingo to let him know you are serious and experienced. The most important thing to site supervisors is speed; if you look like a duffer who will slow things down, you will not be welcome. If you get a "no" from the foreman, you might try talking to the home office, but if you succeed there, you will still have to deal with the super, so gain his confidence as soon as possible. Get to know the workers, have lunch with them, be low-key, and listen. Basically, the crew could care less about your project as long as you do not slow up or endanger them.

When you negotiate, specify what pieces you want, the price, and the time limit for getting stuff out. Because most contractors will want money—*all* the money—up front, get a written contract. Because all jobs go slowly, get as much time as you can. If a contractor is not under great pressure, he may be lenient with the deadlines he grants you to remove pieces, but do not count on such leniency. Be prepared to work

long hours and get all the help you can. You might also contract for several hours of heavy-equipment use, usually at the end of a job, to lift out the heavy pieces you have unfastened or denailed. The contractor may insist that you sign a liability waiver because the dangers are real and insurance companies are very skittish about demolition jobs. Talk to your own insurance company, but if they insure you at all, expect stiff premiums.

ARCHITECTS AND DECORATORS

This group has some of the best taste and the highest prices. Designers often buy old pieces, intending to use them in some future building. Such salvaged artifacts are often so odd or ungainly that only a palace could accommodate them, but designers are generally sentimental about rare finds and hence want high prices to lessen the pain of parting. I do not mean to impugn

so varied a group, but I have never seen a piece go cheaply from their hands nor, for that matter, reasonably; they will, however, willingly design the palace to fit the piece. Being familiar with sources of supply, they may offer good leads to salvage that they do not own, however.

SALVAGE EMPORIUMS

Emporiums are the source most familiar to the general market and, for that matter, to other dealers. Such collections strongly reflect the tastes of the owner, and for all the joyous jumble in most places, dealers tend to specialize. Dealers know well what going prices are, but they too buy impulsively, in areas with which they are unfamiliar. When this happens, the odd piece sometimes fails to move and you may be able to get it for less than asking price. In any event, pieces are marked according to the whim of the collector; negotiate, especially if you intend to buy several pieces.

1-5. In the Southwest many older pieces come from Mexico, such as this yard full of weathered doors and columns.
Architectural Antiques, Ltd.

1-6. These elegantly worked beams, originally from Mexico, are now in a Santa Fe residence.
John Midyette III

Because many emporiums mix old pieces and new reproductions (of old stuff), ask a salesperson how the two groups are distinguished. Light fixtures with gleaming brass can be quite tough to distinguish, particularly because many old fixtures will have been refurbished with new parts. Most dealers will not misrepresent the age of a piece, but if it matters to you, have the bill of sale specify, generally, if an item is old or reproduction.

Salvage prices reflect the dealer's initial purchase price, shipping costs, time and parts necessary to refurbish, and profit. For greater savings ask the dealer if any pieces are available "as is"; the technical information in this book will enable you to refurbish those pieces yourself. Most emporiums have back rooms groaning with still-dusty artifacts.

Antique dealers and scrap yards represent the two extremes of salvage dealers: quite rare items at the former source and common materials at the latter. Antique furniture dealers carry few architectural ar-

tifacts and sometimes regret that they carry any—such pieces may simply not sell because browsers are not looking for that sort of thing. Thus, you may get a bargain in a shop whose furniture prices you could not touch. As for scrap yards, expect anything: materials may be priced by the pound, the foot, the piece or, one suspects, by the weather.

1-7. Steve Israel of Great American Salvage, Montpelier, Vermont.

PUBLIC AUCTIONS

Building auctions are infrequent but worthwhile sources of supply because everyone present has a chance to bid, although participants may need to present a letter of credit or a bank check in advance. Such auctions are widely advertised; their sign-up sheets will notify you of any subsequent auctions.

Arrive at auctions early so that you can get a parking space close to the building, especially important if you are transporting large objects. Assess materials to be sold—figure out how you would remove pieces without breaking them; and make notes of the prices you are prepared to pay for each. The last point is particularly important if you are excitable or on a tight budget.

Plan to remove pieces as soon as practical, which usually means when the sale is over. Not infrequently, sales stipulate that the buyer assumes all responsibility once the gavel comes down. Unless you have many pieces to remove, take them with you that day or evening; a lot of theft occurs on unsecured sites. To prevent confusion, paint the handles of your tools a bright color so that you will know which are yours, imperative if the place is crawling with contractors. The seller may ask you to sign a liability waiver to forestall suits should you injure yourself on the premises.

GOVERNMENTAL AGENCIES

Local and federal agencies hold prodigious amounts of property, usually assumed when taxes were not paid or, in the case of federal holdings, when former owners defaulted on guaranteed loans such as Ginnie Mae or Fannie Mae programs. The usual fate of such buildings is demolition, a particularly loathsome route considering the shortage of good housing stock.

Dealing with such agencies can

1-8. Auctioning a church in Camden, New Jersey.

be difficult. Employees are frequently vague about what properties they hold and unsure about which bureaucrat has the power to dispose of property. Properties disposed of publicly involve lengthy review processes. Public auctions are perhaps the best bet, because those buildings have had their fates decided already and buyers receive clear title. Have a real estate lawyer research the zoning status of any property before you buy. Once you buy such a property, you may renovate it or raze and recycle its materials, depending upon the terms of sale.

As always, there are oddities. One salvager in Brooklyn, New York, simply approached a federal authority on-site and offered five hundred dollars for one of several buildings slated to be torn down. The federal agent had the power to approve such a sale, all perfectly legal. So, as improbable as your request may seem to you, have the courage to ask.

A number of municipalities—Baltimore, Maryland, comes to mind immediately—save easily salvaged parts of demolished buildings and resell them to homeowners rehabilitating inner-city houses at minimal cost. I hope this enlightened policy will spread to other cities.

Houses to be displaced by highways, high rises, and the like may be auctioned off by mailed bids. Terms of such sales are simple in most cases: the high bidder buys the entire property and must remove it within a stated time. Failure to remove it in that time may result in penalties; at the very least, the buyer defaults any moneys paid.

So, happy hunting. Architectural salvaging is not a cheap route to go, but there are considerable savings to be had for your efforts. You join a distinguished family, some of whose members and works are shown herein.

1-9. Mark's grinning friend sits beneath a beam in a kitchen.

1-10. Those who design and build with architectural salvage are not cast in the common mold. Shown here is architect Adolf deRoy Mark of Philadelphia and Carefree, Arizona—bagpiper, calvaryman, and designer extraordinaire.

In northern California, where redwoods come down to the sea, shipyards, warehouses, bridges, and mills were built from the huge trees. Many of these buildings have outlived their usefulness, but the big timber lives on in comtemporary residences. This house overlooking the Pacific was designed and built by Trey Loy of Littleriver, California. Once Loy had constructed the massive frame—but before he closed it in with stud walls—he sandblasted the timbers so they would have a clean, uniform surface.

Windows

Safety Tips

- Gloves and goggles are particularly important when working with glass because of the dangers to eyes and hands.
- Do not strain or lean over glass as you cut it, even to improve your cutting leverage on leaded glass. A slip at close range while applying pressure could mean lacerations.
- Wear a respirator mask when soldering lead or using chemicals; leave a window open or employ a fan to blow away fumes. Do not smoke or eat around chemicals.
- When working with lead, wear gloves to avoid lead poisoning. Solder lead only on a nonflammable surface, and avoid inhaling fumes.
- Because glazed sashes can be heavy, have help removing or installing them. If you are working at any height, rent scaffolding to ensure your safety.
- Store sashes on edge rather than laying them flat; they will take up less room and are less likely to be broken.

Tools

- Goggles and gloves are imperative to safety.
- A first-aid kit is handy to have around; little cuts are common.
- For working with plain glass, buy a glass cutter with a "rapper ball" on the noncutting end; glass pliers if you must snap off small slivers of glass; putty knives for glazing; and needle-nose pliers for pulling out glazing points lodged in tight spots.
- If you are interested in leaded or stained glass, you need medium-weight rubber gloves; a lead cutter; a soldering iron with a stand that frees both your hands; and a lathekin, a flat, spoonlike paddle that enables you to open and close lead strips. Other glass-working tools are shown in figure 2–13.
- Repair and reinstallation of sashes require few specialized tools. See chapter 4 for those commonly used in woodworking.

This hand-painted, enamel-fired window reflects the turn-of-the-century fascination with oriental silk screens. Unusual because it is painted over textured glass, the piece has an eerie, evanescent quality. French, circa 1890.

"Reflections" Antique Stained Glass

After sloshing around all day in the local fen looking for grubs and tasty roots, our distant ancestors wanted nothing more than a warm shelter where they could snore without interruption until hunger drove them out again. The ideal house then had but one opening, both door and window, which could easily be blocked to keep heat in and predators out. Windows came along only after man was relatively advanced and well fed, when the loss of a little heat did not threaten life and slumber.

As the eons spun around and civilizations grew more complex, so did houses and, notably, windows. Generally, the more windows a house had, the richer the householder. Gaping wall holes were shuttered, covered with opaque animal membranes that admitted light, and eventually glazed, fitted with glass. But even after centuries of use, glass remained delicate and rare, and windows were uncommon on northern walls or where prevailing winds blew. Only in the last half century or so, in the golden age of fossil fuels, were large windows on all walls common, so that the citizens of that happy time might sit comfortably on sofa or couch and observe the antics of their neighbors. But times change, and with the passing of cheap energy, we return to the energy-craving and conserving natures of our ancestral bog-hoppers; we want to be warm (or cool) when the climes are severe.

The point of these historical reflections is that windows are, and have always been, heat losers. Even in modern constructions that have two or three thicknesses of glass sandwiched together, windows leak energy at an appalling rate. A single thickness of glass has an R-value of 0.89; two-ply, R-1.89; three-ply,

R-2.70; compared to R-14 for an average insulated wall. (R-value is the resistance of a material to the passage of heat through it; the higher the R-value, the better the insulative qualities of the material.) Since most salvaged windows come from an age of relatively cheap energy, they are not a good bet to install in your home. Worse, old sashes rarely fit tightly to their frames, allowing prodigious amounts of heated or cooled air to escape through infiltration. Window sashes that rattle when the wind blows can lose 3 Btu's per degree difference between inside and outside for every lineal foot of the window perimeter.

The energy efficiency of old sashes can be improved with sash channels (described later in this chapter), by caulking and repairing

glass, by using storm windows, and so on, but the bottom line remains: old windows are not going to be as efficient as new ones. If your climate is mild, if you will be using the window sash inside the house (say, in an interior partition), or if you will be putting old sashes in sheds or unheated outbuildings, buy the old window; otherwise, save your money. The only exception to this rule, and a qualified exception at that, is sandwiching the old sash between glass, such as the stained glass assembly shown in figure 2–31.

There are a number of types of windows, classified primarily by how they open and shut. The most common group of old windows, called *double-hung*, have two sashes that slide in vertical channels. *Casement* windows, which are hinged on one

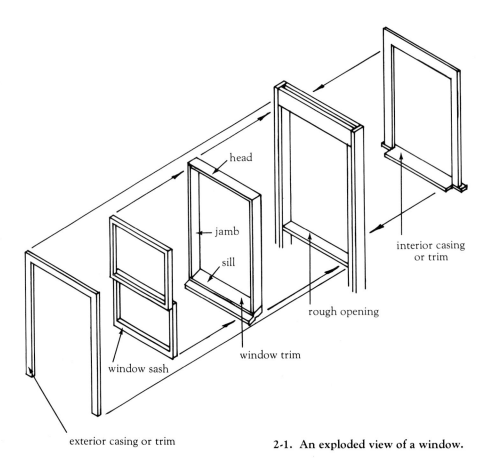

head

jamb

sill

interior casing or trim

rough opening

window trim

window sash

exterior casing or trim

2-1. An exploded view of a window.

side much like doors, are more re-cent developments. Stained and leaded glass are most often in *fixed* windows, which do not open at all. Because double-hung windows are the most common type, we will look closest at their construction; other window types are similarly installed and removed.

Each section of a double-hung window is called a *sash*, hence *upper* and *lower sashes*. Sashes consist of vertical elements called *stiles* and horizontal ones, *rails*; the top rail of the lower sash and the bottom rail of the upper sash are also called *meeting rails*. If the sash has more than one piece of glass in it, the thin strips of wood that separate pieces of glass are called *muntins*. This term is sometimes confused with *mullions*, which are large ver-tical pieces between two or more units in a bank of windows.

Windows may be counterbal-anced with *sash weights* or *sash springs*, or they may not be assisted mechanically at all.

Sashes are contained within a *window frame*, which is set into the *rough opening* in the wall. As shown in figure 2–1, the primary elements of the frame are the two *jambs*, or side pieces; a top piece called a *head* or *frame head* (sometimes called a head jamb, although that term is not used in this book); and a bot-tom piece, or *window sill*, pitched slightly so that water runs off. In double-hung construction, jambs have an *inside stop*, an *outside stop*, and a *parting strip*, which create channels in which the sashes run.

After the window unit is placed in a rough opening in the wall, that unit is leveled, plumbed, and then wedged in tightly with *shims*, tapered pieces of wood. Once shimmed, the frame is nailed into the studs of the rough opening. To cut air infiltration, the gaps between window frame and rough opening are stuffed with insulation or caulked. Finally, the window is *finished off* or *trimmed*.

Trim, or *casing*, is installed around the frame of a window in-side and out to cover the edges of the frame, to blend the unit aesthetically to other materials, and to make the house weathertight. Trim pieces are named for the parts of the frame they cover: side trim is *jamb trim* or *jamb casing*; the top piece is the *head trim* or *header cas-ing*. The outside of the window usually has no bottom piece of trim because its sill juts out. Inside, the bottom of the window is finished off with a *stool*, which fits over the in-side edge of the sill, and an *apron*, which fits beneath the stool.

ASSESSING A WINDOW

By the time they enter the salvage mainstream, most window sashes have been removed from their frames. Even for those windows whose frames are intact, however,

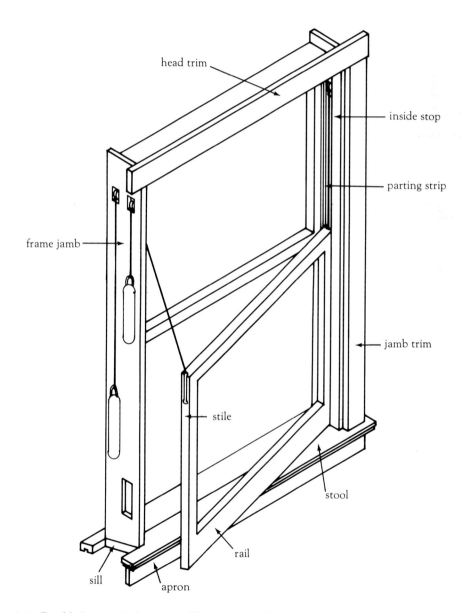

2-2. **Double-hung window parts. This unit is pulley weighted; spring-loaded types are also made.**

the health of the sashes is *the* crucial question.

SASHES

A quick glance at the sash will tell you most of what you need to know. Does it look sound? Is the paint continuous and glazing intact or have both deteriorated? Is rot apparent? Are there gaps where rails meet stiles? Do metal mending plates hold corners or were nails used to knock pieces together? Look along the edge of the sash—is it straight or bowed? Does the entire sash seem flat or warped? Are corners square?

If a sash has been much doctored, pass it by. Only if it is extremely rare or nicely designed are repairs worthwhile. If the sash is reused as a fixed window, a bit of looseness or decay is tolerable, but if the sash will move—in casement or double-hung windows—it must be sturdy.

The weak points of windows are bottom rails, corners, and muntins, if any. Bottom rails often rot from water sitting on a sill, especially if the sill has not been maintained and the bottom of the rail rested on it. Prod the rail with a penknife; if the blade goes in more than ½ inch, do not buy the piece. If you *must* buy it, rot notwithstanding, add on wood as explained in chapter 3; prod with an ice pick to see where rot ends and good wood begins. If less than ¾ inch of solid wood remains around the glass, absolutely forget the sash; not enough old wood is left to hold the new wood.

If rot is localized, say, at one corner, reinforce it with an *epoxy stabilizer*, as described later in this chapter in the section on upgrading window frames.

To test the strength of the sash, place one hand on a rail and the other on a stile; twist your wrists to see if the frame moves. If you can wiggle the corner of the sash,

chances are that the mortise-and-tenon joint that holds rail and stile together has rotted. This joint can be reinforced with dowels or with epoxy stabilizer, but again, pervasive rot should deter you, especially if you would like to reuse the sash as a moving window part.

Often the muntins of older windows become damaged by inept glaziers who used glass tacks that were too big or who gouged the wood when changing glass or stripping paint. If any muntins have been broken down to the glass-level, do not buy the unit. If only part of a muntin has splintered, however, you may be able to rebuild its contours with epoxy or (less acceptable) with wood filler.

Finally, if the sash is structurally sound, are its corners square and free from bowing? A sash slightly too big or out of square can be cut down with a circular saw. If the frame is bowed, however, it will not slide in a straight channel nor fit tightly to a straight stop piece. If the sash has no glass in it, you can weight the wood to bend it the other way, but this operation takes time. If there is glass (probably cracked), remove it before attempting to straighten the sash.

GLAZING

Replacing glass is not difficult, but glass prices have soared in the last few years. If the glass is bowed or otherwise unusual, call a glass supplier and then compare repair costs to the purchase price of new windows. If you reuse old glass with visual imperfections, count on breaking at least one-third of it when cutting; buy extra.

Stained glass repair is markedly more difficult if the damaged piece is towards the center of the composition. Soldering and cutting old lead, as described below, are arduous for a beginner. Because the more esoteric shades and shapes of glass are

expensive and difficult to find, professional glaziers often buy the second piece of a pair, even if badly damaged, to use as a replacement for flaws in the first one.

REMOVING WINDOW FRAMES

Obtain the original frame of a window if you can. Even though the old frame may be too tired to reuse, it will be useful as a template for a new frame. Old frames may also contain useful accessory hardware such as sash pulley weights or springs.

Take pains when removing the frame. If it is in bad shape—rotted sills are common—and there is obvious water damage:

1. Pry off the inside stop and lift out the inner sash.
2. Pry out (which usually means destroy) the parting strip and lift out the outer sash.
3. Remove the trim on one or both sides of the frame.
4. Pry out the frame itself, using a utility bar to pry up nail heads so they can be pulled out.

If you intend to reuse frames, take even greater care when removing them; prying out is particularly hard on frames. A gentler but more time-consuming way to remove units leaves the sashes in place. Begin by loosening paint seals with a putty knife. If the sashes are so swollen that you cannot budge them, use a utility bar to get them started. Pry off inside and outside trim, exposing the edges of the frame. With a putty knife or a chisel, dig out any insulation stuffed between frame and rough opening, thus exposing any nails and shims. Brace the edges of the frame by nailing a furring strip diagonally from corner to corner. Put on goggles and

2-3. Loosen paint seals around the perimeter of sashes and casing with a putty knife.

2-4. Get stubborn swollen sashes started with a utility bar.

use a metal-cutting blade in a reciprocating saw to cut through nail shanks, leaving the two uppermost nails until last. With the help of a friend, cut through the last two nails and lift out the window. Leave the diagonal braces in place until you reuse the unit. If you do not own a reciprocating saw, you may use a hacksaw blade to cut through nail shanks, but a reciprocating saw is preferable for this operation. Its blade will be little bothered by shims obscuring the nails or incidental nails in the way. The time and trouble saved here make renting this saw—if you do not own one—worthwhile.

To upgrade the fit of the sashes in their frames, use new channel inserts, as described later in this chapter. Remove the sashes as described above. If the frames are reusable, again brace them before you cut the nails holding the frame in its opening.

WINDOW REPAIRS

By far the most common window repair is replacing glass. Other worthwhile repairs include: refinishing old frames, especially along their bottom rails; weatherstripping frames; installing new channels; and replacing or reinforcing window sills with epoxy.

REPLACING GLASS

Several tools make glass replacement much easier: *gloves*, because even a professional glazier breaks glass unintentionally; a *glazier's chisel* to remove putty easily (a stiff-bladed putty knife works too); a *glass cutter*; a *metal straightedge* (a framing square will do) to guide the glass cutter; *glazier's pliers*, indispensable if you must cut small pieces of glass; and *goggles*. *Putty*, or glazing compound, is available in most hardware stores.

Begin by removing the old putty. Most old putty can be dislodged by inserting the blade of a glazier's chisel (or putty knife) between the putty and its muntin (sash rail, etc.) and twisting. Because

2-5. Dislodge old putty with a knife.

you need clean, ungouged wood around the glass to produce a straight putty line, take pains not to damage the wood around a light (pane) of glass. Work around the perimeter of each pane, removing the putty to expose the *glazing points*, or tacks, holding the glass in place.

That is the way the job *should* go. Old putty can, however, be tenacious beyond belief, testing your ingenuity and patience. Paint stripper may soften tough putty. Apply stripper to putty when removing paint from the rest of the window. Also effective is a small amount of paint thinner or turpentine poured right onto the pane. Allow the solvent to sit for ten or fifteen minutes, and the putty should soften. Applying heat to recalcitrant putty will work, but you must be careful; before placing the electric putty heater or applying a propane-torch point, cover the glass with a piece of hardboard wrapped in aluminum foil to prevent the glass from breaking as it heats and expands. (Sheet asbestos works well but can cause lung cancer if fibers are inhaled.) If you use open flame, keep it moving so that you do not char the wood.

Remove old glazier's points and lift out any glass still in place. Lightly sand the sash or use the corner of a putty knife to remove putty remnants. Again, take care not to round or obliterate the contour of the wood.

To prevent the dry wood from sucking the oils out of the new putty that you apply, brush a sealant of solvent (turpentine or alcohol) and boiled linseed oil, mixed in equal amounts, onto exposed wood.

After the sealant has dried, spread a thin bed of putty along the wood lip that receives the glass, as shown in figure 2–7. This prevents glass from rattling and stops air infiltration.

To allow for variations of temperature and the shifting of a house,

2-6. Sand away any putty residue but do not round the contours of the sash.

2-7. Before placing the glass into the sash, spread a thin layer of putty.

the length and width of replacement pane should both be 1/8 inch less than the opening in the sash. Before cutting the glass, wipe it with a rag damp with kerosene. Using a straightedge to guide your cut, pull the glass cutter, with an even pressure, toward your body. One pass of the cutter should do it. Once you have scribed the glass, gently rap

the ball of the cutter on the underside of that line. Rap the ball up and down the line and the break will be uniform. When a clear line is visible through the thickness of the glass, hold the cut over the edge of a table and snap free the waste portion of glass. If the waste section is too small to grip, use glass pliers.

Press the replacement glass on

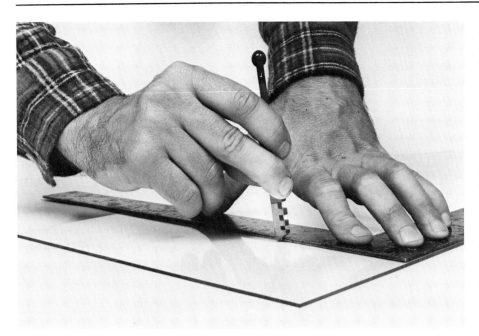

2-8. Cut replacement glass 1/8 in. smaller than the dimensions of the sash opening. After cleaning the glass, cut it with a single pass of a glass cutter.

glass meets wood. Putty the entire perimeter of the glass before trimming excess.

To trim putty, rest one side of the blade on the edge of the muntin (or sash) and the other point of the knife on the glass—a 45-degree angle is optimal. Pull the knife in a steady motion, cutting a **V** into the putty. Go back to clean up corners when you are finished.

If putty pulls free or wads up, the glass is dusty, you are holding the knife blade too high, or the blade is dragging. (A bit of saliva cures the last problem.) Allow the putty to cure for a week before painting it. To seal putty against weather, overpaint onto the glass about 1/16 inch.

REFINISHING WINDOWS

Refinishing wood is discussed at length in chapter 4, but here are some salient concerns and strategies for windows. Wood must, above all, be sound and dry to take a finish. Isolate existing decay by applying preservatives or cutting out and replacing bad spots.

Will your sashes be painted or left natural? If you will paint them, first treat the wood with Cuprinol

the puttied lip. Holding the glass down lightly with one hand, push in the glazing points with the other. Hold your putty knife almost flat against the glass and push each point until it is half buried. Sink a point every 6 inches or so around the perimeter of each pane; there should be at least one point per side. Be careful when pushing in these points: go too far into a mun-

tin and you risk cracking the pane of glass on the other side. Push points in, never hammer them.

When the replacement glass is fixed in place, spread putty generously around its perimeter. Scoop up a handful of putty and knead it until it is soft and pliable. As you work, feed the putty out of your hand as shown in figure 2-9, pressing it into the joints where

2-9. Apply putty generously around the perimeter of the replacement glass after it is in position; press it firmly into the joint for better adherence.

2-10. Holding the putty knife blade at a 45-degree angle, cut away excess material. Pull the knife towards you in a single stroke.

Figures 2-5 to 2-10 originally appeared in *Renovation: A Complete Guide*, here reprinted with permission of the publisher, John Wiley & Sons.

preservative. Sufficiently dried, Cuprinol will receive paint without bleed-through or blistering, although you should check manufacturer's instructions on the label. Creosote and penta, both petroleum-based preservatives, are unacceptable because they will bleed through and are toxic as well. Because window frames are for the most part hidden by trim, they may be safely treated with a preservative but most treatments will smell unless sufficiently dried.

If you leave the wood natural, you have several finish options. Tung oil is perhaps the best all-around finish where moisture is a problem. Your wood should be thoroughly dry. Brush in tung oil cut to 50 percent strength with a solvent, such as alcohol or turpentine. Allow the wood to dry for an hour or two in a warm place, and wipe off excess with a rag: the first coat or two over old, dry wood should yield little residue. Thereafter apply full-strength tung oil once a week; two or three additional coats should saturate the wood. Once tung oil is absorbed, it can be touched up without leaving brush marks on the old finish; more important, the oil will not degrade in contact with moisture. It does, however, have some disadvantages. It will darken wood somewhat. You may have to touch it up semiannually if you live in a very wet climate such as the Pacific Northwest. Finally—and most important—some varieties are very slow to dry. Check the label.

Other clear or natural finishes include spar/marine varnish, a surface coat which should be touched up every year. It is perhaps the best exterior-grade hard finish. Polyurethane is touted as an all-purpose coat, but it clouds when exposed to sustained moisture, and it will peel, leaving the wood vulnerable. Even when used on the interior surfaces of windows, poly will degrade from condensation. Lacquer is an ad-

mirable interior finish but does not wear well around excessive moisture; it therefore should not be used on window surfaces. Linseed oil is generally avoided because it dries so poorly. Shellac is entirely unsuitable around moisture.

Old wood must be sound and dry before refinishing it. After allowing it to stand in a heated room for at least a week or two, repair any major splits. Sand down rough spots and wipe them clean with a tack rag. Sand lightly between coats of paint, lacquer, or polyurethane; you need not sand, however, between coats of penetrating oils.

MAKING WINDOWS MORE WEATHERTIGHT

Weather stripping varies greatly in cost, ease of installation, and permanence. Most products are soft materials that compress against the sashes or frames, thus reducing infiltration. Before adding weather stripping of any kind, upgrade sash movement. Scrape free any excess paint and sand down sash edges (without rounding them); use medium-grade sandpaper. With a piece of candle, wax the edges so they slide better. If you observe nails or screw heads on the sides of the sashes, sink or remove them so they cannot catch in the channels of the frame. Should you want to change the dimensions of sashes, please see the section in chapter 3 that illustrates how door edges are built up and cut down.

The least expensive and permanent weather stripping is *caulking cord*, a roll of soft, puttylike cord pressed into the junctions of sash and frame. Windows cannot be opened while caulking cord is in place. Although it must be changed annually, this product does stop air leaks.

Felt and foam strips are usually resilient substances backed with wood or metal. Because backing is nailed to the inside of the window frame, you can open the window sashes when this weather stripping is in place. But because felt and foam may compress or become sodden, these materials are less effective than caulking cord. They rarely last more than two or three seasons. *Unbacked* felt and foam stripping are even more useless.

Rolled vinyl or tubular gaskets are effective, easy to install, and probably the least expensive types of permanent stripping. Adequately compressed along the perimeters of sashes, they cut air loss while allowing you to open and shut windows. Because strips are almost an inch wide, they are usually installed along the outside of the sashes and painted for concealment.

Metal tension strips and *interlocking metal channels* are more permanent than rolled vinyl, but are better suited to doors (see chapter 3). Problematic to install on windows, metal strips require that you remove sashes from the frame, which usually means destroying the parting strip. Not uncommonly, an installer must also plane down the width of the sashes to accommodate the additional thickness of the metal channels.

Replacement channels, such as those shown in figure 2–12 are probably the best way to reconcile old sashes to any frame, new or old. Fashioned from stainless steel, zinc, aluminum, or heavy-grade vinyl, channels embrace the sides of the sashes. The assembly is fitted into window frames and secured to jambs. Because such channels replace the parting strips and stops that guide sashes, you must remove strips and stops to create a flat frame surface. Likewise, disconnect any sash weights, pulleys and the like that might interfere with the operation of the new channels.

Before fitting old sashes into

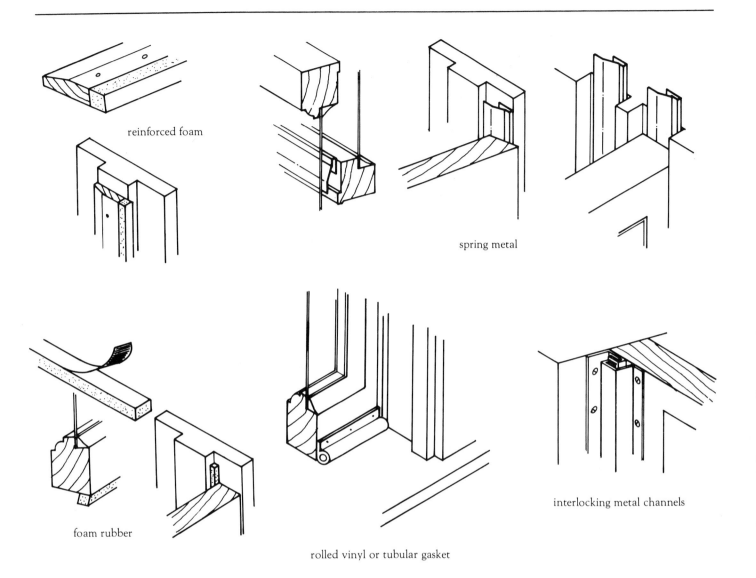

reinforced foam

spring metal

foam rubber

rolled vinyl or tubular gasket

interlocking metal channels

2-11. Types of weather stripping.

replacement channels, square up those sashes. To square up a sash, you should remove any glass; otherwise you may crack it while applying pressure to errant parts. Use bar clamps placed on diagonally opposite corners of the sash. Tighten until your framing square—held on the inside of the sash—tells you to stop. A cheaper way to effect squareness is to square and screw two pieces of wood to the top of your worktable. If those pieces are carefully squared to each other, you have a handy jig into which you can set the sashes. Gently force the sash until it is flush

against the two sides of the jig, then reglue the sash corners. Leave the sash in the jig (tack the free corners to the tabletop) until the glue is dry.

Sash corners must be square and sound, and both sashes must be the same width. (Build up or plane down the wood as described in chapter 3.) The thickness of the sashes is not a problem, however, because replacement channels have spring-loaded center strips that adjust to sash thickness. After placing refurbished sashes into the replacement channels, simply place the whole assembly into the window

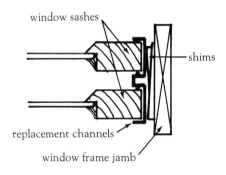

window sashes

shims

replacement channels

window frame jamb

2-12. After reconditioning old window sashes, fit them into replacement channels, which have spring-loaded parting strips to accommodate discrepancies in sash thickness.

frame and shim the backsides of the channels as needed. Pack insulation and caulk, screw the channels to the frame, and replace the trim. Installation takes about three hours per window.

UPGRADING WINDOW FRAMES

Should you decide to reuse old frames, upgrading sashes *and* frames go hand in hand. It should be apparent, thus, that if you take the trouble to square up old sashes, you must also provide a squared frame in which they can run. Begin by stripping old frames of paint, taking special pains to clean up the sash channels. Replace any bad wood and then square the frame. Use the same procedure as in squaring sashes, but first remove the sashes before squaring the frame.

Window sills are the frame part that deteriorates most often, because water rests on or beneath it. Allow the sill to dry thoroughly, then prod it to see how much is rotted. If you can dislodge sections with gentle pressure on a knife blade, replace the section. If, however, the wood is punky but intact, treat it with epoxy resin.

Resins vary, but most are two-part mixtures that set up within ten minutes of mixing. Epoxy can be applied in two ways: by spreading it on the surface of the wood to fill in bad spots or by drilling into the wood and injecting epoxy into those holes. Because it actually reinforces the section, the latter treatment is preferable, although both applications may be appropriate for a single piece.

Into the weakened area, drill 1/4-inch holes at least halfway into the deepest dimension of the piece. That is, drill into sill width or length rather than just through its thickness. Cluster holes no closer than 1/2 inch apart. When you have drilled half a dozen holes, squeeze in

epoxy and allow it to set before drilling more. If possible, the epoxy cores should run with wood grain, but that is not always practicable. If your epoxy kit does not have an injector, drill all the way through the sill and work the mixture in with a putty knife—work fast. The longer the epoxy cures, the better. When the epoxy is dry, it can be sanded and worked. Check the manufacturer's instructions for priming advice.

If the sill is too far gone to be reinforced with epoxy, replace it with pressure-treated wood; wolmanized lumber is best because it can be painted and will resist rot for decades. Many restorers brace the upper part of a frame with diagonal braces nailed to the edges of the frame, thereby keeping header-to-jamb joints from spreading. Then they cut the sill in half. Because most sills are end-nailed through the jambs, you can pry nails from the bottom of the frame jambs. Save the parts of the sill as a template for a new sill.

Replacement sills should pitch downward 10 degrees, away from the house, so that water will shed. (On the inside of the house, that pitch of the sill is covered by a beveled rabbet in the underside of the trim stool—see fig. 4-17.) Along the exterior edge of the sill, cut a 1/4- by 1/4-inch *drip kerf* into the underside. This kerf allows water to drip free instead of clinging to the surface of the wood and backing up under the siding.

Before attaching the new sill to the jambs, reinforce the bottoms of the jambs with epoxy if they are deteriorated. Treat any newly cut wood with preservative. Then nail the assembly together; check for square. End-nail through the backsides of the jambs into the ends of the sill, unless the original construction was otherwise. Use three 10d galvanized box nails for each end; blunt the nail ends (hammer their points) so that they do not split the

ends of the frame jambs. If you reinforce jamb ends with epoxy and find it too hard to nail through, predrill and use three 2 1/2-inch by 8-gauge *brass* wood screws instead.

INSTALLING A WINDOW

Because sashes help keep the parts of the frame from wandering out of square, it is best to install a window with the sashes in the frame. The unit will, of course, then be heavier than a window frame alone. Whether you install the complete unit or just the frame, square up and diagonally brace all corners. Leave the braces in place until the frame is securely nailed to the studs behind.

Several dimensions should concern you. First, the depth of window frame should be equal to that of the thickness of the wall, from the finish wall surface on the inside to the sheathing on the exterior. Check these widths well before installing a window: discrepancies of 1/4 inch are not critical and can be disguised by interior trim, but you must build up or plane down larger amounts. Other dimensions to note are the width and height of the rough opening, which should be 1/2 to 1 inch larger than the outside of the window frame. As rough openings are seldom perfectly plumb or square, shim up discrepancies to make the sides of the window plumb.

With the shims behind both jambs, temporarily center the window in the rough opening. Holding your level to the jambs, adjust those shims—two at each spot—until the jambs are plumb. When you are pleased with the position of the unit, tack-nail through the jambs (and shims) into the rough opening behind, using 12d galvanized casing or finish nails. At this stage nail heads should stick up so that they can be easily removed. To repeat, the inside edges of the frame should be flush with the finish walls; the outside edges of the frame, flush to the sheathing on the building's exterior.

Open and shut the window several times to be sure that you have not overshimmed; the window should not bind. Pack loose fiberglass in the gaps between frame and rough opening and caulk any gaps that you cannot insulate. Use a putty knife to pack insulation.

With the window tack-nailed and packed, apply trim inside and out, using a pair of nails spaced every 10 to 12 inches. The inner nail of each pair secures the trim to the edge of the window frame; the outer nail (through the sheathing or the finished wall) sinks into a stud around the rough opening. On the exterior of the house, use 8d galvanized nails to secure trim; on the interior use 6d finish nails; do not sink any nail heads until you are positive that all trim fits perfectly.

Trimming a window is not physically arduous, but it does require patience and fastidiousness; there are further tips about fitting trim in chapter 4.

STAINED GLASS REPAIRS

If you wish to repair stained glass, above all you must be patient, for materials are often rare and fragile, whereas leaded and soldered connections are unyielding and tough to cut. Few specialized tools beyond those used to repair regular glass are needed, but patiently applying those tools is all telling.

The principal elements of stained glass are the glass itself, often textured and colored; lead *cames*, the strips that hold the glass in place (cames, also called channels, are **H**-shaped or **U**-shaped in

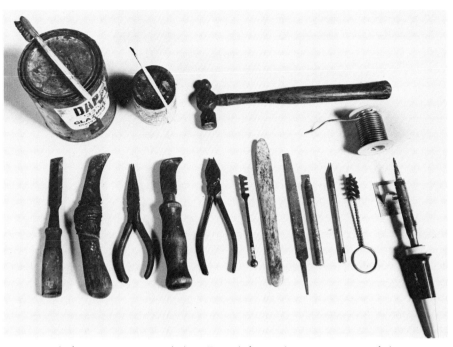

2-13. Tools for repairing stained glass. From left to right: top row: can of glazing compound with an old toothbrush on top, can of flux with brush, ball peen hammer, solder; bottom row: old wood chisel, lead-cutting knife, needle-nose pliers, linoleum knife with its outside edge sharpened, glass pliers, glass cutter, lathekin, file, two utility knives, wire cleaning-brush, soldering iron with stand.

cross section); *solder* to connect the cames; *putty*, which tightens the fit of glass within cames and cuts infiltration; *sashes* routed out to receive the glass assembly; *tacks* to hold the assembly to the sashes; and, for pieces larger than 2 feet in any dimension, *saddle bars*, for reinforcement, which attach to glass by soldered-on copper wires.

Wear gloves and goggles when handling glass. Although the chances of glass flying up into your eyes is scant, the repercussions are serious—eye protection is imperative. When cutting into lead or solder, most workers will strain on tools to make them cut better or will lean close to see what they are doing. A slip of the tool would be dangerous. If you find goggles hot and uncomfortable, at least wear safety glasses. Gloves will prevent cuts and forestall lead poisoning through the skin; medium-weight rubber gloves offer the best compromise of flexibility and impermeability.

If you will be soldering, work in a well-ventilated area and have adequate light. If there are small children or pets around, declare your shop off limits. After each work session, clean up; clean shops are safer ones.

A word about handling glass: move it in a deliberate, even way, especially if it is unsupported by a sash or has obviously buckled. The best way to transport such glass is to tape it (with fiber-reinforced tape) to a piece of plywood or fiberboard. It should be stored, on end, vertically and preferably sandwiched between pieces of plywood. If you must store it horizontally, lay it perfectly flat. When you take glass off the worktable, slide the piece toward the edge of the table and, using the edge of the table as a fulcrum, tip the glass up to a vertical position.

The optimum working area is a large tabletop covered with 1/2-inch fiberboard (Homosote is one brand), which can be cut upon; it also allows you to push in square nails to

2-14. When removing stained glass from a frame, keep it as vertical as possible so it will not slump.

2-15. As you approach your work area with the piece, use the edge of the table as a fulcrum upon which to lower the glass.

hold glass in place. Ideally, one part of the surface should have two pieces of furring strip (1 × 2) nailed or screwed down to form a square corner, which will keep glass squared as you work on it.

REPUTTYING AND CLEANING GLASS

Use putty around the perimeter of a glass assembly, where glass rests on the sash, and in most constructions, beneath individual lead cames as well, so that the glass will not rattle. Even if no major repairs are to be made, you should reputty degraded or missing sections. If you plan on major repairs, reputty when big work is complete.

Reputty the glass from the back side, the side seen from the exterior. Scrape out any obviously loose putty with a utility knife, vacuuming up the debris as you proceed. Once you have started this task, you should not move the piece until putty is again restored. You may find oversized nails holding the glass to the frame, the work of an earlier hapless renovator. Pull out those nails and replace them with glazing points (or tacks), which will not in-

terfere with the application of new putty. Replace putty by working it under the cames with a putty knife; where the edge of a came is not high enough to receive new putty easily, thin the putty slightly with turpentine and brush it under the came with an old toothbrush.

Should your glass still be in the sash during this operation, bevel the large swath of putty around the perimeter of the glass, where it meets the sash—this bevel will help water run off (see fig. 2–10). Reputtying while the glass is still in the sash also increases the danger that you may distort the center of the glass

2-16. To keep a corner square or to bring a skewed one back into shape, screw a right angle of 1 × 2s to the worktable.

2-17. Square nails hold the glass firm to the frame: they need not be driven as deep as standard round-shanked nails.

2-18. If you find oversized nails holding the glass to the frame—the work of an earlier hapless renovator—pull out those nails and replace them with glazing points (or tacks).

2-19. Apply putty beneath lead cames too.

by leaning on it as you work. To prevent this problem, insert a piece of sturdy foam rubber cut to the size of the *glass*—not the sash—under the glass. The foam will compress somewhat, but it will largely support the glass. Backing pieces with such a foam support is a good idea even if the glass is backed with saddle bars.

When putty is dry, use a lathekin to press down the edges of cames that may have become raised by your efforts. Scrape off any putty residue with a razor scraper, and

wash the window well. Although commercial window cleaners should do the trick, try straight vinegar or trisodium phosphate (washing soda) for more stubborn cleanups.

The only long-term remedy for putty deterioration is putting a storm window on the outside of the stained glass sash to intercept weather. If your glass is unsupported by a sash, you can best hang it inside an existing window: solder a heavy perimeter of **U**-shaped lead came around it, with chain loops for

hanging at the top. Such glass can be easily removed should you want to open or clean the window behind.

REINFORCING GLASS

A number of factors may cause glass to sag or buckle. The maker may have failed to install saddle bars. Wires holding the glass to the saddle bar may have come loose. Someone or something may have bumped against the window. The prevailing winds may have pushed it out of shape. For all cases the remedy is flattening the glass and then attaching (or reattaching) it to saddle bars.

Flattening a Bulge

Remove the glass from its sash carefully. After dislodging the putty around its perimeter, pull any nails that hold it. Because the lead will have stretched as the window bulged, removing the piece from the sash may take time. Go around and around the sash, pushing the back of the glass gently until the entire piece comes out.

Lay the glass, bulge up, on a flat surface. There are a number of opinions about how glass should be flat-

2-20. Place bowed pieces, bulge up, on a flat table to work the high spot down.

tened. Some experts advocate putting the glass, perhaps with a piece of plywood above, on a flat section of asphalt driveway. The heat of the sun softens recalcitrant lead, and the piece flattens itself. Other restorers recommend cutting and resoldering cames at all solder points. But perhaps the easiest way to effect a cure is to gradually work down the bulge by hand. Starting at the middle of the glass, apply uniform pressure with your hands over the face of the glass.

This last method may take two or three hours to flatten a moderately sized (say, 1½- by 1½-feet) piece with a bulge of 2 or more inches. Virtually nothing will seem to happen for the first hour of your labors, but in the second hour, pieces of glass will slip back into the channels of the lead cames. Wear gloves during this operation, because handling lead for so long can make you ill. If you notice the edge of a came blocking the reentry of a piece of glass into its channel, pry up the lead with a pocketknife. When the task is over, flatten the lead with a lathekin.

2-21. To remove glass from its frame, first loosen the wires soldered to the glass that tie around the saddle bar.

Reattaching to a Saddle Bar

If wires holding glass to the saddle bar have pulled free from the glass,

remove the glass from its sash. Trying to resolder wire to glass with a bar in the way is too difficult. Before removing the glass from the sash, lightly pencil in where the saddle bars cross lead cames. These pencil marks indicate where to solder connector wires.

Use 2-inch-long pieces of copper wire, folded roughly in half and spaced every 4 to 6 inches along the path of the saddle bar, as connector wires. Sand the surface of the lead, apply flux to the spot, and, holding the solder and soldering iron close

to, but not directly on, the spot, melt a drop or two of solder onto the spot. To attach the wire, reheat the drop of solder just placed and insert the wire, holding it in place for a second or two until the solder hardens.

When all wires are soldered into place, reinsert the glass into the sash and twist those wires around saddle bars. Twist the wire three or four times and snip off excess so that less than a ½ inch of wire sticks up. Reapply the nails and putty around the perimeter of the window.

Soldering Tips

2-22. Hold the tip of the soldering iron and the end of the solder just above the juncture to be soldered, so that a slight mound of melted solder forms.

The soldering iron must be the right temperature, which is learned only by practice. If too hot, the solder pools; if too cold, the solder balls up and skitters around the surface of the glass; if just the right temperature, the solder mounds uniformly. Do not hold the iron on a lead came for too long though, because you may crack the glass.

Practice cutting and soldering on scrap windows first. You will find that getting solder to stick to lead is not so easy. Sand all lead well so that any corrosion or dirt is scrubbed away, leaving only shiny metal. Apply flux. Actually applying the lead is easy enough to describe—the end of the soldering iron and the end of the solder barely touch the lead—but doing it is another thing. Quite often the lead will melt, which is not a disaster, but not the desired effect either. Thus, if a piece of glass is only slightly damaged, leave it alone.

Installing New Saddle Bars

Any glass assembly larger than 2 feet wide or high should have saddle bars. If your piece is smaller than that and has buckled, add saddle bars anyway. Use 3/16-inch steel rod for saddle bars. After cutting the rod—but before inserting it into the sides of the sash—prime it with a rust-preventive primer such as Rustoleum. In most cases black will be the least noticeable color. Space bars more or less evenly across the face of the piece; you will, however, get the best visual effect by positioning bars so that they coincide with major lead seams. Move the bar stock across the sash until you are pleased with the position of the metal, and then, holding the bar steady with one hand, trace its path across sash and cames. The pencil marks on the cames will show you where to solder the copper fastening wires (as described above) and, on the sash, where to drill into the sides of the frame.

Remove the glass from the sash.

Using a 3/16-inch drill bit, drill all the way through the sides of the sash, in about 3/8 inch from the lip on which the glass rests. To make sure that drilled holes are perpendicular, use a drilling jig (see fig. 3-35). Once the holes are drilled, cut the rod to length: the width of the sash *minus* 1 inch. Insert the rod into the holes just drilled; seal the rod on either end with 3/16-inch dowel plugs, 1/2 inch long. Glue the plugs or, if you envision removing saddle bars at some future time, forgo dowel plugs and just shoot a bit of silicone caulking in after rods are in place. Now you are ready to reinsert the glass and tie its fastening wires to the saddle bars.

A simpler but somewhat less sightly way to add a saddle bar is to screw it onto the outside of the sash. Use 3/16-inch angle bars (**L** shaped), with predrilled holes that will receive 6-gauge wood screws. Screws should be at least 3/4 inch long so they seat adequately in the sash. Less permanent is round rod nailed onto the outside of the sash with 4-gauge staples (which look somewhat like croquet bends). Either method allows you to leave the glass in the sash.

REPLACING GLASS

Two methods can be used to remove damaged glass. You can pry up the lead around that piece, or you can cut out sections of glass, leaving the lead around them intact, until you get to the damaged piece(s). The first method, called "lift out" or "open lead" repair, is most appropriate where the lead cames are wide, as is common in church windows. The other method, "cutting apart," is easiest if the lead is narrow.

Lift-Out Repair

If the damaged glass is beyond saving, break it gently so that you can pull free the shards; removing a glass section will make lifting its lead much easier. Lift up the lead on one side—the back side of the glass—so that your repair will be less noticeable. Although almost any flat tool will do, a lathekin is perhaps best for this work; square-jawed pliers also work well, as does the tang of a flat file. Work the entire perimeter of the piece, gradually working up the lead so that its flanges do not tear. At corners cut the lead with a knife so you can peel flanges back.

Trace around the unlifted flange of the lead to establish the pattern of the replacement glass. Glass should rest upon lead at least 1/16 inch all around, but cut the glass slightly small so that you do not have to wrestle it into place; you can always fill up any looseness with putty. Once the glass is in place, very slowly press the flanges of lead cames back down with a lathekin. Take it easy, for this is the point at

2-23. If your glass has wide lead cames, you can replace glass by carefully prying up the edge of the came.

2-24. Once the new piece has been cut and placed, smooth down the lead with a lathekin or some such flat-bladed tool.

which tears often occur; solder cut corners and any tears that occur.

It is possible, though not advisable, to do this operation with the glass still in the sash.

Cut-Apart Repair

When a broken piece of glass is in the interior of a window and lead cames are too narrow to pry up, you will have to cut apart leaded sections and remove undamaged, intervening glass, gradually working your way toward the damaged piece. The cut-apart method should be attempted only after the glass has been removed from its sash; cutting cames means leaning upon the cutting tool, which could damage any glass not fully supported by a tabletop.

The purpose of this strategy is to leave the lead intact around as many sections of glass as possible. Cut the lead at the corners of the pieces and lift out sections one by one until you arrive at the damaged piece. If the damage is close to the border of the assembly, you need

not cut too much. Otherwise, cutting is a time-consuming, tedious job: you often encounter solder at corners of came sections, which is harder to cut than lead.

Place the cutting tool (in our photo series, a linoleum knife with a sharpened outside edge) on the solder joint. Rock the tool until it "eats" into the metal; wiggle the blade. Because old glass is often very tightly fitted into the lead, be careful not to press too hard. Once all the corners of a side have been cut, turn the piece over very carefully and cut the back sides of those same corners.

When you have completely severed the corners of a section, pull out the glass. Continue with each section until you reach the damaged piece.

Note: It is permissible to heat the solder in lieu of, or in addition to, cutting it; but every melted section must be reattached later on.

Replace the damaged glass, then refit sections in the reverse order that you removed them. If any of the lead has become twisted or

crimped, clean up its edges with a flat file. It will probably be necessary to file down a lot of the lead channels, in fact, because they will have stretched as you handled them. Some gaps may be left at corners, however, because these can be built up with solder.

USEFUL TIPS FOR STAINED GLASS REPAIR

Cut textured glass from its smooth back side.

To blend newly soldered sections to old, darken new lead and solder with *zinc chloride*, applied with a cotton swab. Zinc chloride is available at most glass-supply stores.

To disguise new putty, mix lampblack with it. The resultant dull gray mix will look like lead itself.

To repair an old window whose perimeter lead has corroded, peel and cut the old lead off while holding glass in place with square-cut nails, as shown in figure 2–17. This perimeter lead is usually **U**-shaped

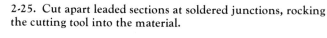

2-25. Cut apart leaded sections at soldered junctions, rocking the cutting tool into the material.

2-26. If the edge stripping has deteriorated, simply pull the lead free and lift out sections of glass.

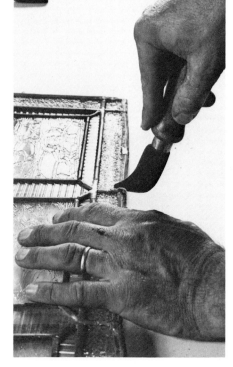

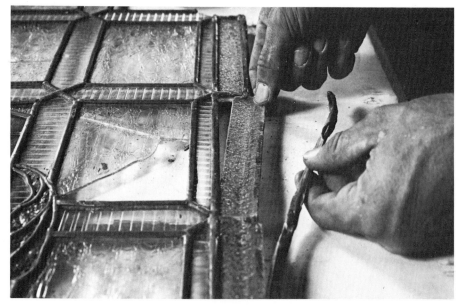

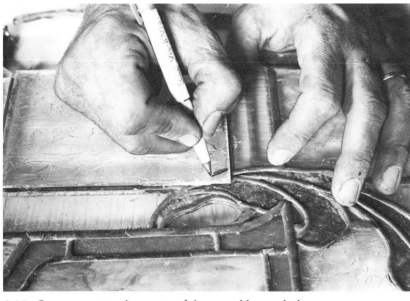

2-27. Once you get to the center of the assembly, mark the replacement piece.

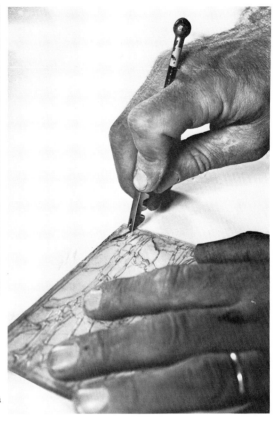

2-28. If the glass is textured, cut it from the back side, which is smoother.

2-29. If, during reassembly, you find that some of the lead cames have compressed, open them with a file.

2-30. Hold pieces reassembled in place with square-cut nails. Apply flux in advance of soldering.

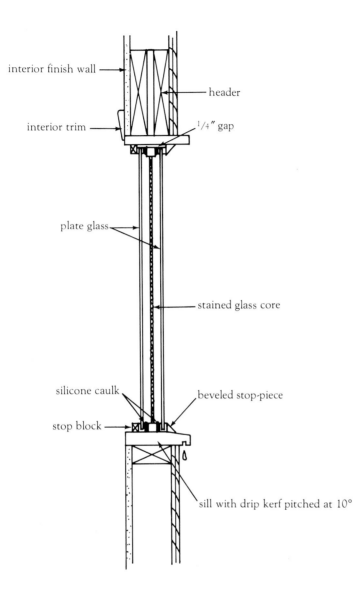

interior finish wall

header

interior trim

1/4″ gap

plate glass

stained glass core

silicone caulk

beveled stop-piece

stop block

sill with drip kerf pitched at 10°

2-31. Side view of a stained glass thermal window.

in cross section; use new **U**-channel to seal the edges; fill gaps between glass and lead with putty.

Old windows are the best sources of repair glass; buy a pair if one is damaged and one is good.

If your glass has a crack that gaps cleanly at least $1/16$ inch between pieces, disguise the gap by cutting the top flange off a strip of **H**-shaped lead came. Push the heart of the lead into the crack and solder the cutoff part of the came to the back side of the glass; merely soldering its ends will hold the came in place.

A very simple stained glass thermopane can be constructed as shown in figure 2–31. Particularly important is slightly undersizing the pieces of glass to allow for expansion and shifting in the house. Note too the silicone caulking, which keeps glass from rattling. Beveled wood strips are not strictly necessary; they can also be cut square and sealed with caulking. Be very careful not to break glass when tacking strips into place: use a magnetic tack hammer to start nails, or hold onto small nails by sticking them through a piece of cardboard. Once you have hammered the nail in, merely tear the cardboard free.

This particularly nice application of salvage uses two pieces, an ornamental masonry block (a Mexican "ox eye") and a specially cut section of glass. The cast-concrete block is set into an adobe wall and plaster is run flush to its inside edge. The glass is set within the lip of the block with silicone caulk. Both outside (over the woodpile) and inside, this window breaks up a large expanse of wall and delights the eye.

John Midyette III

An floral pattern in etched glass, used in an exterior door on a second-story porch.

Eric Bauer

A nice interplay of textures: an elegant leaded glass casement window set in roughsawn siding, beneath a split-shake roof.

Ken McKenzie

These doors were from six small-pane window sashes that were probably European. The builder had oak door frames with through-mortise corners fabricated; the handles are also salvage, although the lock mechanisms themselves are new. Both doors open out onto a deck.

Mike Greenberg

Should you forget, in the midst of all this elegant reuse, what the original articles looked like, here is the backyard of Sunrise Salvage Company in Berkeley, California.

These Palladian windows, originally used on a building exterior, now grace an interior partition, allowing light into the stairwell behind.

David Dickson, design; Richard McElhiny, photo

An impressive array in the main dining hall of Saint Orres Inn in Gualala, California. Designer-builder Eric Black kept the windows in proportion—even in this 30-ft.-high room—by oversizing the trim (1 × 8s) around each bank of windows.

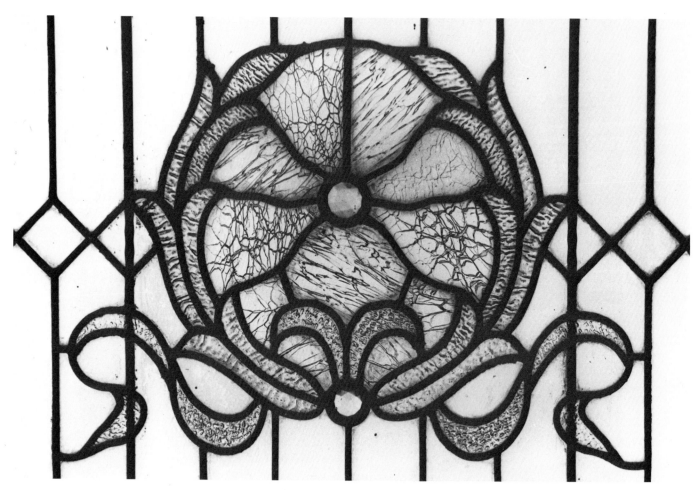

An English neoclassical floral motif, cracked glass with faceted jewels; circa 1900.
"Reflections" Antique Stained Glass.

Adolf deRoy Mark placed this solid brass porthole in the second-story bathroom of a Philadelphia town house.

Facing page: This pair of clear "granite" glass sashes works well as a tea screen. Each is 49 in. × 24 in., mounted in original mahogany. The austere, geometric design dates them to about 1910. The four circles in the center of each panel are blown rondel centers.
"Reflections" Antique Stained Glass.

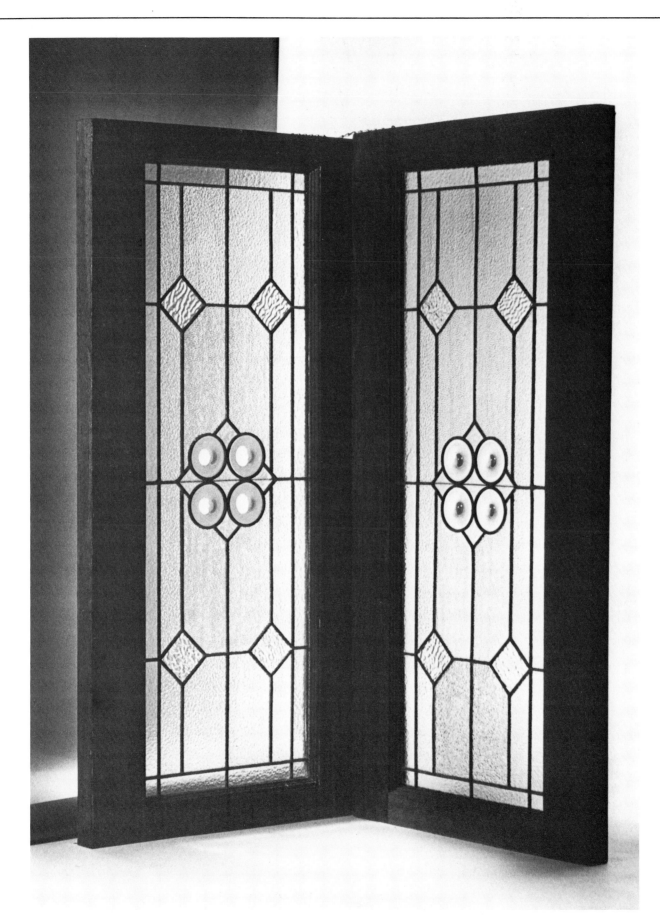

Doors

Safety Tips

- Use a voltage tester to make sure that electricity is off if you are removing or installing door casings (see figures 4–1 to 4–3). The chance of encountering a hot wire is slight, but electricians sometimes route wires around door casings.
- Before sawing, drilling, or cutting around a doorway, survey it with a metal detector, so you will know of hidden nails. An inexpensive "stud finder" will suffice.
- Wear goggles when using any power tools. Using a router, which requires your being close to the machine, is particularly hazardous if you do not wear safety glasses or goggles.
- Adequately secure doors (for example, clamp down) before working on them with power tools.
- Store doors on edge, under cover if necessary.

Tools

Few special tools are required for removing or hanging doors; those listed below are necessary if you want to rework a door, say, to enlarge it.
- Jack planes, usually, 14 inches long, are longer than most hand planes, thus giving you a straight edge less influenced by "local" contours.
- Butt markers make setting hinges much easier.
- Use a router if you patch holes with solid wood; a depth gauge will help you determine the accurate thickness of patches.
- A doweling jig keeps a drill bit perpendicular, crucially important if you are reinforcing a door with dowels.
- Bar clamps are long enough to draw together a door along its length; hand screws will hold smaller areas flat while gluing.
- Belt sanders are preferred for removing a lot of wood; sand with the grain. If only preparing stock for finishing, use an orbital or block sander.

These old Zaquan doors have center doors that open to admit usual human traffic to the central court. Typical of the many haciendas throughout Mexico, the "outer" doors open to admit horses and carriages into the courtyard.

John Midyette III

Old doors are unquestionably the most commonly salvaged architectural items. Simply constructed in most cases, they are little affected by decades of use and are easily removed and stored. And, perhaps most important, the average new door—of plywood, cardboard, and glue—is so ghastly that a sensible builder would not even consider using it. To be sure, nicely made modern doors do exist, but they cost so much that many people opt for old ones.

ASSESSING THE ELDERLY DOOR

In the days before plywood, all doors were constructed from solid stock; today, the best ones still are. The problem with wood, so far as doors are concerned, is that it expands and contracts with changes in temperature and humidity. Doors must be tightly fitted to a door frame if they are to keep out weather, so fitting the door loosely is no answer. On the other hand, a door fitted too tightly expands and swells, and it will be difficult to operate in warmer months.

The solution to this dilemma is to construct a frame-and-panel door, with a heavier frame slotted out to receive somewhat thinner panels. Solid-wood panels still expand and contract, but they do so within the confines of the frame, the edges of the panel concealed by slots in the frames and by any decorative molding that its builder uses. A panel thus floats freely—is not glued—within the frame.

The construction of panel doors is important to the salvager because it is at wood joints that doors most often fail. The most common cause of door failure is in settling, the weight of the door itself causing *stiles* and *rails* (the vertical and horizontal parts of the frame) to separate. This sagging may also be compounded by twisting as the door no longer meets the door *casing* properly (see fig. 3–40). A skewed door may, for example, scrape along the floor or abrade the side of the casing.

Exterior doors are particularly susceptible to water damage, especially along the bottom rail, which rests on the door sill. If the sill pitch is not at least a 10-degree angle away from the house, water will collect, making the sill and bottom rail of the door punky and unsound.

Other causes of door failings include poorly sized or installed hinges or the shifting of the house. In either case the door does not strike its frame squarely.

Splitting is generally limited to the panel of a door, usually caused by the finish surface not being maintained: water soaks the wood, and it cracks. A less common cause occurs when the panel is too big for the frame. When it swells, it has no place to go; thus the wood fiber is compressed, ultimately weakening it.

Other causes of door failure are as varied as the carelessness that causes them. Latter-day renovators hack and shorten doors with little appreciation for structure, frequently cutting through the rail's tenon (the "finger" of a mortise-and-tenon joint) or driving so many nails through the corner of an old door that the wood splits within a season or two. These types of botches are readily apparent and need no further examples.

Whether you buy a door depends upon its condition and the use that you intend. Most important, is it an interior door or an exterior door? The latter is 1⅝ inches or more thick; interior doors are simply too flimsy to be used outside, even if you live in a mild climate. Moreover, the molding of exterior doors is frequently shaped so that it will shed rain. An exterior door can be used inside the house, but its greater weight will make hanging more difficult. (If you decide to go that route, be sure to use a correctly sized hinge, as outlined in fig. 3–43.) If you intend to cut up the door and use it as, say, paneling, you can use almost any type of door.

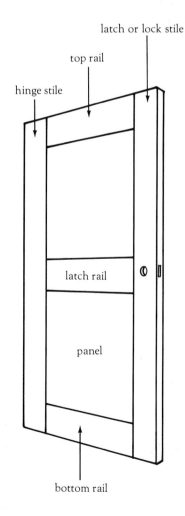

3-1. Parts of a panel door.

To examine the structure of the door, carefully probe the bottom rail and the bottoms of the door stiles with a pocketknife. Is the wood sound? If not, probe until the wood is uniformly sound and then measure up from that point to determine the total usable height of the door. If the door is too small for your purposes, you have essentially two options. You can reinforce the decayed wood with an epoxy stabilizer, or you can remove the rot and add on a new section. If the rot is slight and you will be painting the door, the former choice is easiest; if you want a natural finish, however, you should add new wood, a task of some complexity.

If the door structure is basically sound, check it with a long, straight board to see if all edges are straight and, across the face of the door, if it is warped. Apply a framing square to corners to see if they are square. Doors must be square and true before being rehung or the task becomes absurdly complicated. Hence you must measure again to see if there is enough usable door for your purposes after trimming out-of-square corners.

Correcting a warped door is not difficult, but the cure does not always take. Lay the door flat across two sawhorses, with its curve up, and weight the high spot down with bricks or the like. That may work, but if the door has been warped over many years, wood fibers may be deformed and will not be amenable to such quick cures. Steaming a door brings it back to shape, but that requires special equipment and is generally not worth the trouble.

It is possible to bring a door back into square by drawing it up with bar clamps, but door parts that have taken decades to settle may be held in that errant position by built-up finishes, lodged dirt, and the ministrations of earlier carpenters. If the rail/stile joints are loose, clamping into shape is probably practicable, but if the joints of the door

3-2. Heavy mesquite doors with bone inlay, from Morelia, Mexico.
Architectural Antiques, Ltd.

seem quite tight (though out of square), it is probably best to forget clamping unless you are a very experienced carpenter and are willing to take the whole assembly apart.

If any of the door tenons are broken—you can probably wiggle that section of the frame with your hand—repairs will be quite complex. Pass that door by.

If the door has hardware that you do not like or hinges and latches in the wrong places, you will have to remove such items and fill in the holes. Such repair is involved, but eminently within the capability of a conscientious amateur. Hardware is rarely a reason for not buying a door, unless it has really been butchered. If you are buying a door and have other hardware in mind, however, check the width of the door stiles to be sure that the new hardware will fit.

Likewise, cosmetic repair rarely disqualifies a prospect. Do take a sample scraping from an inconspicuous spot to see how many layers of paint there are, though, especially if you will remove paint by hand. Dipping the door to strip it is an alternative, but an unacceptable one if the door is open grained or finely detailed: wood may split after a sustained immersion in hot stripping liquid.

If the original door casing (discussed in chapter 4) is available, purchase it. The motifs of trimwork sometimes recur on the door and at the very least, the trim will be of the same architectural era as the door. If the door is still hung from that casing, by all means take it, because you will have spared yourself the chore of cutting hinges into a new frame.

Finally, will an old door be an energy-loser? I advised against using old window units in chapter 2—they waste too much heat. Here the advice is equivocal. Although no old door can match the R-value of a new, insulated door (1-inch-thick wood is R-1.56; insulated-core doors, R-6 or -7), old ones can be upgraded significantly with storm doors and weather stripping. Infiltration *around* the perimeter of a door loses more energy than the passage of heat *through* the door.

REMOVING AND STORING DOORS

Removing doors requires only a hammer and an old screwdriver in most cases. After chipping away any paint that may be covering the top of the hinge pin, drive the pin up and out. To keep the door in place until the last moment, remove the top hinge pin last. If the door is particularly heavy, have a helper hold it while you knock out the pins or shim up the bottom of the door so that it will not fall when the hinges are out. Removing the hinge pins while the door is shut is also a good strategy.

Hinges are occasionally so decrepit or paint-encrusted that pins cannot be driven out, or the pins may be fixed. In that event unscrew the hinge leaves themselves, again leaving the top set until last. Where screw heads are stripped, redefine the screw slots with a used chisel or screwdriver. Wearing safety goggles, strike the stripped openings with the tool. If that does not work, rent or borrow an impact driver, a machinist's tool especially designed to free tight nuts or screws.

Storing doors has few mysteries. Stand them perfectly upright in a dry place, with wooden blocks underneath if the floor is concrete or otherwise slightly damp. Dry old doors will easily wick moisture from a damp spot and become spoiled. If you must store them outside, wrap them entirely in sheet plastic (polyethylene). To prevent doors from warping when stacked, first remove doorknobs and, if storing the doors flat, do not place objects of any weight on the stack.

REBUILDING AND RECONDITIONING OLD DOORS

First strip any paint from the door. Besides being necessary for subsequent refinishing, stripped wood shows you the real extent of the repairs to be done, including any cracks or metal that were masked by paint.

A few words about metal. Nails, screws, and metal mending plates are rarely more than stopgap measures that will work loose in time. Afterwards the door will be in worse shape than it was originally. Should you hit metal with your saw blade or drill bit, you may ruin the cutting edge and possibly injure yourself. After stripping, carefully survey the door, even using a stud finder (a small magnet used to locate the nails in studs) to find hidden metal. When you make your repairs, use wood and glue; this will truly bond repaired sections together and be as strong (or stronger) than the wood itself.

The most common ways to recondition a door for reuse are cutting and squaring its edges; reinforcing its corners; patching holes; and increasing the size of the door with additional wood. Repairing glass is discussed in the preceding chapter on windows.

SQUARING A DOOR

One of the simpler tasks is cutting down a door that is a trifle out of square (say, ½ inch per 2 feet). The door should be basically sound and should not need to be clamped and glued. Wear goggles. Use a carbide-tipped blade in your circular saw, and cut only after you have surveyed for metal.

Start on the *hinge stile* of the door, the vertical part of the door into which hinges are mortised (cut in). Because the axis of each hinge must be perfectly aligned if hinges are to operate correctly, the hinge stile must be perfectly straight and its edge, square.

Never cut off any more than you must. Measure out from the inside edge of the stile at several points to locate the cutting line. Align a straight board or a taut string through these marks, and mark the cutting line with a pencil or simply snap a chalkline.

The blade of the saw must be perpendicular to the face of the door if the resulting edge is to be square. Because the panels of most doors are set below the edges of the door frame, there is a danger that the sole plate (the bottom) of the saw may tilt down into panels. To provide a uniformly flat cutting surface, place a flat board—say, a 1 × 8—over the edge of the door; run the saw atop that. You will, of course, have to increase the depth of cut of the saw to accommodate the increased thickness of the 1 × 8. Check your cut when you are finished to be sure that it is in fact straight.

Next square the *top* and *bottom* rails of the door to the hinge stile. Use a framing square, its *tongue* (the

short leg) aligned to the stile and its *blade* (the long leg) along the rails. Mark with a pencil as shown in figure 3–4 and reverse the legs of the framing square to be sure that your markings are true. Cut as before, using a runner board beneath your saw to ensure square-cut edges.

The last element to be cut is the *latch stile* (along the latch side of the door). Measure out from the outside edge of the hinge stile every foot or so, and snap a chalkline through those marks. Again use a runner board beneath the circular saw, but this time the cut should not be 90 degrees, but 87 or 88 degrees; adjust the angle of the saw blade accordingly. This small inward bevel allows the latch stile to shut tightly without bumping its inside edge along the frame *jamb* (side). This bevel is less critical if the door is not thick (1⅛ inches or less) or if there is more than a ¹⁄₁₆-inch gap between door and door frame; the bevel cut is essential, however, if the door is a thick, exterior type. You can also just cut the edge square and bevel it later with a jack plane.

Many carpenters prefer to delay cutting down or beveling the latch stile until the door is hung. If the

door frame is not perfectly square, you may want to cut down the stile slightly irregular to match the oddity of the frame. Likewise, in extreme cases where you fit a door to an existing door frame that is badly out of square, you may want to cut down only the hinge stile, hang the door, and then swing it to see where other door parts will hit.

REINFORCING CORNERS

To strengthen corners that have worked loose, first remove any nails, screws, or molding that may interfere with squaring the section. Next, pry apart the stile and rail slightly so that you can scrape out the gap, especially any paint that may be present which could prevent the glue from bonding.

The joint cleaned, squirt white carpenter's glue in, then draw the pieces together with a bar clamp, being sure to protect the wood with a block of scrap. If you lack such a clamp, an acceptable makeshift clamp may be devised by laying the door flat on a worktable and nailing two strips, one on either side of the

3-3. After measuring out from the inside edge of the hinge stile, align a taut string (or a very straight board) through the measurements and mark your cutting line.

3-4. To square the top and bottom rails of the door, align one leg of a framing square to the hinge stile and mark off the rails.

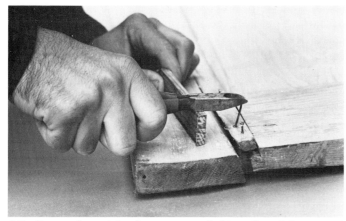

3-5. Corner damage is often compounded by a "repair" consisting of a banging in a few nails; remove such metal.

3-6. Glue loose pieces or those joints that have pulled apart; clamp as needed but protect the finish wood with a scrap piece beneath the clamp's jaws.

door, into the tabletop. Drive tapered wedges between the door and those strips, thus forcing the parts of the door together.

That done, drill new holes into the corner and insert ⅜-inch dowels. How many dowels you fit into the corner of a door varies: five, in an **X** pattern, is right in most cases. No dowel should be closer than 1 inch

3-7. Drill in dowels to reinforce corners.

to the edge of the door, or splits could occur. The drill bit should be held perpendicular to the face of the door; there are special jigs to hold bits just so (fig. 3–35), but judging by eye is sufficient here. Add glue to the holes, and gently rap in the dowels with a hammer or mallet. When the glue is dry, remove the clamps and saw off the excess dowel. Take care not to score the face of the door with the saw, however; stop short and plane or sand off the rest of the dowel until it is flush. Sand and refinish.

PATCHING HOLES

Most older doors are fabricated from several kinds of wood, often a poplar or pine core overlaid with a fancy hardwood veneer. The reason for doing this is, of course, economy but also to reduce the weight of a door; poplar is a particularly stable wood as well. Whereas most face veneers are ⅛ to 3/16 inch thick, the veneer along a door stile is often ¾ inch thick to allow the installer to mortise in hinges.

Although you could repair only the thin face veneer of a door where it has been cut into or abraded away, such replacement veneer may wear out or chip through use. Use a solid stock, at least ⅜ inch thick, and you will have a truly permanent

patch. Besides, the real art of patching is matching the grain of new and old woods, a process that cannot be rushed. Cleaning the old flaw and cutting the new patch are almost secondary.

We will consider three kinds of patches: a surface patch; a mortise patch, in which an old mortise lock has been removed and its hole must be filled; and an edge patch, often done in tandem with a mortise patch, to finish off the door edge. Keep in mind that whatever the nature of the patch, it must support the reuse you intend. That is, if you intend to insert a new lock assembly in a given spot, that spot must be solid wood.

Surface Patches

A patch repair assumes that there is solid wood into which you can rout and on which the patch will sit. If that is not the case—and it often is not where a mortise lock has been removed—prepare a mortise patch first.

Begin by looking over the door, noting all the repairs that you must make and being especially watchful for small nails that might ruin the cutting edge of a chisel or router bit. If the door has ornamental trim that is flawed or would interfere with using a router (or any other tool), gingerly pry off such trim and store

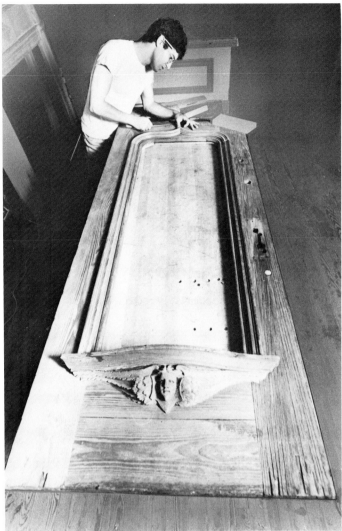

3-9. Remove any ornamental molding that would interfere with operating a power tool on the face of the door: pry off pieces carefully so that you do not damage them.

3-8. Survey the entire door before repairing any part of it. In addition to holes caused by removed hardware, this door had pronounced splitting along its bottom rail.

3-10. Nail pincers are best for nails that barely stick up or that are too brittle or small to be gripped by hammer claws.

it where it will not become damaged.

The purpose of patching is to fool the eye. Select replacement stock that matches the original wood as closely as possible, including its grain. Use a number of small patches rather than one large one, if possible. Cut diamond-shaped patches, whose sides run diagonally across the grain of the door; a diamond patch is much easier to blend in than a square or rectangular one.

The door being repaired should be already stripped: old stains and weathering will obscure wood grain. If the door is as yet unstripped and you want to get started anyway, scrape down a section with a cabinet scraper. Many publications have extensive photos of wood grain, which should help you identify the type of wood you have before you. But even professionals may be fooled. If you are unsure what type of wood you have, you can send a small sample to the Wood Identification Laboratory, USDA Forest Products Laboratory, P.O. Box 5130, Madison, WI 53705; it will take about six weeks to get an answer. A passable patch can be made, however, by matching grain as closely as you can by eye. Our craftsman hunted for pieces of ash whose grain matched pretty well. Refinished, the patches were invisible.

Small holes such as nail holes or screw holes do not require such attention: they can be plugged with small sections of hardwood dowels later on. Never use wood filler; it does not receive stain well.

Noting the grain around the hole to be patched, cut several sections of replacement wood. Cut pieces roughly to thickness (in our example, ½ inch thick) and slide the replacement sections over the hole until grain lines align. Mark off the width of the patch and then, using a combination square, draw the

3-11. Mark off the approximate width of the patch on stock with color and grain that closely match the area to be filled.

3-12. Use a combination square to create the diamond-shaped patch.

diagonal lines (figs. 3–11 and 3–12).

Cut out the diamond-shaped patch and position it over the hole one last time. *Note:* It is important that edges of the patch not coincide with any strong grain lines; if they do, cut a new patch slightly larger. Such grain lines will split as you fit the patch; moreover, the patch will not blend well.

For the best fit, bevel the underside of the patch slightly with a plane or a sanding block. Hold the patch in a vise for this operation; it is too small to hold by hand. The bevel need not be large—only 2 or 3 degrees—just a slight taper so that the top of the patch is a little wider. When you bevel the edge of the patch with a plane, note the grain of the wood and plane in a direction that will not catch the grain. When you are finished, lightly mark the patch so you will know which side is to face down—the bevel is so slight that it will not be apparent.

Place the patch over the hole, again aligning grain lines, and clamp it down. With a scriber or a very sharp knife, trace around the edge of the patch. This is tricky because the blade will want to follow the grain of the wood somewhat. As you scribe, hold the knife at an angle more severe than the bevel; thus, the knife point will follow the bottom edge of the patch. Loosen the clamp, remove the patch, and darken in the scribed lines with a very sharp pencil. It is easy to lose a scribed line; if you do, reposition the patch and trace it again.

It takes time to patch successfully; you cannot rush the task. Go around the outline of the patch with a chisel, flat face of the tool towards the outside of the area, as shown in figure 3–15. You need not hammer on the chisel at this point; just press it down by hand. Then strengthen the chisel lines with dark pencil. Now you are ready to rout out most of the patch hole. Wear goggles or safety glasses when using the router.

Use a straight, double-fluted router bit for this task, setting its depth against the thickness of the patch as shown in figure 3–16. Getting the depth of the router bit just

3-13. Check the grain patterns of the patch.

3-14. After carefully aligning the grain of the patch to that of the door, gently clamp down the patch so it will not move while you scribe around it. If you bevel the patch, be sure to hold your scriber to the *bottom* edges of the patch.

3-17. Test the patch fit, planing it very gradually, until you can seat the piece one-third its thickness without having to force it.

3-15. Because a scribed line is often faint, strengthen its outline with a chisel and then, for good measure, with a dark pencil.

3-16. To minimize later sanding or planing down the patch, set the router depth to the exact thickness of the patch; test the depth of cut on scrap wood.

right is an important part of the operation: if the hole is not deep enough, you will have to sand away some of the surface of the patch, especially undesirable if you selected your patch because its patina matched that of the door. So test the depth of the router bit on scrap to be sure.

Remember, the surface of the door must be perfectly flat if your

router is to produce a uniformly deep hole; remove any trim and pull up any nails that could interfere with the operation of the router.

You will not be able to rout the entire hole. The corners must be cleaned out with a chisel. As you chisel, tilt the blade just a little—say, 2 or 3 degrees—so that you backcut the edges of the hole. Your goal is to cut an essentially square-

edged hole, but a tool held perfectly perpendicular tends to ride into the hole, resulting in a less than square cut. Be patient—this hand-chiseling will take some time.

When pleased with the hole, tap the patch into it just a bit to see where the patch binds. Trim as necessary with the chisel, fitting the patch repeatedly until the edges of the patch and those of the hole are a good match. Blow out the hole as you work so that shavings do not accumulate. When you can tap the patch down into the hole about one-third of the way, you are ready to glue. (If a patch will fit one-third of the way in with gentle coaxing, it will fit all the way.)

Use exterior-grade glue for all repairs to exterior doors and, because of its superior bonding, for all sections of thin veneer that have sprung. Use white carpenter's glue for interior repairs. Spread glue around the inside of the hole, including its sides. Gently tap the patch into position. With the aid of a piece of scrap to prevent marring, force the patch all the way in with a C-clamp. Make sure that pressure is evenly applied to all parts of the patch. Wipe up any excess glue and allow the patch to bond.

The patch should stick up above the surface of the door no more

3-18. Spread glue on all sides of the hole.

3-20. If you routed the hole to the perfect depth, you may not have to sand. In most cases, however, light sanding is necessary.

than 1/32 inch, so it can be sanded smooth without much work. If you did not measure the depth accurately and the patch sticks up higher than 1/32 inch, plane it down with a block plane to the proper height before sanding. It is best to sand down open-grained woods such as oak and ash; close-grained woods such as maple can be planed down.

3-19. Using a scrap block to prevent marring, tighten down the patch with a C-clamp.

In either case a plane blade can catch on the corners of a diamond-shaped patch; be careful. Before refinishing a patched area, go over it with a cabinet scraper once or twice to clean up any glue residue that may have resulted when you wiped up excess.

Mortise Patches

A patch for a mortise hole is a rectangular block cut to fit as tightly as possible; it can be of virtually any wood. The size of the mortise-lock case (if it is still around) will be a good indicator of the hole size, but in any event measure the hole carefully to ascertain its exact dimensions. As such holes are often tapered slightly, square up the mortise with a 1/2-inch chisel or whatever size tool seems right.

Cut the block to size. It should not be flush to the edge of the door; finishing the edge is usually a separate operation, as described below. So when deciding the depth of the block, subtract the thickness of the patch (usually 1/2 inch to 3/4 inch thick) you will use to finish off the door edge.

Fit the block into the hole, chisel as needed, and when you are satisfied, smear white glue all around the inside of the hole. Tap

the patch block in. This straightforward procedure is not difficult; the fit should be tight. Surface patches are applied over the mortise patch after the glue has dried. In addition to camouflaging the mortise holes, surface patches provide mechanical joints when they are routed into the mortise patch, holding the block firmly in place.

3-21. All that remains of an old lock assembly is the mortise cut into the door stile.

3-22. Square up the mortise as best you can with a straight chisel, the better to receive a patch block with square corners.

3-23. After you have dry-fit a patch into the mortise, spread glue liberally.

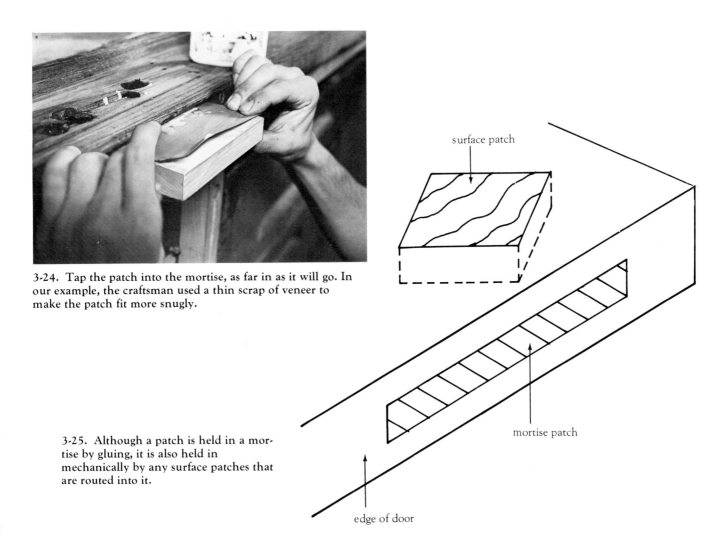

3-24. Tap the patch into the mortise, as far in as it will go. In our example, the craftsman used a thin scrap of veneer to make the patch fit more snugly.

surface patch

mortise patch

edge of door

3-25. Although a patch is held in a mortise by gluing, it is also held in mechanically by any surface patches that are routed into it.

Edge Patches

Once a mortise hole has been filled with a block and surface patches have been applied, you are ready to repair the edge of the door. The edge of the door must be reasonably square and sound; if it is rounded or deteriorated, cut off a slight amount (about 1/4 inch) so that you can patch to a square edge. The reason for this, as you will see, is that an edge patch is not as wide as the door is thick; if such a patch were as wide, there would be new wood peering out from both sides, difficult to blend in and subject to wear.

The edge patch is a long, rectangular piece whose dimensions are determined by those of the door. It should be about 1/2 inch longer than the hole it is covering so that the end of the patch can be cut into solid wood. Its width should be about 1/4 inch less than the thickness of the door, so that 1/8 inch of the door edge conceals the patch on both sides. The patch should be 1/2 to 3/4 inch thick.

Like the surface patch, the edge patch is fitted in by a router with a straight bit. The trick to the operation is a sufficiently wide—and level—base on which to rest the router.

Set the door on edge and stabilize it so that it will not move while you are working on it. You can use a number of clamping arrangements; perhaps the easiest is just to tighten two adjustable wooden clamps to the bottom stile of the door. (Such clamps are also called parallel clamps or hand screws.)

To either side of the area to be routed out, clamp two absolutely straight boards to serve as a base for the router. Those base guides need not be flush to the edge of the door, as the router depth can be adjusted, but the board edges *must* be parallel to each other and to the edge of the door. After clamping these straight boards to the door, check for parallelism with a square.

Recheck the dimensions of the patching piece. Although it is desirable to match the grain of the patch to that of the door edge, matching is not so critical here as it is on the door face. Remember that an edge patch is not quite as wide as the door is thick.

After cutting out the patch, bevel its edges slightly with a plane, as described in the preceding section on surface patches. Hold the patch onto the edge of the door and scribe around it with a scribing knife. Darken the scribed lines with a pencil; this outline will be a guide for the router cut that follows. Set the router bit depth so that, when the tool is resting on the edges of the clamped-on guides, the cut into the door edge will match the thickness of the patch (that is, bit depth should equal the measurement from the top of the guide to the door edge plus the depth of the patch). Take several readings with a depth gauge to make sure. After routing, clean out the corners of the outline with a straight chisel. Test-fit the patch, glue, and tap it down with a mallet, as described for surface patches.

After allowing the glue around the patch to dry completely, plane or sand down the new wood until the edge is perfectly flat. The door is now ready to receive any new hardware.

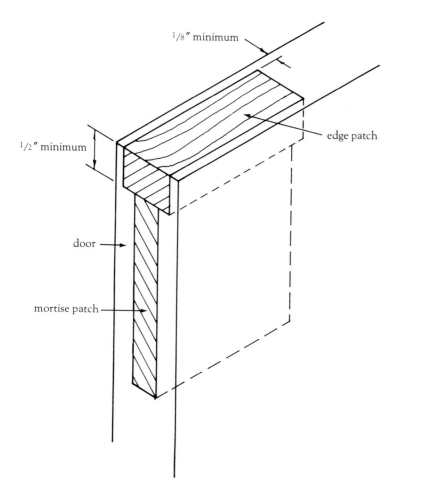

1/8" minimum

1/2" minimum

edge patch

door

mortise patch

3-26. The mortise patch is not quite as deep as the hole it fills so that an edge patch can finish off the door edge.

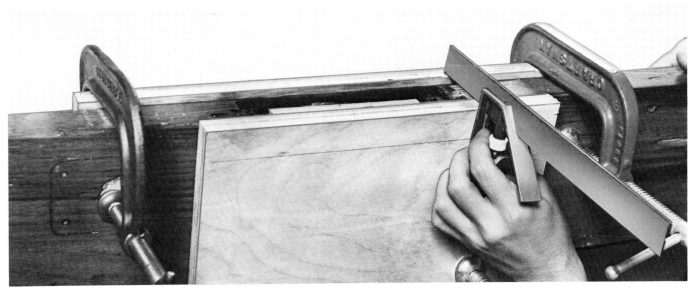

3-27. Because the edge of a door is too narrow to balance a router on, build up that edge by clamping on guides, in this case, pieces of scrap plywood.

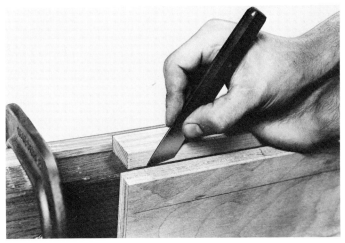

3-28. Trace the outline of that patch onto the door edge.

3-29. To determine how deep you should set your router, measure down—from the top of the clamped guides to the edge of the door—and add the thickness of your edge patch.

3-30. After testing the router depth on a piece of scrap, rout out the hole for the patch.

INCREASING THE SIZE OF A DOOR

Adding wood to a door to increase its length or width is by far the most complex task described in this section. The elements of the job are straightforward, but your measuring, cutting, and fitting must be extremely accurate, within 1/32 inch in most cases. Some specialized equipment is also needed; a router with a slot-cutting bit; sets of bar clamps, C-clamps, and handscrews; a power drill, and a doweling jig to keep the drill bit perpendicular to the stock; a table saw to rip down splines; a heavy-duty belt sander; access to a thickness planer; and a host of hand tools—in short, a small woodworking shop. You may be able to subcontract cutting the stock (to be added) but you will still need a table saw for the many little adjustments to be made.

The door to be enlarged must be sound and square, including its edges. If necessary, rip down the door to make it square. The door also must not be warped in any way.

The final size of the door depends on the size of the doorway. If there is presently only a rough opening (just wall studs framed out, without any finish casing), that opening should be about 2½ inches wider and longer than the door to allow for the thickness of shims and the door frame to follow. If the doorway is presently framed and finished and you are merely replacing an old door, allow 1/16-inch clearance on each side of the door. As much as ½-inch clearance is sometimes left beneath the door, especially if carpet is to follow or if the floor slants somewhat; 3/16 inch is typically left between the bottom of a door and a wooden finish floor.

If the doorway is finished but is slightly out of square, you can cut down or build up the door slightly to fit those odd angles. To figure out just how much wood you must add or subtract, lay out the dimensions of the doorway—including its odd angles—onto graph paper first. An appropriately scaled cutout of door dimensions will quickly show what alterations you must make.

Because added-on wood can be quite conspicuous, match new wood as closely as possible to the original. Wood type, color, and grain patterns are important; finish can be matched later. If possible, use old wood with a patina similar to that with which you are working; salvagers often buy an old pair of doors, using the second to build up or otherwise repair the first. Some disparity between old and new wood may result on even closely matched woods, however; in that event you may elect to add ornamental strips over joints, as depicted in figure 3-39.

Splining

A *spline* is a long, thin strip of wood that fits into grooves cut into two pieces of wood being joined. Once glued together, a splined joint is strong along its length, resisting lateral movement; the joint is thus appropriate to the edges of doors, which meet resistance each time a door is closed.

Splines are preferably ripped from plywood sheets, but may also be from hardwood that you have around your shop. Customarily, two splines are used to prevent lateral movement of the piece to be added. The size of the splines depends upon the thickness of the door you are adding to, but splines ¼ by 1 inch should suffice for 2- or 3-inch doors. If your door is only about 1 inch thick, it lacks the heft to cut slots into—simply dowel on edges instead. If the strips you are adding to the door are less than 1 inch thick, do not bother to spline; just glue the strips well, countersinking a 1½-inch woodscrew every 18 inches or so. Conceal screw heads with plugs.

If you intend to spline all four edges of a door, lengthen the door first. Spline just one edge at a time.

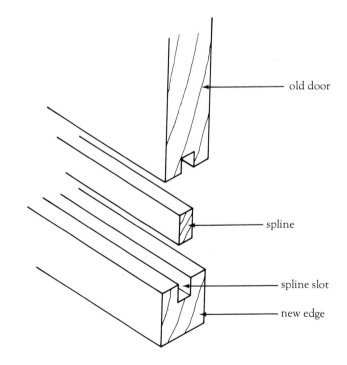

3-31. Cut slots for splined joints with a dado blade in a table saw or with a rabbeting bit in a router.

Measure the thickness of the door; a slot should be cut at approximately one-third of that measurement from each face of the door. The depth of the slot should be half the width of the spline. It should be wide enough to accommodate the thickness of the spline. Mark the dimensions of the slot on both the edge of the door and the piece to be added.

Before actually doing any routing, test-cut slots into scrap. Wear goggles when using the router. Use a slot-cutting bit for cutting slots, keeping the router running at top speed. If the machine is not heavy enough to do the job without straining, make several passes. Be sure to keep the router base flat so that all cuts will be parallel.

Cut slots to marked dimensions into the door edge. Test-fit a spline to make sure each slot is the correct depth; if slightly off, you can vary the depth of the corresponding slot in the piece to be added on. Then cut the corresponding slots in the piece to be added. Apply glue liberally to the slots, fit in the splines, and pull the edge-strips towards the door with bar clamps straddling the door. (If splines do not go easily into slots, tap them in gently with a mallet.) Because an edge so clamped will tend to pull up, keep the added-on strip flat by using a jig made from C-clamps and a piece of scrap, as shown in figures 3–33 and 3–34; or use wooden hand screws, as shown in figure 3–38. Wipe up excess glue.

Once the glue has dried, remove the clamps. Cut off the protruding ends of the splines. When all edges, including the sides, are done, sand down or plane (with a jack plane) the added-on edges until their faces are flush to the door. Because the thickness of the stock should have been within 1/32 inch to the thickness of the door, you should not have to plane down that much stock.

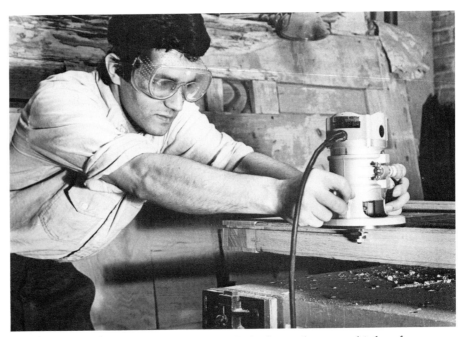

3-32. Cut the spline slots with a router, each slot being about one-third up from a door face. Be sure to hold the base of the router flat to a face of the door.

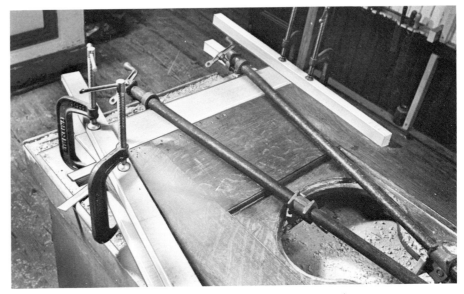

3-33. Long bar-clamps straddle the door and pull the new edge fast to it.

3-34. A close-up of the glued edge with its splines sticking out, before trimming. The strip that the C-clamps are holding down keeps the newly added edge from pulling up as it is being pulled tight with the bar clamps.

61

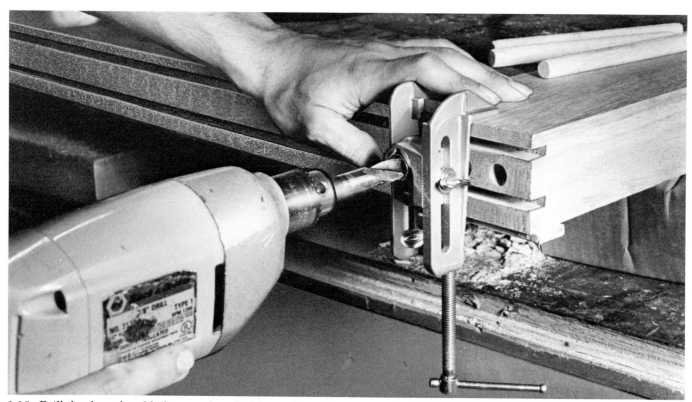

3-35. Drill the three dowel holes at each end of door sides with the aid of a doweling jig, to ensure perpendicular drilling.

Splining and Doweling

Adding wood to the sides of a door is essentially the same as adding it to the ends, but the edges along sides should also be doweled for additional strength. Three dowels should be added to the top and to the bottom of each side. In our case, hardwood dowels were 3/8 inch by 4 inches, spaced 3/8 inch apart and centered vertically. The size and placement of the dowels is determined by the thickness of the stock and, in this case, by the presence of splines. There should be at least 1/4 inch of wood between dowel holes and splines, and space between dowel holes should equal the diameter of the dowels. Keep in mind that dowels *and* splines are used only on a 2- or 3-inch-thick door; thinner doors cannot accommodate both operations.

Cut the two slots for the splines into the sides of the door, as described in the section above. Then locate the positions of the dowels. You must use a doweling jig to be sure that the holes drilled will be perpendicular to the door edge. If even one hole is misaligned, your efforts to dowel pieces together will fail. Once dowel holes are drilled into both ends of the door edge, locate holes in the edge-strip you intend to add. The easiest way to do this is to use center finders, little metal points the same diameter as the dowels. Insert the center finders into the holes drilled in the door. Hold the strip being added on against the edge of the door, rap the strip lightly—and the points will make impressions onto the face of the strip. Those point impressions are the centers of the holes you must drill into the edge-strip.

After routing spline slots, dry-fitting the splines for fit, and drilling dowel holes into the edge-strip, you are ready to join the new section to the edge of the door. Have a lot of clamps and a helper handy. Once glue starts to dry you must not tarry.

Dowels will go in most easily if they are fluted (have grooves cut into their sides so glue can pass) and if their ends are beveled slightly. Bevel dowel ends with a file.

3-36. The completed holes.

Work on the sides of the door first. Shoot glue into the holes and spread it evenly inside with broom-straws or thin slivers of wood. Rap the dowels in as far as they will go, but do not blunt the ends of the beveled dowels. If you do, rebevel them.

When the dowels are rapped in, they should all be perpendicular to the edge of the door. If any are not, allow the glue to dry and drill out the errant dowel; if you try to force a crooked dowel into place, it will simply snap. If the dowels are the same length, they should also be sticking out of the door an equal height. If any are too high, their ends can be cut off, but first measure (with a depth gauge) the matching holes drilled into the add-on strip. If a receiving hole is deep

enough, you need not bother to whittle down the dowel.

Next add glue to the spline slots in the door and to those in the edge-strip. Fit the splines into the edge-strip. Splines should fit tightly but should not need to be forced into place. Add glue to the dowel holes in the strip; spread that glue well.

Now comes a tricky part. With the aid of a helper, lift the strip that you are adding to the door. Carefully fit the holes drilled in that strip onto the dowels sticking out of the door—it will take some maneuvering. Using a bar clamp at either end of the door (with scrap between the jaws of the clamp and the finish wood, to prevent marring), pull each end of the strip in gradually and uniformly. Invariably, the

dowels will "shriek" as they rub against the holes, but keep your courage and continue tightening the clamps. As the edge-strip approaches the edge of the door, the splines will engage the slots in the door, as shown in figure 3–38. To aid this step and to keep the edge-strip from pulling up, use adjustable wooden clamps (hand screws) as shown. Using two bar clamps at each end—one above the door and one beneath—will also counteract the tendency of an edge to misalign.

The last half inch or so of pulling in the edge can be quite anxious, but if you have measured and drilled correctly, the dowels will fit despite their resistance. Turning clamps on both ends at the same rate is the key to success. When the added-on edge is snug against that

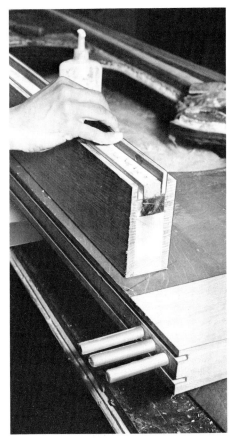

3-37. Tap dowels into holes in door sides. Next, spread glue in all spline slots and insert splines in the edge-strip.

3-38. As the new edge approaches the door, its splines engage.

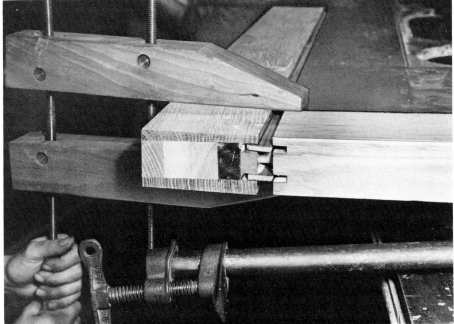

of the door, wipe up excess glue and take a breather.

FINISHING DOORS

Chapter 4, *Woodwork,* discusses wood finishes at length, so only the highlights are covered here.

Hand-stripping a door is the method least destructive to wood; methylene chloride (the active ingredient in Zip-Strip and the like) is the best chemical to use. (Apply it only with natural-bristle brushes; nylon and poly brushes will disintegrate.) Dip-stripping a door is not advisable because the liquid agents soak into the wood and cause it to swell and, as it dries, to crack. Detail can also be ruined in this manner.

If you strip your door in a lye bath, it must be neutralized by rinsing it with straight vinegar before any refinishing; otherwise, the lye will interfere with whatever paint or natural finish you use. Nonlye strippers should also be removed by rinsing well with water.

A dry, old door will benefit from a coating of one-third boiled linseed oil and two-thirds solvent such as turpentine or mineral spirits. Brush the mixture on and wipe off any excess. Allow the door to dry until there is absolutely no oily feeling; wait a month and you will surely be safe. Then lightly sand the wood. Apply a good grade of stain sealer or polyurethane, exterior grade if it is an outside door. You can use all-oil finishes, such as tung oil, in lieu of above applications, but such oils tend to darken wood and you cannot apply other finishes (such as polyurethane) over

3-39. A late-Victorian door, the size of which was increased by the methods depicted in the preceding sections. To further blend original and new wood, the craftsman added beading over the edge joints. When the door is stained and finished, the new work will be all but indistinguishable from the old.

Work by DiBartolomeo Woodworking; door from Architectural Antiques Exchange

them. Whatever you use, check the label of the product to learn the range of its uses.

When applying finishes to exterior doors, be scrupulous about sealing the ends of doors, especially the bottom rails, for they are prone to rot if not sealed adequately.

REUSING DOORS

Since most doors are reused simply as doors, let us consider how they ought to be hung. We will assume that the door has already been reconditioned as described in the preceding section. There are two procedures to consider: when a door frame already exists and the door need only be hung, and when the door frame must be assembled and hung as well. But first a few terms and concepts.

For those unfamiliar with framing carpentry, wood-frame walls are constructed primarily of 2 × 4 lumber, occasionally of 2 × 6s. The vertical members of a wood-frame wall are *studs*, bounded on top and bottom by *plates* (the bottom plate is sometimes called a *sole* plate or *shoe*). Where there are openings in walls, it is necessary to double up the lumber around, for greater support. Such *rough openings* include shortened studs, or *jack studs*, on each side, and a *header*, lumber running across the top of the opening, which may or may not be doubled.

Because of quirks in framing or irregularities in lumber itself, rough openings are rarely perfectly square—*never* would be closer to the truth. Therefore, it is necessary to fit the finished *door frame* to the rough opening with thin *shims*, tapered pieces between frame and opening; cedar shingles are the most common shims.

The door frame consists of several pieces: two side pieces, or *jambs*, and one across the top, a

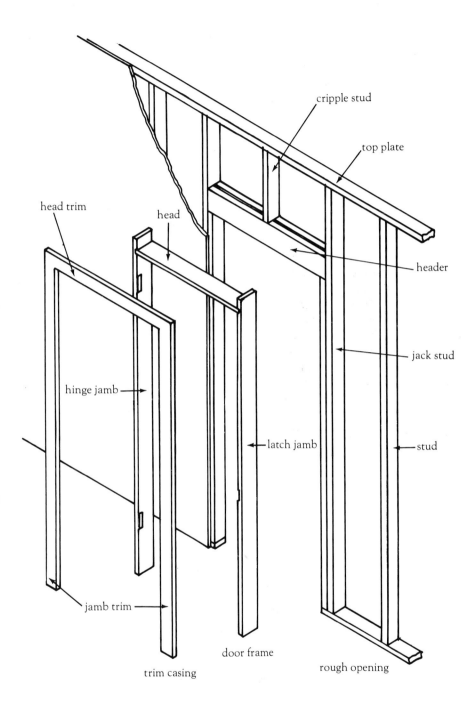

3-40. **Anatomy of a doorway.**

head (or frame head). The term "jamb" is sometimes used for all pieces of the frame, that is, "side jambs" and "head jamb," but this use is confusing; in the section that follows, "jamb" refers only to a side piece. The head of the frame is usually joined to each jamb with a rabbet or dado joint, in addition to nails and sometimes glue. The frame

65

is nailed, through the shims behind, to the rough opening.

Doors are hung with hinges off one of the frame jambs; the latch or lock catches are cut into the jamb on the other side. The parts of a frame-constructed door were defined earlier (fig. 3–1), but we will repeat them here. The vertical elements are *stiles*; the horizontal parts, *rails*; the panel inserts are, simply enough, *panels*. The door stile into which hinges are cut is called a *hinge stile*; the stile into which the latch or lock is set, the *latch stile*.

Finally, the gaps between the frame and the rough opening are covered with *trim*. The piece that runs across the top of the doorway is called *head trim*; the pieces on each side, *jamb trim*. The trim around a doorway is also referred to as *casing*; the terms "head casing" and "jamb casing" used accordingly. The last pieces of trim are the *door stops*, or *stop-pieces*, which fit around the inside of the door frame. As their names suggest, they keep a door from swinging too far into the frame.

WORKING WITH A FINISHED DOORWAY

If a doorway already has its frame and trim in place, it is referred to as "finished." Hanging a door to a finished doorway is relatively simple if you reconnoiter beforehand; it can be irritating if you do not.

Apply your carpenter's level to the jambs of the door frame to see if they are plumb and to the head to see if it is level. Then check the corners of the doorway with a framing square to see if the jambs meet the head in a right angle. Apply your level to the floor around the doorway as well—is there any slope on which the door might bind? Your primary concern in these investigations is that the hinge jamb be plumb, for the door will not operate correctly if its hinge stile is not plumb. If the hinge jamb is not plumb, you will have to vary the depth at which you set the two hinges. If the hinge jamb is plumb but the head or floor are not level, you may want to trim the top and bottom of the door to make the fit

exact. If the latch stile of a door must be cut down to fit, that operation is usually left until the door is hung and the edge of the latch jamb can be traced directly onto the latch stile.

Sizing the Door and the Hinges

After applying your level and square to the doorway, take accurate readings with your tape measure. There should be 1/16-inch clearance (1/8 inch is acceptable) on each side of the door, except the bottom, which should clear the floor by at least 1/8 inch (1/4 inch is acceptable), or 1/2 inch if you intend to lay carpet.

Hinges are sized according to the size of the door. The most commonly used hinges are *loose-pin butt-mortise hinges*, whose pins can be pulled, allowing you to pull hinges apart and work with each hinge leaf

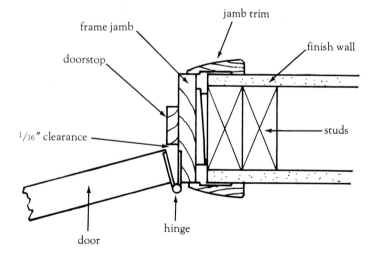

3-41. Top view of door casing in cross section.

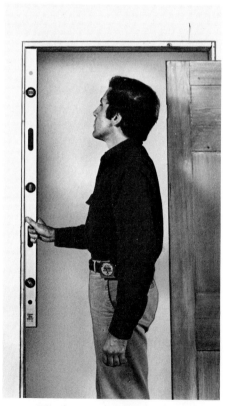

3-42. The first step in hanging any door is to check the doorway to see if it is plumb; the longer the level, the more accurate the reading.

separately. Because one leaf of a hinge is mortised into the door stile and the other into the frame jamb, being able to work with each leaf separately greatly facilitates hanging the door.

Most exterior doors require three hinges; most interior doors, two. When you use two hinges, the top of the top hinge is set 7 inches from the top of the door; the bottom of the bottom hinge, 11 inches from the bottom of the door. If you use three hinges, the top and bottom hinges are spaced as above and the middle hinge is placed equidistant between them.

Figure 3–43 provides recommended hinge sizes.

Setting the Door

With the door cut to size, temporarily wedge it in the door frame so that you can mark hinge locations on to the door and the frame at the same time. If there are already hinge positions cut into the frame, you can probably use those; otherwise, they should be filled in.

Stand the door in the doorway. If there are door stops around the inside of the frame, let the door rest against them; if there are no stops, tack on some temporary 1 × 2 strips. Shim the door tight so that the hinge stile of the door is flush against the hinge jamb of the frame. Use at least three shims: one beneath the door, one centered between the frame head and the top of the door, and one midway along the latch jamb and latch stile. The shims at top and bottom should represent the final position of the door, with ⅟₁₆-inch clearance from the frame head and ½ inch (or whatever you choose) between the bottom of the door and the floor.

The door so affixed, measure down 7 inches from the top of the door, up 11 inches from the bottom of the door, and if setting an exterior door, to the point equidistant between these top and bottom mea-

surements, to locate hinges. Use a pencil or a scribing knife to mark positions on door and frame at the same time. Be very careful that you mark exactly the same locations on each, or hinge leaves will not match.

Then pull out the shims, set the door to one side, and, with a hinge leaf placed between the marks you

scribed, trace around the leaf. The edge of each leaf must be perfectly parallel to the edge of the door if it is to work properly. Note, however, that hinge leaves are *set back* at least ⅛ inch (¼ inch is more common) from the edge of the door and from the edge of the frame to prevent the inside edge of the door from binding against the door stop when shut.

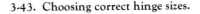

Door		Hinge size
Width	Thickness	
up to 32 in.	1⅛–1⅜ in.	3 ½ in.
32–37 in.	1⅛–1⅜ in.	4 in.
up to 32 in.	1⅜–1⅞ in.	4½ in.
32–37 in.	1⅜–1⅞ in.	5 in.
37–43 in.	1⅜–1⅞ in.	5 in. *extra heavy*
up to 43 in.	greater than 1⅞ in.	5 in. *extra heavy*
greater than 43 in.	greater than 1⅞ in.	6 in. *extra heavy*

3-43. Choosing correct hinge sizes.

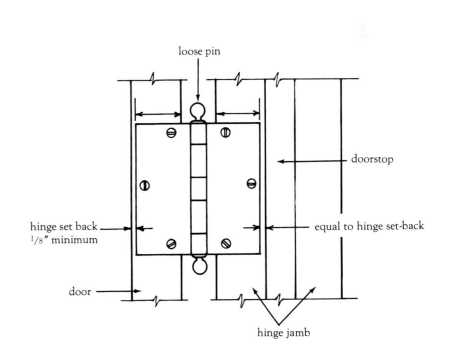

3-44. Hinge leaves are set back slightly from the edge of a door so that it shuts without binding.

Mortising the Hinges

The act of cutting hinges into the door frame or door is called *mortising the hinges*, or *letting-in the hinges*. The area of wood that you cut out is called the *mortise* or the *gain*. In most cases the hinge leaves, when let in, should be flush with the surrounding wood. The only exception to this rule is when hanging a door to an out-of-plumb frame. Then, one leaf should be left a little higher, so that the door will lean away slightly.

The easiest way to mortise out the gains is to use a *butt gauge*, a sort of flat, three-sided chisel that outlines the hinge leaf in one motion; you then chisel out the area within the outline to the depth of the leaf thickness. A more common way to do the job is simply with a straight chisel and a mallet, as shown in figures 3–45 to 3–48.

Trace and score inside the penciled outline of the hinge leaf with a

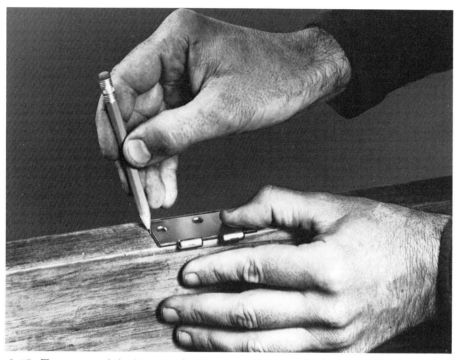

3-45. Trace around the hinge leaf with a very sharp pencil or a scribing knife.

3-46. With a straight chisel, trace around the outline of the leaf; then cut a series of parallel, shallow cuts, to promote a mortise of even depth.

3-47. Keeping the beveled face of the chisel blade down, pare out the hinge gain.

3-48. To make sure that the hinge gain is the perfect depth, keep fitting the hinge leaf; when the leaf is flush to the edge of the door, screw it down.

straight chisel, its bevel facing toward the area to be cut. Be especially careful when the chisel blade is parallel to the wood grain as splits are a danger. Using shallow, parallel cuts, carefully pare away the wood within the outline, checking periodically with the hinge leaf to test its fit. Be sure not to seat the hinge too deep or the door will not shut properly and in time the hinges will pull free.

Use the same procedure to cut the gains into the door frame. This job is more awkward, however, especially the bottom hinge leaf, roughly a foot above the floor. Take your time and be especially careful when paring out within outlines.

Once your chiseling is done, place the hinge leaves in their mortises and mark the centers of the hinge screws with a nail point or an awl. Screw the hinges in firmly, but use only one screw per leaf at this point. Lift the door and stand it in the frame to see how the hinge leaves on the door mesh with those on the frame.

Note: There should be ¹⁄₁₆-inch gaps on each side and over the top of the door. If the gap along the hinge side is too great (and that along the latch side is too small), set the hinges slightly deeper. If the gap on the hinge side is too small, the hinges are too deep; unscrew screws and build the mortise up with pieces of sandpaper beneath each hinge leaf.

If you are pleased with the way the door fits, pull the hinge pins and screw in all the remaining screws. Reset the door, open and shut it repeatedly. If the clearances around the door seem right but the door sticks somewhat on the latch side, remove the door and plane a 2- or 3-degree bevel into the latch stile of the door. For this task use a jack plane, whose long base ensures a uniformly flat surface, rather than a block plane, which, with its small base, responds to "local" bumps and valleys along the edge of a door.

Dealing with a Warped Frame

When surveying the door frame, you may have noticed a warp: the edge was not a flat plane. A door hung in such a frame will show an irregular edge when shut. There is no easy solution to this problem. You could make the frame flat by prying it off, building it up beneath with shims, and artfully reattaching the trim—but it is not worth the trouble and the corners of the casing will probably tattle. Perhaps the easiest cure is to pull up and reset the door stops so that the entire door edge will at least fall within the frame, not stick out beyond it. Doorstops are usually held in place by only a few finish nails. Use a putty knife to pry up the stops; reattach with 4d finish nails.

Adding Doorstops and Metal Tension Strips

If your door frame has no doorstops, they can be easily fashioned from ½- by 1½-inch clear pine. Shut the door so that it is flush with the edge of the frame; then tack on the stops from the other side, making them flush to the back face of the door. Attach stops with 4d finish nails placed every 12 inches or so. For best-looking results, miter the corners of the stops. You only tack the stops until you have set the other door hardware, because you may later have to reset the stop-pieces.

Should you wish to add metal tension strips to improve the weathertightness of an exterior door, now is the time to do so. Tack one piece of folded metal strip to each of the three sides of a door frame, just outside the stop-pieces. Then tack matching pieces of metal to the perimeter of the door itself. When the door closes, the pieces of metal compress, stopping air infiltration.

WORKING WITH AN UNFINISHED DOORWAY

An unfinished doorway, as described earlier, is also called a rough opening. The finish surfaces of the walls (Sheetrock, plaster, whatever) will be installed, but the 2 × 4 rough framing around the opening will be visible. Your job, then, is to install a door frame, hang the door to it, and apply the finish trim.

There are basically two ways to hang a door after making the frame: You can install the frame, shim the door in the frame temporarily, mark hinges, and cut in hinges. Or you can "hang" the door onto the frame jamb *before* installing the frame. The first method is essentially that described in the previous section on finished doorways; a good method, except that you must work at awkward angles cutting hinges once the frame is in place. The second method is favored by many good carpenters because all hinges can be mortised on the workbench, and the fit of frame to door is better. We will consider this second method in the section that follows. (If you elect to make the frame and install it before hanging the door, the section immediately below on making the door frame has the specifics; skip the section on mortising hinges.)

Making the Door Frame

Door frames, as noted above, consist of two jambs (sides) and a head (top), with a stop-piece usually nailed on later. Most often, the head is dado-joined or rabbeted to the two side pieces and afterwards bolstered with nails through the back of the jambs; in some constructions, glue is also used. Frame stock is usually 1 inch thick (actual size, ¾ inch).

The frame stock should be slightly wider than the surrounding walls—including finish surfaces—are thick. For 2 × 4 walls covered with ½-inch Sheetrock, therefore, rip

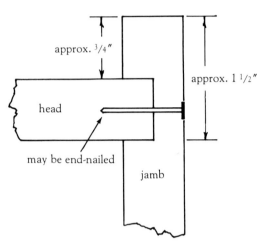

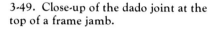

3-49. Close-up of the dado joint at the top of a frame jamb.

frames out of 1 × 6 pine stock. To allow for irregularities, leave an extra ⅛ inch on the width of the frame, which will allow the trim that follows to straddle any imperfections in the finish wall. In any event the extra ⅛ inch can always be planed down later.

The width and height of the frame to be assembled depend largely upon the dimensions of the door. The inside width of the frame should be the width of the door plus ³⁄₁₆ inch—¹⁄₁₆-inch clearance on both sides of the door and an extra ¹⁄₁₆ inch for error. The frame head is dadoed into the jambs to a depth of ⅜ inch on both sides. The length of the head stock therefore equals the width of the door *plus* ¾ inch (dados) *plus* ³⁄₁₆ inch (clearance).

The height of the frame jambs, which rest on top of the finish floor, equals: the height of the door *plus* clearances above (¹⁄₁₆ inch) and below (usually ⅛ inch, see p. 66) *plus* another 1½ inches to accommodate the dado joint (see fig. 3-49). The rough opening in the wall is usually 2½ inches higher and wider than the door, providing enough room to fit the door and the frame, as well as a little extra space that is shimmed up for a tight fit.

All of these measurements are

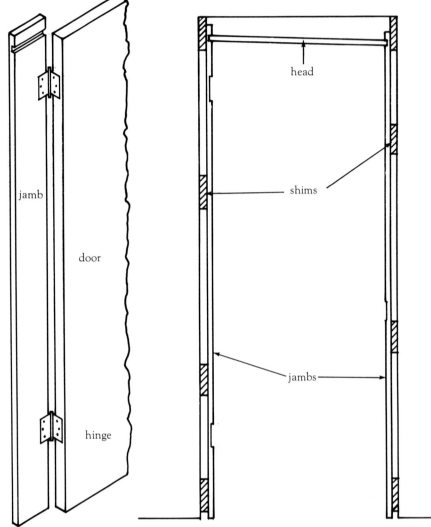

3-50. By hanging a door to a frame jamb before attaching that frame to its rough opening, you can vary the position of the frame. Although the head piece is usually level, it may be skewed slightly to accommodate an eccentric door.

straightforward and easy to calculate, but they become slightly complicated if yours is an old house and the floors slope. In that event one of the jambs must be a trifle longer. To establish an inside height for the door frame, measure up from the *high side* of the floor and add whatever clearance beneath. By measuring up from the high side, you ensure that the door will not stick.

Constructing the frame is not difficult. All the cuts are square across the face of the stock. The dado slots in the jambs are most

easily done with a router or a table saw. If you use a router, use a double-fluted straight bit to cut a ¾-by ¾-inch slot into the jambs. If you use a table saw, a combination of dado blades will give the exact width of cuts or a regular blade making several passes will do the trick. Whatever method you use, test all cuts beforehand; improper depth of cut will affect the width of the assembled frame.

Before assembling the pieces of the frame, however, first "hang" the door to the hinge jamb, as described below.

Mortising Hinges

Lay the door on your worktable and place the hinge jamb, dado joint up, next to the hinge stile of the door. Allowing 1/16-inch clearance between the top of the door and the underside of the head (when it is assembled), measure down 7 inches from the top of the door to locate the top of the jamb and the face of the door. Mark the bottom hinge so that the bottom of the hinge is 11 inches from the bottom of the door plus a clearance of, usually, 1/8 inch (see page 66). If hanging an exterior door, mark the position of the third hinge equidistant from the top and bottom hinges.

3-51. Mark the hinge positions on the inside of the jamb and the face of the door; the marks on the door face will be transferred to the edge of the door when the hinges are to be mortised in. Note the dado slot in the top of the jamb.

It does not matter whether you trace and cut hinge leaves into the jamb or into the door first. In this case we set the door on edge, extended the hinge marks to the edge of the door, and mortised those first. Then we cut hinge gains into the frame jamb, as described earlier.

Test the success of your hinge-fitting by fitting jamb to door and inserting hinge pins. The door should not bind. This is a straightforward operation because all work is done on a tabletop, at a comfortable working height. Now pull the hinge pins, thus separating jamb and door, so that you can hang the frame in the rough opening.

Hanging the Frame

First assemble the frame by end-nailing the head through the back of each jamb; use three 6d common nails on each side. Galvanized nails hold better but are not critical. If you blunt nail points by hammering them slightly, you will minimize the chance of splitting the jambs made thin by the dado slots cut into them. Glue is not imperative, but if you do use it, give it time to dry thoroughly.

Before attaching the frame to the rough opening, refresh your memory of that opening by applying your level. The frame must be plumb—especially the hinge jamb—if the door is to hang correctly. To temporarily hold the frame in place within the rough opening, slide shims beneath the bottom of each jamb and behind the top of each jamb about where the head joins.

Secure the hinge jamb first. Without making the jamb bow, gently insert pairs of shims along the length of each hinge jamb. Use a pair of shims at each point, with their tapers reversed, to ensure that the jamb lies flat. It is customary to use five pairs of shims behind each jamb, more or less equally spaced, making sure to place a pair of shims behind each hinge. On the latch jamb, shim behind the latch strike-plate. Keep sighting for plumb with your level; when the hinge jamb is plumb from top to bottom, tack-nail it, with 8d finish nails, through each pair of shims and into the rough opening behind.

With one side of the frame attached, lay a straightedge across the opening and adjust the edge of the latch jamb so it is flush to the surface of the finish wall. Temporarily place a few shims behind the latch jamb, but only lightly tack them into place.

3-52. To temporarily lodge the frame in the rough opening, slide shims beneath the bottom of each jamb and behind the top of each jamb.

3-53. Make the frame jamb plumb by sliding pairs of tapered shims (usually cedar shingles) between the jamb and the stud behind. Adjust the shims and check with your level until the jamb is perfectly plumb.

3-54. The edge of the door frame should be more or less flush to the wall surfaces; check this with a straight board.

Now, although the latch jamb is still not secured, reattach the door by inserting the hinge pins. Swing the door and see if it moves smoothly. If it does not, the hinge jamb is only tack-nailed; readjust it. If all is well, you can now manipulate the still unsecured latch jamb so that it closely fits the hanging door. For the greatest ease in any hanging, the door should have been squared beforehand, but the beauty of this method is that the frame can be adjusted to minor discrepancies.

To find the final position for the latch jamb, swing the door shut and—with the aid of a helper—tack-nail temporary stops to the inside of the jamb frame. To establish the 1/16-inch clearance, push small shims between the edge of the door and the latch jamb; 4d nails are useful as spacers here because their shanks are 1/16-inch diameter. With those small shims in place, adjust the larger shims between the latch jamb and the rough opening. From behind the door, tack those larger shims into place.

Swing open (or remove) the door so that you can see if the latch jamb is plumb. If you squared the door beforehand, the jamb should be plumb. If the jamb is not plumb but fits the edge of the door closely (and is visually pleasing), tack it up. Shut the door once more to see if the clearances are uniform all around. If so, drive nails all the way in, using a nail set. (There are no shims over the frame head, for if there were and the header sagged from loads above, those shims would carry the load downward, causing the frame head to bind the top of the door.)

With the frame secured and the door hung, you are now ready to install other door hardware, such as handles and locks, and then trim.

3-55. A door with squared corners is the easiest to hang, but because only one side of the frame is secured so far, you can adjust the door frame slightly to accommodate oddities of a door.

3-56. To establish the final position of the other jamb, use two sets of shims: little ones to establish the 1/16-in. clearance between door edge and frame, and large shims to position the frame within the rough opening.

These nicely articulated, early-Victorian (c. 1860) mahogany pieces were probably originally cabinet doors, perhaps on a chifforobe. Their size—each is 70 in. high × 32 in. wide—and the joinery visible at corners suggest that they are not regular doors that were cut down. Simply hinged together, they make a pleasant room screen.

Gargoyles, Ltd.

Facing page: One of the more interesting rooms in Allen Brown's castle (fig. 1-1) features a 30-ft.-long wall paneled in chestnut. In the course of Mr. Brown's search for materials, he uncovered thirteen doors of the stuff, most of which were covered with paint. Once stripped, the lot yielded seven doors in good shape and six five-panel doors that were too far gone to be reused as doors; those he had milled down into 5/8-in. boards.

Chestnut has been an extinct tree since the turn of the century, and is incredibly valuable, so Mr. Brown thought long about his cache of wood and what uses he would make of it. Eventually he decided to alternate the seven intact doors with the milled-down lumber. After applying Sheetrock to his study wall, he simply chalklined its surface so that the doors would be leveled and of a same height, and nailed the doors up, into studs, with 16d finish nails.

Because his seven sound doors had a cumulative width of less than 20 ft., he spaced them about 22 in. apart and filled in the spaces between with the milled-down stock. To bring that stock up to the thickness of the doors, he first nailed up a horizontal undergrid of furring strips and then nailed the stock to that. To echo the beveled panels of the doors, he ripped 45-degree bevels into the 5/8-in. stock. Although the operation sounds difficult, its execution was simple: Mr. Brown left stock edges ragged and old lock holes alone, simply covering all edges with more of the milled-down wood. "The nice thing about working with wormy chestnut," he noted, "is that you can knock a lot of holes into it and never notice." When he completes the wall, he will seal it with a clear, natural finish.

Allen Brown

Used in a restrained manner, panel doors can be cut down to enhance other architectural elements. After locating a radiator on the floor of a bay, the designer boxed in the area with a window seat, the top of which was laminated maple, with panels made from cut-down doors.

R. Lear Design

Facing page: This old-looking door is actually a new one fashioned from old wood, its corners reinforced by through bolts.

Mike Greenberg

Legs missing from old tub often cause a problem, here solved by boxing in the tub, once again with cut-down panel doors. The tub is first supported by a 2 × 2 frame, the paneling being attached to that frame with 8d finish nails.

R. Lear Design

These wonderfully worked late-eigh-
teenth-century doors came from a burned
monastary near Mexico.
John Midyette III

This seventeenth-century mesquite door is effectively set into an adobe arch; the "goat fencing" is fashioned from cedar saplings.

John Midyette III

Woodwork

Safety Tips

- Before you cut or drill into attached woodwork, test with a voltage tester to make sure electricity has been turned off. For that matter, you should use the voltage tester before any ambitious prying off of woodwork, because a pry bar could sever a cable routed behind woodwork.
- Wear goggles when chiseling or using power tools.
- Remove nails from trim as soon as it has been removed. The volume of removed trim quickly adds up, reducing working space and making footing unsure.
- Support elaborate or heavy pieces of woodwork before you disassemble or remove them.
- When working over your head for extended periods, rent scaffolding; your work will be safer and more productive.
- When stripping woodwork:
  read all labels before starting
  goggles, gloves, and long-sleeved clothing are a must
  provide adequate ventilation
  no smoking around chemicals
  brush on chemicals away from yourself to avoid splashing them on you
  dispose of chemicals, rags, and waste paper so they are not fire hazards
  do not combine chemicals unless the manufacturer specifically advises you to do so

Carved pine panel, twentieth-century Southwestern.

John Midyette III

Tools

Few special tools are required for removing pieces. Restoring pieces is another matter, however—the more extensive your repairs, the better equipped your shop must be.

- Goggles, gloves, and a hard hat are imperative to large demolition tasks. A voltage tester will assure that you will not get shocked.
- A reciprocating saw with an offset attachment will allow you to fit a metal-cutting blade behind attached trim and sever the nails holding the piece(s) up.
- A truck spring, ground flat on one end and sharp on the other, is a handy homemade prying device. Wear goggles when striking it with a hammer, however.
- Several measuring and layout tools are worth noting: a chalkline for marking a straight line on a broad expanse; an adjustable bevel for noting angles exactly; marking gauges for scribing lines parallel to a board edge.
- For cutting woodwork angles exactly, a miter box and miter saw work well but nothing tops a miter trimmer, which chops a perfect cut, much as a paper cutter does.
- Shave hooks are scraping tools with contoured heads and replaceable blades, suitable for all but the most ornate moldings.

Wood is alive. Though cut down and sawed up into uniform sizes, its grain has wildness and dynamism and, in its hues, life. Woodworking, dealing with such unique patterns and colors, is an exacting and complex craft. Although drawn to the beauty of wood, however, salvagers are less concerned with how woodwork is fabricated than how those pieces can be removed intact and reused creatively. Apart from the section on refinishing, most of the technical information in this chapter shows details of attachment.

The terms trim, molding, and casing are used more or less interchangeably throughout this chapter; it will be helpful to discriminate among them. *Trim* is the best word for general use; *molding*, also a general term, implies trim that is shaped or molded; *casing* refers to trim assemblies around doors and windows. *Head casing* runs over the top of a door or window; *side casing*, or *jamb casing* (or just *jambs*), indicates trim along sides.

ASSESSMENT

Few hard and fast rules apply to assessing and buying a piece. If you can remove it without destroying it—and you can afford it—buy it. Because woodwork is usually nailed or screwed down, there are no moving parts that wear out and little chance that there has been hard wear. Do pieces complement or contrast with a decor you have in mind? Take photos of the rooms you are decorating when you visit salvage emporiums.

If woodwork has been bundled, untie it and look closely. Do all pieces in the bundle match? Are there parts missing? Simple geometric shapes that have broken off may be easily replaced, but parts of a complex molding may be tough to find. If wood is painted, examine its back side: pine, spruce, fir, and other softwoods may not be worth the trouble to strip and refinish. If you can gouge the wood with your thumb, the piece is probably a nondescript softwood. By gently shaving up a small section of paint with a penknife, you can determine how many layers of paint it has and hence how arduous stripping will be.

If the woodwork has a natural finish, are all parts of the same hue? It is not uncommon for some sections of paneling to be bleached by the sun, making them fainter than those located, say, behind a door.

Is the woodwork the right size for your intended use? Door, window, and room trim generally can be cut down if they are slightly oversized. Particularly wide trim cannot be shortened too much, however, or it will look squat and ill proportioned. Slightly short trim can be lengthened by bevel-splicing on additional trim of the same stock, but assume that you would have to refinish the entire length of trim to disguise the seam. Mantel size is particularly important: many building codes state that the sides of a wooden mantel may not be closer than 8 inches to the fireplace opening, nor mantel tops closer than 12 inches.

Cabinets and stand-up pantry shelves require careful measurement, although they can be built up with plinths beneath, with molding where cabinet sections join or abut the ceiling. While taking measurements, apply your framing square to both the room and the cabinets to see if both are square; older units are often built in place, unsquare. Again, accommodating the units to your rooms may not be a problem, but the more oddities to accommodate, the more time-consuming and expensive the job.

The edges and ends of woodwork are particularly telling: they are often the most worn areas and the most easily damaged during removal. Prod the back side of any damaged area with a penknife to see if it is sound enough to hold a nail; otherwise, subtract that area from total usable length.

REMOVING WOODWORK

Contracting to remove trim yourself is risky business, because once you have paid for the pleasure, any trim that you break is your own loss. Using the correct tools and the methods described here will minimize breakage, but a certain amount is all but inevitable. Moreover, taking out paneling, trim, and the like is time-consuming, one of the reasons why many salvage pros bid on only those parts that are easily removed, such as doors and windows. Your woodwork may also be stolen. Often unsecured, buildings being dismantled are prey to vandals and thieves; if you cannot get your woodwork out within a day or two, do not buy it. Furthermore, if the place is crawling with other salvagers, your pieces may be damaged by other contractors as they carry out articles. Finally, you may get hurt in such a roily atmosphere; at the very least, get a tetanus shot.

When is it worth your while to remove woodwork? First of all, when the price is so low that you cannot pass it by. Second, when you get some assurance that you can take time to do the job right. If the house is in a safe neighborhood or you can remove pieces without hassling with other contractors, your task will be easier. Third, and perhaps most important, when the woodwork is relatively easy to remove.

Door and window trim *should* be attached by 6d or 8d finishing or casing nails, spaced in pairs every foot or so. Larger nails are unnecessary and, in fact, many carpenters use 4d and 6d nails. Overnailing—using too many nails or nails that are too large—is the sign of an inept carpenter. If the piece has any common nails (whose heads are large and cannot be sunk), beware: overnailed woodwork yields about double the wastage and may take a third more time to remove.

Try to pry up one jamb of door trim or a cap rail (top rail) of wainscoting to see how thick the wood is and how it is attached. Most building auctioneers will not let you test-pry, but there is no harm in asking. In general, the thicker the wood, the greater its worth and ease in removal. Finally, if your salvage agreement allows you to gut finish surfaces to remove woodwork (see fig. 4–6), your efforts will be much more productive. Should you gain the contract to remove the wood, be sure to *shut off electricity* to affected areas *before you begin* (see accompanying box on using a voltage tester).

Here follow general tips about removing architectural woodwork; additional specifics of attachment and tips about removal may be found in the following section on reinstallation specifics.

Architectural woodwork is usually attached with nails to the studs it traverses. Where woodwork runs horizontally, it crosses a great many studs; when it runs vertically, such as door-jamb trim, it is nailed into the rough opening around that doorway. Woodwork is also nailed into the edges of door or window frames; in the case of crown molding, to joists above; or, on occasion, to masonry materials behind. But whatever the material behind, the salvager's job is to remove those nails or screws with as little damage to the architectural woodwork as possible.

Conceptually, removal is not difficult, but in fact, the salvager pits his or her wits against the original carpenter, whose job it was to secure the pieces well and to disguise those attachments so that they would be invisible. Trim, after all, is designed to conceal the seams of a building. The original carpenter may have also used smaller pieces of trim or even plaster to blend materials, making detection even more difficult.

The basic tools for demolition are few but important. A *flat bar* or *utility bar* is the most versatile tool, at once a nail-puller, pry bar, crude chisel, and, when need be, a hammer. A stout *knife* is indispensible for cutting through paint and establishing the edge of trim. *Putty knives* or *joint knives* enable you to pry up the edges of trim gradually so that you can drive *shims*, tapering pieces of shingle, between trim and wall. An automotive *leaf spring* ground down on one end is an invaluable homemade tool for gently popping up woodwork. *Cat's paws, wrecking bars, hammers, screwdrivers,* and the like should be in any basic tool collection. A *reciprocating saw* with a metal-cutting blade (preferably with an offset attachment) is far more effective than a *hacksaw* when cutting nails in tight spaces.

Safety is, as always, of primary importance. Get a tetanus shot before starting. Determine whose insurance is covering you. It may be wise to add a temporary "contractor's risk" insurance to your own personal coverage. Wear goggles, gloves, a hard hat, heavy boots, and a respirator mask on the job.

Organize your work site. Sweep debris aside as it accumulates. One salvager I met pulls up a floor board along a far wall and sweeps plaster down into the basement of the house being demolished. At the end of each day, clean up and transport your woodwork to a safe place.

Very important: As you lower each piece of trim, pull out nails immediately. This task can easily be done by an inexperienced helper but is imperative to your safety. If you must jump down from a ladder in a hurry, you want no boards with nails sticking out. This rule has *no* exceptions: remove nails immediately!

You must have safe footing at all times. Rent scaffolding if necessary; it will save a lot of time if you are removing crown molding or ceiling medallions. Stout planks laid across sawhorses will work if your ceilings are 10 feet or less; boards should overhang horses by at least 1 foot.

Always disconnect electricity to affected areas and check all outlets and switches with a voltage tester *before* proceeding.

Because the crucial part of removal is prying up the first half inch or so of a section, take your time. Score along the edge of trim with a penknife to break the paint seal. Prod gently into the finish wall surface so that you know exactly where the wall ends and the trim begins; that is, figure out where you can rap in shims and wedges. Start prying at one end of the trim, using a hammer to drive a putty knife behind the trim; then slip another knife behind that. If you may not damage finish surfaces, slide scraps between any tools and those surfaces.

By driving both knives in, almost up to their handles, you

Using a Voltage Tester

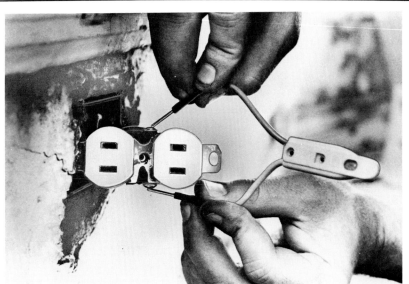

4-2. This test should tell you if a receptacle is "live." It sometimes happens, however, that a receptacle is defective and does not transmit current. To be doubly sure, therefore, unscrew the machine screws holding the receptable to its work box and—being careful not to touch the sides of the receptable—pull the receptacle out of the box. Touch your tester to screws on both sides of the receptacle.

4-1. Before cutting into any finish surface, turn off electrical current to the affected areas. Then test the outlets nearby with a voltage tester. Being careful not to touch the bare-wire prongs of the voltage tester, insert those prongs into the receptacle. If the tester lights, the outlet is still live—*do not* proceed until you have isolated the circuit and cut off power.

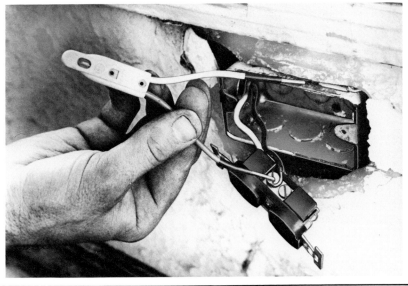

4-3. Finally, with the receptacle still pulled out of the box, touch the prongs of the voltage tester to the side screws and to the metal box itself. If your tester is operable and does not light during any of the above steps, the receptacle is indeed "dead" and you may handle it without danger.

create a gap behind the trim; tap very slender shims into that gap. When the shims are driven in, the knives will fall out; reinsert them further along the trim, gradually working up the trim with shims along the entire length before trying to pry up further with a utility bar. With the entire length of the piece elevated a half inch or so, you will be able to see the nails holding the piece. Using the utility bar, pry up trim as near to nailing points as possible.

What will happen to the finish surfaces around the woodwork? Scraps slid between tools and finish surfaces will protect those you may not damage; doing this, however, will make the operation somewhat tedious. If you may demolish the walls around the woodwork, the job will go much more quickly, for you do not have to grope around finding the trim edge. Simply break plaster around the perimeter of the piece and then hammer your utility bar behind the trim. Or insert the claws of a hammer after the trim is partially raised. If a wall has been replastered several times since the trim was put up—not uncommon in old houses—breaking up the plaster may be the *only* way to remove trim without breaking it.

If you can, get underneath or behind woodwork such as flooring or paneling. Then you can clearly see what sections are nailed into and how to safely exert more leverage.

As you work, listen and look. Trim can always crack at the last minute because of nails you do not notice or flaws in the wood itself. If a piece of wood squeals unduly, it is telling you something.

Fragile trim is best pried up with the method just described—carefully wedging along the length, prying up little by little. If trim is sturdy, however, pry up a half inch or so at a given spot and then, with a flat bar covering the trim to cushion the blow, whack it back down. Leave the nail head sticking up; it can be easily pulled. Either method is good, but choose the one that raises nails most easily without destroying trim.

Document the trim so you will remember where all parts came from. Take pictures of the room overall and close-ups of pertinent details; at the very least, take notes on graph paper. As you pull each piece down, staple or tack embossed plastic tape to the back side of the piece. (Such tape has adhesive on the back, but that will not adhere to dusty wood; tack it instead.) Number pieces E_1, E_2, E_3, and so on.

To minimize loss and confusion—especially important with complex molding—take off sections of molding in the largest pieces possible. A crown molding, for example, may consist of three or four separate elements; try to pry up the large nails holding the entire assembly to the ceiling line, if possible. Of course, the more complex a trim assembly, the heavier it will be; get help lowering it.

4-4. To pry up trim along its entire length, begin by inserting a wood chisel or stiff-bladed putty knife behind the trim.

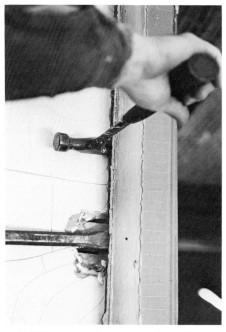

4-6. Where you do not care about finish surfaces or the trim is particularly delicate, break through the plaster (or drywall) to insert tools behind the trim more easily.

4-5. With the trim raised slightly by the chisel, insert a flat bar or a hammer claw. Work up and down the entire length of the trim piece.

4-7. Another way to remove a piece is to pry it up only slightly and then, using a flat bar to cushion the blow, knock the piece back down—thus leaving the nail head sticking up.

STRIPPING AND REFINISHING WOODWORK

Wood finishing fills several volumes; here follows an overview of the processes and materials commonly used. The key to successful wood finishing is stripping and sanding off old finishes and wiping away residue with a tack rag before applying new finish. Keep in mind that a new finish will highlight scratches and the like, so be careful to sand only with the grain, especially during final stages. (The only exception to this rule is when you want to remove a lot of wood, such as when refinishing floors.) Most finishes will adhere better if you sand lightly between coats and wipe with a tack rag, but follow manufacturer's instructions on the label.

Experiment with strippers before committing yourself. It may be that the old finish can be removed with a common solvent such as turpentine, which is considerably cheaper than, say, methylene chloride. Test different strippers on inconspicuous spots and choose the least expensive stripper that you find effective.

STRIPPING WOOD

Stripping wood is not difficult to master, but it takes patience and persistence to do it right. Your choice, basically, is to use chemicals or to apply heat; in either case treat the tool or material carefully because the risk of fire is real.

When working with chemicals, apply them generously, touching up areas that dry before they are scraped; allow fifteen to twenty minutes for the chemical to work. If, as you work, wood becomes fibrous and soft, use less stripper and scrape it off sooner. Rinse wood according to manufacturer's instructions before continuing. If you are using a

4-8. Dentists' tools are well suited to stripping finely detailed woodwork.

heat gun—do not use heat guns *and* chemicals unless the solvent manufacturer says it is safe—keep the gun moving so that you do not char the wood.

Choose a tool appropriate to the contour of the wood. If you are cleaning large, flat areas, a stiff-bladed *floor scraper* or *joint knife* will do the trick; cabinet scrapers also work. If, on the other hand, the woodwork is molded (shaped), the scraper blade should be shaped to fit: commercially available *shave hooks* will fit the shapes of most trim. If you have many board feet of a certain trim pattern to clean, it may be worthwhile to record that pattern with a *profile gauge*; have a metal worker fabricate scrapers with that contour from 18-gauge sheet steel. If your woodwork is really detailed, nothing beats *dentists' tools* for close work, but they will be expensive; try to cadge a used set.

Rubber gloves and goggles are indispensable tools. Because some strippers will rot rubber, look for cloth-covered rubber gloves; they are not so pliable as rubber gloves,

but they will last longer. Steel wool, sponges, and buckets are imperative for cleanup.

Natural-bristle brushes are the most versatile for applying stripper; synthetic fibers such as nylon may dissolve. Again, the label of the chemical should advise you.

Immersion Stripping

Having someone strip your woodwork in a tank of solvent will save you a lot of work, but results vary widely according to the expertise of the stripper and the chemicals used. Ask for references of previous work and look at pieces dipped. The primary objection to this method is that wood becomes saturated and may crack and split when dry; large expanses of wood (such as paneling or doors) are particularly susceptible to splitting.

Rinse all pieces well after stripping, allowing them to dry thoroughly before refinishing. If your stripper has a lye-based solvent, rinse wood with full-strength vinegar before proceeding. Vinegar

4-9. Immersion stripping.

Allen Brown

will neutralize any residual lye, which will streak the wood and may cause the new finish to blister.

Stripping at Home

Read the labels of the chemicals you will be using; note especially medical advice. Should misfortune strike, you may be panic-stricken or otherwise unable to take the time to read a label. Know what to do in advance; have the numbers of fire departments and poison information centers close at hand. Open windows and spread newspapers or tarps. If you have sawhorses, use them; stripping from a standing position is much easier than crouching to do the job. After donning gloves and goggles, apply stripper generously to the wood. Brush in one direction—away from yourself—only. After giving the stripper fifteen to twenty minutes to work,

4-10. Apply stripper to the object to be stripped, brushing away from yourself.

4-11. After allowing time for the chemical to work, scrape up dissolved finish.

4-12. Clean tools often.

scrape the sludge that results; wipe the tool blade often, on paper towels. Spots or gouges that retain paint or finish should be dabbed with fresh stripper and then scrubbed with No. 3 steel wool; rinse the steel wool in an appropriate solvent. Wipe woodwork clean with paper towels or newspaper, then rinse. If you are stripping with methylene chloride, rinse with water; if with most other strippers, use alcohol to clean up. Read the label of the product. If wood becomes fibrous, allow it to dry before any further touch-up stripping.

After the wood has dried, but before you apply new finish, sand the surface with fine sandpaper. If that sandpaper becomes quickly gummed, the surface is not clean. Scrape and sand the piece until residue from the old finish is gone.

4-13. When most of the finish has been removed, clean up troublesome areas with steel wool.

4-14. Wood strippers.

Stripper	Use	Comments
Mild Strippers		
turpentine	cuts wax, grease and dirt	apply turpentine with a soft rag; use cotton swabs for tight spots
washing soda, trisodium phosphate, ammoniated cleaners	partially remove shellac and varnish; will cut mildew and some glues	varies according to degree of dilution; mild abrasive
mineral spirits	dissolves shellac and varnish	mild
denatured alcohol	dissolves shellac and varnish, some other clear finishes	relatively strong, cut it with mineral spirits or lacquer thinner
prepaint deglosser	scuffs existing finish to prepare for new finish	mild abrasive that obviates sanding between coats; check label to see if it will work on your finish
Strong Strippers		
methylene chloride	can strip all finishes, including oil-based paints, clear finishes	perhaps the most versatile and easiest to use; water-soluble; nonflammable; good for indoors, but still must have adequate ventilation; using a wallpaper steamer will speed up action of chemical—but do *not* use a heat gun
methanol, acetone, benzol, toluol	will dissolve most finishes	these are bases for a number of solvent-thinned, quite volatile strippers; better used outdoors than in; fire risk is great
heating gun	removes paints, less effective on clear finishes	give very effective results without the mess and expense of chemicals; best are those *without* an open flame; keep the gun moving for best results; avoid using near glass, as it will crack; *do not use with flammable chemicals*

CRACKS AND SPLITS

Take care of cracks and splits before refinishing the woodwork, preferably before staining it. When fixing splits, try to avoid using metal connectors such as mending plates, nails, and screws if possible, because they weaken the wood and will work loose in time. Gluing and clamping is a far better way to fix things.

Filling

If a crack is stable and not likely to spread, fill it, allow the filler to dry thoroughly, sand, and refinish. A number of commercial fillers are available, but most are so "homogenized" in color and texture that they are obvious fills. Perhaps the best way to fill a crack is to mix the filler yourself, using equal parts of white glue and fine sawdust from the wood you repair.

If possible, mix several batches of filler with different ratios of sawdust and glue. Allow them to dry so you can see exactly what the final texture will be. You may also add stains to filler if the object being repaired is to be stained. With a putty knife or a penknife, work the filler into cracks, mounding the filler slightly so you can sand away excess later. This mixture sands very well and matches wood color quite nicely.

Large Splits

Try to clamp and glue splits, working white carpenter's glue into tight spots; use a hypodermic needle or something similar (Brookstone Company makes plastic "needles" for the purpose). If the split is too wide—say more than 2 inches—dowel the pieces together, as shown in figures 3–35 to 3–38.

Surface Flaws

A hole or flaw in the surface of a panel can be fixed with a diamond-shaped patch cut from similar stock, as shown in figures 3–11 to 3–13. Although wood putty fills surface flaws, the blemishes will be obvious. Patching and repairing with solid wood is a bit of work, but once sanded and stained, the patch will be all but invisible.

REFINISHING

Once woodwork is stripped, dried, and repaired, sand it well; the most appropriate tool is a *block sander*, a tool small enough to be held in one hand. *Orbital sanders* are okay for relatively large, flat expanses of wood, but a block sander is most versatile for trim or slightly contoured surfaces. *Belt sanders* are, in most cases, too powerful to use on architectural trimmings. The usual progression of sandpapers to use is No. 90 grit, then No. 120 grit, and finally, No. 150 or 220 grit. Steel wool is used primarily to sand between coats of finish or when you want a furniture-quality finish.

To sand in tight areas, fold the sandpaper and use its creased edge. Wrapping paper around a dowel will enable you to sand concave areas; a blackboard eraser makes a resilient block for sanding larger expanses. On the last sanding pass before finishing, wipe surfaces clean with a tack rag or a cloth dampened with turpentine.

Stain before applying finishes. Because most stains are oil based, they soak in well and will be compatible with most finishes. If your staining job is a large one, mix all cans of stain beforehand so they will be uniform. Keep stirring the stain as you work, to keep pigments suspended. Apply most stains with a rag and wipe up excess. Adequate ventilation is imperative.

Should you wish to remove a stain from a piece of wood, dab the spot with dilute bleach or, that failing, use a mild oxalic acid solution (1 ounce acid to 1 quart water), which is available at most paint stores. Wear goggles and gloves.

Stripping may leave wood finish relatively lifeless and dry. The finish you choose will perk up the appearance of the wood somewhat, but after—or instead of—staining, some professionals prefer to rejuvenate the material with a diluted oil treatment before finishing. Following manufacturer's instructions, mix 15 to 25 percent of boiled linseed oil (tung oil, whatever oil you choose) in an appropriate medium of turpentine, alcohol, or other solvent. If you will be using a hard finish (see chart below), give the wood only one such treatment. Rub in the oil well, wipe off excess, and allow it to dry until there is no oiliness to the touch. Read the labels of the oil, thinner, and finish cans that you will be using to make sure that all materials are compatible.

It is general practice to thin the first coat of a clear finish so that it soaks in well. Cutting that first coat 50 percent with turpentine should work. After brushing on the first coat and allowing it to dry, sand lightly with fine steel wool and wipe with a tack rag. When applying finish with a brush, paint the outside of trim edges first and then smooth out the finish toward the center. Work from top to bottom on vertical pieces. Apply finish in long, steady strokes and avoid the temptation to touch up sections that have started to dry.

The accompanying chart lists the most commonly used finishes, roughly divided into *penetrants*, which soak into the wood, and *surface finishes*, which soak in less but provide a more impervious layer. Lemon oil, antiquing or polishing oil, linseed oil, and shellac are generally used on furniture or architectural woodwork but not on floors; the other finishes may be used on floors, exceptions noted, and on woodwork.

Counter-top Finishes

How you apply finishes to wood counter tops is as important as what you apply, particularly where counters contain a sink and standing water could be a problem. Treat not only the surface of the wood, but also the edges and the underside, soaking edges especially with an oil-based finish. Wood is very beautiful, but it is not well suited to be a counter top because hot pots will scorch it and water, undeterred, will split and rot it.

Perhaps the best finish for wooden counter tops is tung oil. There are three types of tung oil. Polymerized tung oil has the most additives of the three and dries most quickly; tungseed oil is half to two-thirds thinner and is intermediate in drying time; pure tung oil will stabilize after a week or two of drying but will never entirely dry. Any

Wood Finishes

Penetrants
Lemon oil brings out rich color in wood, resists moisture somewhat, has fair to poor durability. Because this substance remains somewhat oily to the touch, it must be cut with mineral spirits and alcohol and allowed to dry before applying another finish over it. Lemon oil cannot be applied over wax.

Antiquing or polishing oil can be buffed to a high sheen and may be used as a finish coat. It has fair to poor water resistance and durability. This finish is incompatible with shellac.

Boiled linseed oil is a good conditioner of dry wood. Cut it with half mineral spirits or turpentine before applying a surface finish over it. Although it brings out the color in wood, linseed oil is not particularly durable or moisture resistant.

Tung oil is very durable and water resistant, *the* finish to use near moisture, although it should be touched up periodically where moisture is extreme. Tung is easy to touch up and greatly enhances wood color, although the wood will darken in time. After it is thoroughly dry, it may be waxed if you like, but tung oil is usually not compatible with hard finishes.

Stains are not intended to be finish coats and must be sealed with a compatible surface finish after the stain has dried. Or they may be waxed.

Stain sealers (also called penetrating seals) are designed to stain and seal floors in one operation. They are usually a matte finish that can be touched up easily, waxed, or further sealed with a compatible surface finish.

Surface Finishes
Butcher's wax is not a lasting finish, but it can be reapplied and buffed up three or four times a year. It is particularly suitable for old softwood floors, where a hard finish would crack and dull. It can also be applied over hardwood.

Shellac is perhaps the least permanent of the hard finishes. It abrades easily and so should not be used on floors. Shellac resists water poorly, turning milky and discoloring.

Varnish varies greatly, some types being suitable for marine use, some for furniture, others for floors, and so on. Although it is glossy and reasonably durable, varnish is often waxed for even greater durability. Cut the first coat slightly with turpentine so it will sink in and adhere better. Difficult to touch up, varnish will not adhere to oily undercoats.

Lacquer is similar to varnish except that, because of its ethereal solvent base, it dries very quickly (in about an hour) and may thus be tricky to apply. Because new coats dissolve old ones somewhat, lacquer can be successfully touched up.

Polyurethane is a clear, plastic finish that is durable and reasonably water resistant, although it will cloud up if exposed to continuous moisture. Easily applied with a brush, it is perhaps the best all-around floor finish, although it is not easily touched up. It works better, all in all, on hardwood floors, because flexing and bending of softwood may dull a finish. Thin earliest coats so they will adhere better. Check labels carefully: many polys are not compatible with those made by different manufacturers.

tung oil will cause wood to darken in time.

For those concerned about the possible toxicity of wood finishes around food, vegetable oil can be an effective finish, although its application is somewhat tedious. The oil must be heated hot to the touch, lavished on with a rag, allowed to set for at least fifteen minutes, rubbed to remove excess, and rubbed again once every half hour for two hours; repeat treatments once a month. Some users contend that a counter so treated will have a slightly rancid smell, but this point is debatable. Mineral oil can be similarly applied.

Watco oil, a linseed-oil resin, is also used on counters, although there are reports that tin cans left on a counter so treated may leave rings. Linseed oil is less durable and water resistant than tung oil but takes as long to dry. Polyurethane is an acceptable finish if you keep it wiped dry and avoid nicking it.

REINSTALLATION SPECIFICS

This section examines reinstallation and reuse of the various woodwork elements. Readers who need yet more background information about reinstallation should consult the Bibliography. Commonly reused elements such as door and window trim are discussed at length, but one could, for example, write books about installing cabinets.

When reinstalling woodwork, you will have to cut and refit extensively. A *miter-saw* and an *adjustable miter box* enable you to make accurate cuts; saws should have eleven to twenty teeth per inch. The preferred tool for this kind of work, however, is the *miter trimmer*, which allows you to shave off minute amounts of wood and maintain a perfectly clean edge.

Because woodwork is often lightweight (being milled to ¾- or ½-inch thickness), it must be kept dry and stored where it will not get wet. Never install woodwork over uncured plaster and, where practicable, do not even bring trim into a house that is yet to be plastered; wood will absorb moisture and warp. Use the longest, best-looking trim in the most conspicuous areas; hide shorter pieces behind doors and the like. If you strip and refinish wood *before* you cut and refit it, you will save time later—you must still touch up ends that are newly cut, but in general, you will not have to worry about getting stain on newly painted walls.

Sizing nails is an important task and, to some, a worrisome one. Nails must be as small as possible, yet firmly affix woodwork to the framing (usually studs) behind the finish walls. Use 6d or 8d finish or casing nails for most jobs. For casing around doors and windows—which must be nailed into the edges of the frame *and* into the studs of the rough opening (see fig. 4-15)—use 4d nails along the inside edges of the casing and 6d nails along the outer edges. Do not nail closer than ½ inch to the edge of any trim.

Never use more nails than a minimum: a pair every 12 to 16 inches around casings is sufficient; every 16 inches along crown molding, and so on. Sink all finish and casing nails ⅛ inch below the surface to complete the task; use a *nail set* for this operation.

DOOR TRIM

Install door trim after the frames of the units have been plumbed and leveled in their rough openings, shimmed fast, and nailed securely. Door trim, or casing, thus covers the gaps between frames and the finish walls. Install such trim before baseboards, paneling, and crown molding.

The secret of casing doors is *not* trying to align the inside edges of casing to the inside edges of the frame; instead, *set back*, or *reveal*, the casing edge ¼ inch so that a small strip of frame is still visible. The reason for this reveal is that wood is rarely straight these days and it is all but impossible to align two nonstraight edges. Your ¼-inch reveal will not be a uniform ¼ inch either, but your eye will be fooled. So, begin installing casing by scrib-

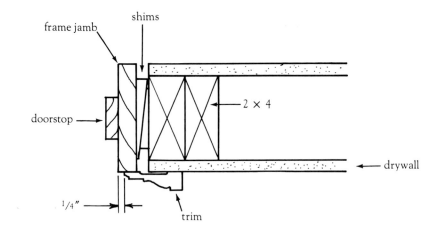

4-15. The trim (here shown installed on only one side, for clarity) straddles and covers the gap between the edge of the frame jamb and the end of the finish wall. The 1/4-in. setback of the trim is called a "reveal."

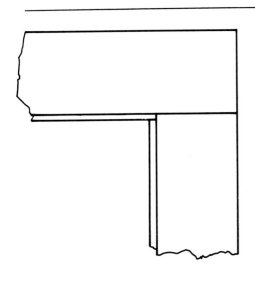

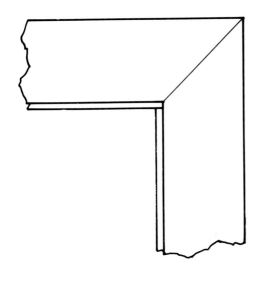

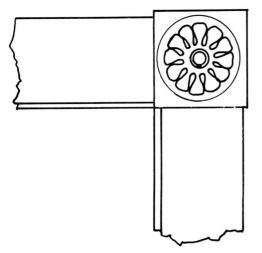

4-16. Trim corner details. From top: miter joint, butt joint, corner block or rosette.

ing a very faint line—set back ¼ inch—around the inside edge of the frame.

Casing corners meet in one of three ways: pieces are cut at 45-degree angles or *mitered*; jamb trim *butts* to underside of the head trim; or jamb and head meet at a *rosette*, an essentially square corner block to which trim butts. Because a mitered corner is the most common (and complex) of the three, we will examine it most closely.

Fit jamb trim first. If your finished floors are down, the bottoms of door jambs will sit directly on floors. Otherwise, put a scrap of finish flooring beneath the trim, so that jambs will be the right height when finish floors are installed.

Align the inside edge of the jamb trim to the reveal line that you scribed earlier on the frame jamb. Where the inside edge of that trim crosses the reveal line scribed along the frame head, mark the trim with a knife. Cut a 45-degree miter through that mark. Do the same for the jamb on the opposite side of the frame.

Tack-nail the jambs in place, again aligning their inside edges to the reveal lines scribed.

If the corners of the frame are perfectly square, you need only measure and cut a piece of head trim with a 45-degree cut on each end. In reality, corners are seldom perfectly square, so measure the distances between the two outer and inner points of the jamb pieces. Transfer these measurements to the head piece. Another way to record the angles you need is to hold a straight board across the tops of the jambs and open an *adjustable bevel* until it fits the angle. If you need to shave down the head trim once it is cut, use a block plane.

Nail up the trim with a pair of nails—a 4d and a 6d—every 12 inches or so. For the best-looking results, place nail pairs at the same height. Draw corner joints tight by driving a 4d finish nail into the ends

of the trim, one down from the top, and one in from the side. Sink all holes.

Butted corners begin the same way as mitered ones: align jamb stock to the reveal lines scribed into frame jambs. As above, mark the jamb trim where it crosses the reveal line scribed into the head of the frame. Instead of cutting a 45-degree angle through those marks, however, simply cut square across the trim boards.

The head trim merely sits atop the ends of the jamb trim. Make the head trim just a shade longer than the outside measurements of the jamb trim, say ⅛ inch, and cut the ends of the head trim slightly more than 90 degrees. This barely oblique angle will look square once it is in place. Because a viewer looks up at the top of a door frame, a squarely cut corner will look less than square, odd as that seems.

After installing trim, check the corners. If trim does not fit perfectly when reinstalled in its new location, fill gaps with spackling compound if trim is to be painted. If it will be finished with a clear finish, mix sawdust from the trim with an equal amount of white glue to make a wood filler; mix stain as required to match the final finish of the wood. The best way to solve this problem, however, is to cut corners correctly in the first place. Because casings receive a lot of wear, they should always be finished; left unsealed, they will be grimy within six months.

WINDOW TRIM

Window casings are similar to those around doors. Like doors, they should be installed after the frame is complete, but before other trim. They also require ¼-inch reveal lines. And their construction is very much like that for door trim, except for the bottom details: window jamb trim sits on a *stool*, a piece of casing specially cut to cover the beveled edge of the window sill. (The window sill, as described in chapter 2, is the bottom piece of the window frame, pitched at a 10-degree angle to shed water.)

We will assume two things for the operations that follow. First, reveal lines have been scribed along the edges of the frame head and jambs. Second, the inside edges of the window frame are flush to the finish wall surfaces in the living space. If such edges stick in too far, plane them down; if not far enough, build them up with ripped-down strips of ¾-inch pine or dimension lumber.

Install the stool first. Cutting the stool requires several sets of measurements and cuts, so its installation takes some time. Purchase specially milled window-stool stock, with a 10-degree bevel already cut into its underside, from a lumberyard. The stock comes in varying widths, but in most cases the installer has to cut down its width slightly.

Measure the inside width of the window frame, from the inside of one frame jamb to the other. Using a try square, mark this measurement squarely across the face of the stock.

From each end of the sill, measure out from the bottom rail of the window sash to the edge of the sill. Transfer these marks to the underside of the stool stock, measuring from the shoulder of the bevel out. When the stock is cut down to correct size, its inside edge will fit snugly to the bottom rail of the window sash. Using the two sets of measurements gathered so far, cut out the stool and test its fit inside the window frame; use a backsaw for best results, holding its blade perpendicular to the stock. If you must rip down the width of the stool stock, do so on a table saw, after placing the stock facedown.

The last set of measurements and cuts trim the "ears" that stick out at each end. Each ear should be at least ½ inch longer than the jamb trim is wide: ¼ inch extra for the amount that the trim is set back from the inside of the frame, and at least ¼ inch extra for the amount of the ear that sticks out beyond the jamb trim. (This last amount is traditional; one could cut the ear flush to the edge of the jamb trim, but that detailing would not look as good.) Make these final cuts and tack the stool in place. It should be perfectly level—if not, shim up its low sides.

If this explanation of measuring and cutting a stool seems unduly complex, reread the section while looking at a window stool in your dwelling; the doing is not that hard.

After installing the stool, install the jambs and head of the window trim as you would door casing; the

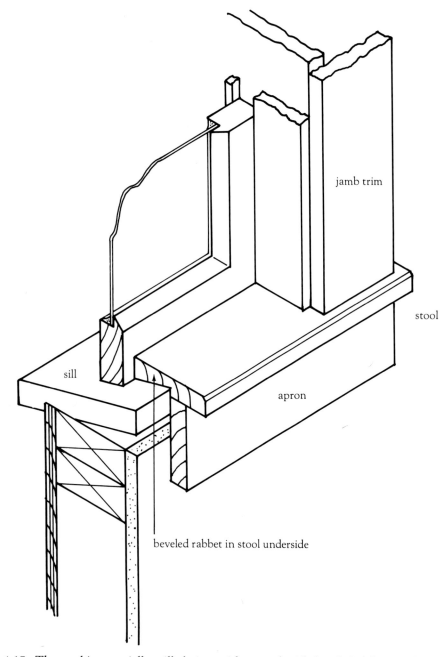

4-17. The stool is a specially milled piece with an underside beveled to fit over the inside of the sill. Note that the jamb trim is again set back in a 1/4-in. reveal.

jamb trim

stool

sill

apron

beveled rabbet in stool underside

jambs rest on the top of the stool and the head atop the jambs. The inside edges of head and jambs are set back ¼ inch from the edges of the window frame. The *apron*, the small piece that fits beneath the stool, should be installed after the stool, so that the weight of the jambs does not cause the stool to settle. The apron should be an inch or two shorter than the total length of the stool, for visual effect.

Nail up window casing with 4d and 6d finish nails, as described in the section on door trim above.

If you are installing side-by-side windows with a wide *mullion* in between, butt the top of that mullion to the underside of the head trim, which should be a single piece. If the trim is molded, however, double-miter the top of the mullion so that its compound shapes match those of the head molding.

BASEBOARDS, CROWN MOLDING, AND ALL BETWEEN

This section presents terms and shows the usual ways of attaching other types of trim; also, it suggests some of the uses possible when only a fragment of trim survives. Victorian ornamentation is especially good to reuse because it is often so gaudy that only two or three pieces of it will suffice for an entire room. You might, for example, highlight the opening around a stereo niche or a built-in wardrobe. Use a chalkline to help lay out long pieces.

Crown Molding

Crown molding is often a composite molding and may not fit well when refitted to your ceiling. You can choose from three methods to make it fit. Nail it in place as best you can and fill gaps with joint compound or plaster. Or, have the back side of the trim recut on a table saw so that the trim angle is greater than 90 degrees— say, 100 degrees. This oblique angle will straddle any oddities in an out-of-square corner. Or, measure the *exact* wall/ceiling

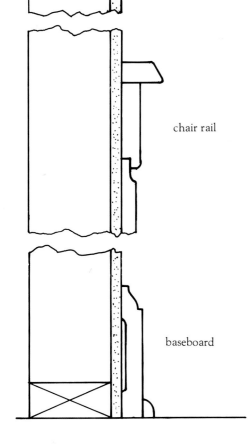

crown molding

chair rail

baseboard

4-18. Crown molding, chair rail, wainscoting, and baseboard trim.

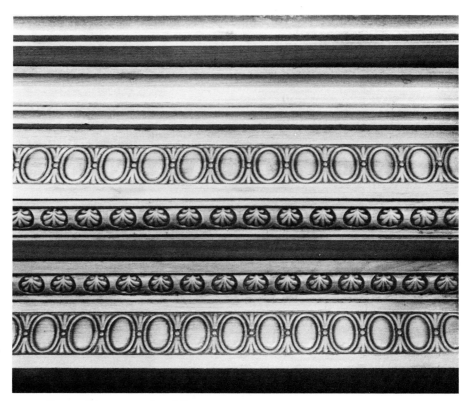

4-19. Egg-and-dart pressed molding.

angle with an adjustable bevel along several points and recut that exact angle with a table saw. Of the three choices, the second is intermediate in results and difficulty; the last method will be the best looking and the most difficult; the first is facile, but will not look good after plastic materials (plaster, joint compound) dry.

Crown molding should be nailed into each stud or joist that it crosses. Attach it to the structure with no nails larger than 8d finish. If there is wooden lath behind plaster, you may use shorter nails. Even less jarring on finish surfaces is trim attached with drywall screws, although you will need to predrill and countersink holes so that the screw heads will be below the surface of the molding. Fill holes with spackling compound, wood filler, and so on. Such screws should sink at least ½ inch into structural members. Use the longest pieces of crown molding where they are most visible. Join pieces with 45-degree bevel cuts centered over the stud centers.

Finally, wooden crown molding more than 6 inches wide may require additional nailer blocks let into the tops of studs and the ends of joists.

Baseboard Trim

Baseboards run along the base of walls, butting right up to door trim. Old baseboard trim works well because it is dry and will not shrink. Its lower edge may rest upon finish flooring, although that joint is usually covered by a piece of quarter-round molding, or shoe.

Nail baseboards into every stud they cross using 6d or 8d nails at each stud. Locate the nails at least ¾ inch from the edges. Angled-in nails hold best. As with crown molding, bevel-join sections over stud centers.

Outside corners, which stick out into a room, should be miter-cut so that the two 45-degree cuts form a perfectly square (90-degree) corner. Inside corners may be butted together if the trim is plain; coped (trace the contour of one piece onto the other) if complex. Improve corner joints by end-nailing 4d nails through each board of the joint.

Paneling and Wainscoting

Paneling and wainscoting manufactured fifty years ago are much different from that made today. Old pieces were, first of all, solid wood, often of one piece, whereas today's sheet materials are reprocessed wood, reglued in cross-grained plies. Present-day panels are superior in one respect: they will not split because of changes in temperature. Because larger sections of solid wood

will expand and contract, old-time panels were not nailed down; rather, they were allowed to "float" within a grid of heavier *rails* (horizontal frame members) and *stiles* (vertical members).

Knowledge of such construction is important to the salvager during removal and reinstallation. When removing old paneling or wainscoting, start by carefully prying off the *top rail*, also called the *chair rail* or *cap rail*, of panels. Removing this rail gives you access to the panels themselves; they can sometimes be slid up and out, without further prying. But, before removing anything else, carefully measure the components in place: how far apart the stiles are, how much space is between panel edges and stiles (for expansion), where half panels or corner pieces should go, and so on. After taking these measurements, which should be recorded on graph paper, dismantle the assembly.

Panels are sometimes tack-nailed with 2d or 4d nails in upper corners; such nails merely hold panels in place before the stiles and rails are fully mounted. Slide a stiff putty

4-20. This figure is a mystery: measuring 22 in. × 16 in. this carved walnut panel seems to be Italian, possibly as early as the eighteenth century.

Urban Archaeology

4-21. Stained ash fretwork, late-nineteenth-century American, 30 in. × 14 in.
Architectural Antiques Exchange

knife behind nailing points to pry up and remove such small nails. If you can, slide out panels before prying off rails and stiles, for those thicker members are nailed down with larger nails, usually 8d finish. If you have difficulty removing panels and getting a clear shot at rails and stiles, pry off the baseboard next; should you nick the baseboard while prying it up, such flaws will be less conspicuous.

When laying out pieces for reinstallation, use a chalkline extensively; snap lines onto drywall or plaster surfaces, for they will be covered up by paneling. Use a level to set rails level and stiles plumb. Avoid the temptation to align the edges of paneling to trim already in place—that method will produce terrible results. Instead, plumb stiles

and panel edges and, where they abut existing trim, cut the paneling to make it fit. Use the largest sections of paneling where they will be most visible.

As you lay out individual panels, you may tack them up with a 4d nail in each corner. Do not, however, use mastic on the back of panels, for such adhesive will not permit wood movement. Remember to leave at least 3/16-inch gaps (or whatever was there originally) between panel edges and frame members. Stiles and rails should be nailed securely to studs or blocking in the wall behind; this is no problem for rails, but since stiles run parallel to studs, you may have to nail on 1 × 2 furring strips first. This building-out can be concealed by using a wider cap rail.

Fretwork

Fretwork most often refers to assemblies of turned wood installed over doorways. Fretwork is gay and decorative, allowing light and air to circulate over a doorway, particularly appropriate when ceilings are high and one does not want a solid section of wall that would lower that height. Fretwork is a distant cousin of the bead curtains of the Middle East.

When you purchase fretwork, you will rarely find all parts present, but new fret patterns can easily be arranged from incomplete ones. Before installing fretwork over doors or hanging it in front of windows, make it rigid by nailing on a 1 × 2 frame, stained to match the perimeter of the surrounding casing.

STAIRCASE ASSEMBLIES

Balusters, railings, and newel posts are the superstructure of a stair, the parts above the steps. Being so ornamental and easily removed, they are much in demand.

Balusters

Before you remove anything, number all parts with a china pencil (if the woodwork is painted glossy) or with embossed plastic tape (the kind of tape that you can punch names and numbers into) so you will know how all parts should be reassembled. Many stair parts are closely fitted, and each varies slightly. Remove balusters before other stair parts. Most commonly, they are fitted into the top of stair treads. Pry off the end-nosing of treads with a chisel and simply slip

the bottoms of balusters out. If those bottoms are nailed and you cannot locate and pull out those nails, saw off the small tenon at the bottom of the baluster.

On occasion the top of the baluster may be tacked to the underside of the handrail. Those top nails will pull out when you twist the bottom of the piece free. Or, where both the bottom and top of a baluster are tack-nailed into place, there may be small pieces of blocking between each baluster top. Pry out blocking and, with a hacksaw blade, cut through those small nails.

Balusters, especially those along porches, may be held in place by rails above and below. Leave such balusters in place if possible; instead, detach each end of the railings as described below.

Rails and Posts

Handrails are largely free-standing. If, however, as you remove balusters, you note that the handrail is sagging, prop it up so it does not collapse and crack. Handrails attach to a newel post at the bottom of a stair in most cases; at their upper reaches, they are nailed (or

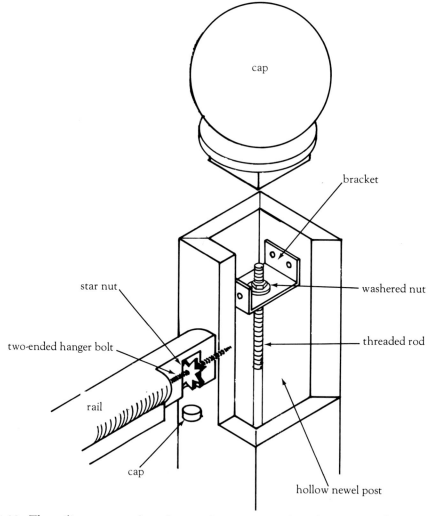

4-22. By alternating balusters in an interior wall opening, this designer created an ornamental breezeway. Because no stresses are placed upon the balusters, they are simply toenailed in place with finish nails.

Nat Kaplan

4-23. The railing may attach to the newel post in a number of ways, one of the more common being a star nut centered in the end of the railing. The post itself may be screwed to the bottom stair or may have a rod-and-plate assembly that runs through the post.

screwed) to a wall, to a bracket beneath, or to a newel or railing that services the upstairs.

By far the most common attachment on the upper end of the railing is a nail-and-bracket combination. Unscrew the screws holding the railing to the bracket; use an impact driver with a screwdriver bit to loosen seized screws. Then strike the underside of the railing with a mallet, which should drive out any nails angled into the wall. (Have someone catch the rail as you drive it free.) If that does not work, the rail may be screwed in; look for plugs. If all else fails, cut the end of the rail free, using a reciprocating saw with a nail-cutting blade.

Rails attach to newel posts in a number of ways. Most common is the starred nut connection shown in figure 4–23. That nut can be backed off by striking it counterclockwise with a screwdriver point—if you can find the nut, that is. Often, the plug covering it has become obscured by many layers of finish and polish. If the post is hollow (tap its sides to see), try to pry off its cap so that you may disconnect the handrail from within. The rail may also join the post by ending in a cap atop the post. Once you have disconnected the upper end of the rail, rock it slightly from side to side to see what kind of joint you have at the post. Strike the joint with a rubber mallet to drive it apart somewhat. (Many salvagers in a hurry simply break free the rail/post joint; try not to do that.)

Newel posts also show a variety of mountings. Perhaps the most common is a hollow post with a long threaded rod running down its center. The nut on the upper end of the rod is snug against a bracket within the post; the lower nut may be visible from the floor beneath, sticking out through the underside of the subflooring. To gain access to the inside of the post, strike the cap of the post with a rubber mallet until the cap flies off. The bottom of

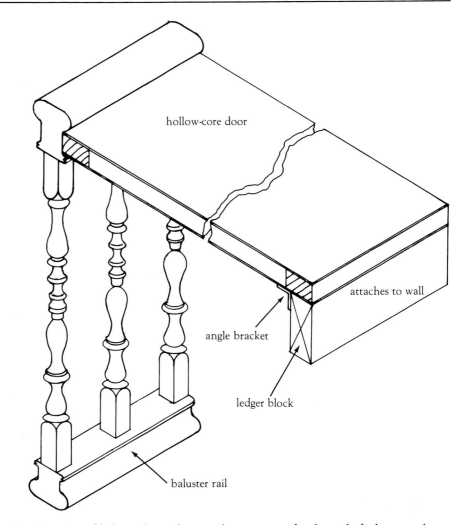

4-24. A section of balustrade can be reused as a support for the end of a homemade desk. The top is a hollow-core door, supported on two sides by ledger blocks nailed or screwed to the wall.

the post may be further affixed, either by being bolted to the last step or screwed at an angle to the floor. Remove the appropriate connectors.

Examples of Reuse

Staircase assemblies may be reused intact, but such use is not common in new construction because fitting the unique dimensions of a staircase to an existing building is a major undertaking. More commonly, staircase parts are used piecemeal in innovative ways.

Balusters are very versatile. Squat ones, intended originally for building exteriors, can support great weights and thus double as furniture

elements, as shown in the color section. Conversely, interior balusters may be used to good effect outside, as shown in figure 4–22, where the designer uses them decoratively, to provide privacy for an interior court. Balusters may also be cut down and used individually as table legs, sawed and drilled to be reincarnated as candleholders, or used as ornate pegs upon which to hang pots or coats.

Perhaps the most ingenuous use I have seen is shown in figure 4–24, in which a section of outdoor baluster with rails supports the end of a homemade desk. The desk top is a hollow-core door supported on two sides by wooden ledger-strips, leveled and bolted with ¼- by 2-inch bolts (or screws) into each stud crossed. After the door is laid across those strips, the section of baluster is affixed on a third side of the door by sinking four ¼-inch bolts, evenly spaced, through the top railing into the end of the door. Angle-nail or screw the bottom rail into the floor and the assembly becomes rigid. Screw the desk top (from beneath) to the two supporting strips. A shortened section of baluster can be somewhat spindly, but attachments to the desk top and to the two wall-mounted strips stiffen things up.

A final tip: if you do not want to use the full length of a hollow core door, cut it down and then re-insert its solid-wood edging along the end of the new cut; otherwise, you will have nothing solid to bolt into. Most solid-wood doors are in-appropriate because they are panel doors, hardly a flat writing surface. One could use a sheet of plywood as a top, but that will lack the pleasing thickness of a door edge. Modifying a hollow-core door is both econom-ical and visually pleasing.

MANTELS

Mantels, which surround fireplaces, were often elaborate in Victorian times, with fancy scrollwork, mir-rors, beveled glass, carved gro-tesques, and so on. Other built-in pieces, such as mirror stands and hall seats, almost as ornate, were mounted to the framing in a similar manner.

How easily a mantel may be removed depends upon what it is at-tached to and whether finish wall surfaces were installed before or after the mantel. We will look at mantels attached to stud walls first.

While a friend holds a flashlight inside the firebox, scan the perime-ter of the mantel, looking for light shining through behind the mantel. If you can see light, the mantel was probably installed after the finish

surfaces; such mantels will be relatively easy to take off because you can slip a flat bar behind. If the plaster or drywall lock the mantel in place, however, you should destroy those surfaces with a utility bar, to expose the edges of the mantel.

That done, slip the flat bar behind the mantel at several points and jimmy the piece gently. At this point you are not trying to pry up the mantel, putting just enough pressure on the nails so that their heads depress slightly in the wood, thereby cracking the paint over them. These cracks make it easier for you to discern nail location. You must know where nails are so that you can pry near them; otherwise you increase the chance of breakage.

Nails located, pry up gently around the perimeter of the mantel, slipping in cedar shingles to hold the piece out from the wall. If nails do not pull out easily and you fear that the wood may crack, cut

through nail shanks (wear goggles) with a metal-cutting blade in a reciprocating saw or strike with a flat cold chisel.

The firebox side of the mantel usually has few nails. If it has any, they are probably square-cuts, driven into mortar joints. Cut through them.

If the entire mantel is attached to brick, either an all-brick wall or an extended flue area, square-cut nails were likely used. These nails do not pull out easily, but as they are most often driven into mortar joints, striking their shanks with a chisel is usually enough to loosen the mortar around them. Other-wise, use cedar shims to raise the mantel slightly and try to cut through the nail shanks with a reciprocating saw.

Useful tools for the above opera-tion are a slate hook and the home-made truck-spring chisel shown in figure 4–32; both are flat and will

4-25. Mantel.
Gargoyles, Ltd.

100

reach behind a mantel nailed tight to a wall. A slate hook was designed to reach beneath pieces of slate roofing and cut through nail shanks, but it is handy for salvaging too. Square-cut nails are likely to burr the cutting edges of the tools, however. Wear goggles.

If the mantel is screwed or bolted to the wall, you have two choices. Delicately chisel through the mantel face until you locate the bolts or screws, and unscrew them; cutting through their shanks will be hard. Or you can pry the mantel off without unscrewing the attachers, which will splinter the wood slightly. Neither method is preferable. It will be easy to cover damaged spots with ornamental rosettes or other elements that fit into the overall design of the mantel.

How you remount a mantel depends upon its size and the surface to which you attach it. The average mantel has a light shelf that is fashioned from stock 2 inches thick or less, which sticks out into the room no more than 6 inches; it is no trouble to mount. If yours is thicker or has an overmantel (an elaborate superstructure above the mantel), use the methods described at the end of this section.

Fire codes may dictate the placement of your mantel; consult your local fire department or pertinent building code inspector. Common usage is that the sides of a wooden mantel be no closer than 8 inches to the opening of a firebox, nor the breastpiece (the top) any closer than 12 inches.

To mount an average lightweight mantel to a stud-frame wall, first locate the studs. Most mantels will cross at least two studs and probably three; additionally, there may be doubled-up studs around the masonry firebox. Using 8d finish nails, nail vertically every 16 inches into studs; if you think the mantel shelf needs a bit more support, use 10d finish nails near that shelf.

You can also use 2½-inch wood screws, which will attach the mantel even more solidly, but you will have to use a drill-and-countersink bit to sink screw heads and a plug-cutter to cut plugs from the same stock as the mantel. Similarly, you might use washered bolts, the preferred method for attaching to masonry surfaces, but these actually provide more support than you need for a lightweight wooden mantel.

To attach to masonry, plumb (with a level) the holes that you will drill through the face of the mantel: three bolts, evenly spaced across the top of the mantel, and at least two bolts in each side panel. Predrill through the mantel first, with a 3/16-inch bit (or whatever the diameter of the bolt you use) and then, holding the mantel against the masonry wall, pencil those holes onto the masonry. Set the mantel aside and, with a carbide-tipped masonry bit in a heavy drill, drill the holes for the lead sleeves that will fit into the masonry. Finally, to attach the mantel, align drilled holes and tighten bolts into the lead sleeves; sleeves will expand and hold fast. You will, of course, need to cover bolt heads with plugs of some kind.

The last method for attaching lightweight mantels is with hanging brackets, as shown in figure 4–27. One set of brackets attaches to the wall and one to the back of the mantel. Carefully level the brackets on the wall and smear a bit of lipstick on the outer tab of each. Hold the mantel roughly in place so the lipstick will mark the back of the mantel, indicating the position of the matching brackets. This is an easy method in some ways, but aligning brackets can be frustrating.

The back of the mantel should lie flat when attached; you need not cushion it. If it has minor irregularities, however, a 1/16-inch bead of construction adhesive or caulking around the perimeter of the mantel will help. Plaster was sometimes used in the old days.

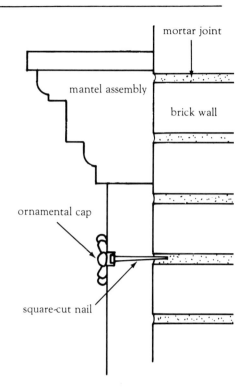

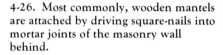

4-26. Most commonly, wooden mantels are attached by driving square-nails into mortar joints of the masonry wall behind.

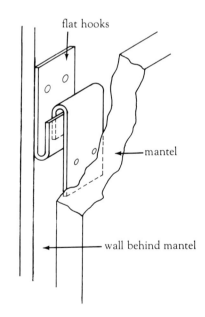

4-27. Lightweight mantels may be attached with mantel hooks, two-piece hardware that attaches to both mantel and the wall behind, which work especially well if the wall is stud framed.

Heavy or oversized mantels can be attached with the washered bolts described above. Increase bolt spacing to 12 inches (vertically) if you have doubts. If the shelf of the mantel is particularly large, however, or if you plan to display weighty objects upon it, you will need additional support. Use a long, threaded rod to tie the shelf to the wall (see figs. 9–27 and 9–28).

Using a doweling jig (fig. 3–35) to keep your bit perpendicular to the edge of the mantel, drill a hole all the way through the width of the piece: a ¼-inch hole should do in most cases; use ⅜ inch for extra-heavy mantels. If you are attaching to masonry, insert the threaded rod, cementing one end of it into the masonry hole with masonry epoxy (Thoro-Grip is one such product). The other end of the rod—that near the outer edge of the mantel shelf—is drawn tight with a washered nut (fig. 4–28). If you attach to a stud wall, simply use long, washered lag bolts buried at least 1½ inches into studs. If you do not think the existing structural framing provides enough support, let in additional blocking to bolt to.

CABINETS AND BUILT-IN PANTRIES

Cabinets these days are fabricated mostly from plywood, assembled in a shop, and transported to a site. In the old days, solid wood was more commonly used and cabinets were often built on-site. In either case the installer had to fit essentially square cabinets to often out-of-square floors and walls.

Base or bottom cabinets sit on a *plinth*, a simple platform whose pieces can be tapered to accommodate tilts in the floor; the top of the plinth, however, is level, so that the base unit is installed on a flat, level surface. Plinths are usually constructed from 2 × 4s on edge, which raise the undersides of cabinets enough to provide toe room beneath. Using a plinth makes installation much easier.

Because walls are rarely plumb, upper cabinets are shimmed to walls until the front faces of those cabinets are plumb. They are then nailed, screwed, or bolted to the framing behind. On rare occasions upper cabinets are screwed into joists above for greater support. It is imperative that cabinet faces be plumbed, rather than just bolted flat to existing walls, because cabinet doors may not work correctly if walls are not plumb; aligning the edges of different cabinet sections could also be problematic.

Once upper and lower cabinets are positioned, counter tops are

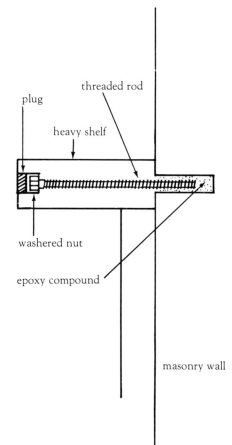

threaded rod

plug

heavy shelf

washered nut

epoxy compound

masonry wall

4-28. Use threaded rods to support oversized shelves that would not be adequately supported by the mantel breastpiece beneath.

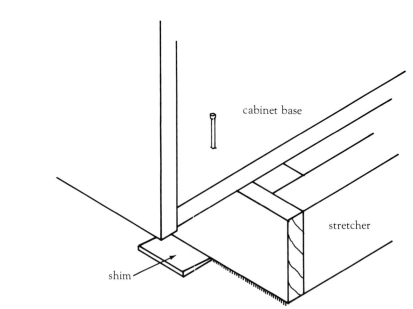

cabinet base

stretcher

shim

4-29. Bottom cabinets rest on plinths, which can be cut on an angle or shimmed to correct floors that slope (cutaway cross-section view).

fastened, sinks and spigots are connected, and so on. As with all finish carpentry, seams and edges are concealed in some fashion to make the total effect pleasing and visually coherent. Molding is applied where cabinets meet floors, walls, ceilings, appliances, and other cabinet sections. Removing this molding is perhaps the first task of the salvager removing cabinets—after shutting off water and electricity to the affected area, that is.

Base Cabinets

Remove base units first so that you will be able to stand beneath upper sections when removing them; otherwise the bases will be in your way and you might strain your back when wrestling upper cabinets down.

Disconnect electricity and water and free the pipes servicing the sink (if any), as discussed in chapter 7. Loosen sink mounting clips, scrape away plumber's putty, and lift out the sink. You do not have to remove cabinet doors, but they are less likely to become sprung or damaged if you do. Unscrew hinges from the cabinet body, leaving hinges still attached to doors for easier reinstallation. If any shelves can be taken out, do so. Do not remove counter tops if you can help it, for they are probably holding units together, keeping them square and rigid.

Grab one end of the base cabinet and see if you can shake it at all. Most are nailed to their plinths, and the plinths are toe-nailed into the floor below, but otherwise they are free-standing. There may be a few nails, no larger than 8d finish, angle-nailed from the back of the base into the walls behind or through the back of the counter into the walls. Look closely for angle braces or nail heads (if any) along the perimeter of the bases; pry at those points.

Slide your utility bar between the cabinet and finish surfaces—or destroy finish surfaces to clearly reveal cabinet edges—and between the bottom of the base and its plinth. Making a new plinth is not difficult, so destroy it if you must. If the cabinet is overnailed to the wall behind, little will happen during the first half hour or so of your ministrations, but eventually your prying will pay off and you will be able to slip shims behind the unit. Pry out the entire unit evenly to minimize wood splits. Should you split any cabinet frame parts that have been nailed to studs, you can reinforce those pieces later.

When the base units are freed, remove any nails sticking out, and set the bases out of the way.

Upper Sections

After removing doors and any molding that obscures the edges of the cabinets, prop up upper sections with 2 × 4s set diagonally to the floor. Notch the upper ends of the 2 × 4s and tack-nail the braces to the floor. These braces will keep the cabinets in place while you remove the screws holding units in place. The most common mounting detail for uppers is the mounting rail shown in figure 4–30. Joined to the cabinet frame, that rail is screwed or nailed into studs behind.

If the mounting rail has been painted, screws or nail heads may be hard to find. Strip the paint with a chemical stripper or, at the very least, with a floor-scraping tool. Dig

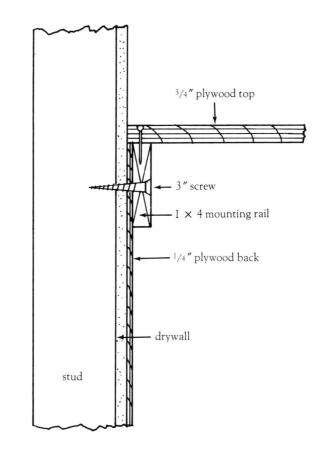

3/4″ plywood top

3″ screw

1 × 4 mounting rail

1/4″ plywood back

drywall

stud

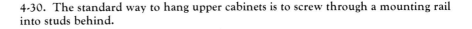

4-30. The standard way to hang upper cabinets is to screw through a mounting rail into studs behind.

out any wood putty and, if necessary, use an impact driver with a screw bit to loosen screws that threaten to strip.

Should the mounting bars be nailed into place, try digging out heads with a cat's paw. If that does not work, slide a utility bar between the mounting rail and the wall at shimming points. Pry the units just enough so that you gain access to the nail head.

Occasionally salvagers find a cabinet back fashioned from a sheet of ¾-inch plywood or solid lumber, without mounting rails. Such large backs mean that the carpenter nailed or screwed directly through the back, into studs at various points, so finding attachers may be difficult. The carpenter may also have attached the cabinet to a 1 × 6 that was let in to the stud behind. Again, you can try to pry the back loose from the wall or you can scrape any paint away to detect screw heads more easily.

Remounting Tips

Review this book's Bibliography for titles about fabricating and hanging cabinets.

Use type-W Sheetrock screws to remount cabinets. With a magnetic screw bit in your power drill, driving screws is effortless and can be done almost one-handedly.

Before remounting salvaged cabinets, make sure that mounting rails have not been weakened;

rescrew them to the cabinet frame as needed.

Use a long board and a level to assess your walls and floors for plumb and level. Anticipating shimming or plinth-building in advance will prevent trouble later. If you intend to reframe walls or level floors anyhow as part of a larger renovation, do so before it is time to install cabinets.

FLOORING

Flooring that has been correctly nailed into joists—and not indiscriminately into subflooring—can be taken up with a minimum of waste. Simply looking at the floor will tell you a lot: if you see no nails, you probably have tongue-and-groove flooring whose nails, being angled through the tongues, are concealed. If nails are visible (face-nailed), they should be nailed uniformly, in rows every 16 inches or every 24 inches. If visible nails are erratically placed, the floorer may have been inexperienced; hence materials may be hard to salvage.

To take up flooring, slide a wrecking bar underneath boards, as close to the nailing points as possible; work up each board along its entire length, rather than raising just one end first. Prying up boards is easy enough once you have the first course or two of boards up, but you may have to destroy those first few courses. One way to save even those first few courses, however, is to destroy the finish surfaces along a wall running parallel with the flooring. Being able to get the head of your wrecking bar between studs will give you enough "purchase" to pry up the very first course of boards. Another way to minimize breakage is to get beneath the floor and, working near joists, tap up flooring so that you can slide a wrecking bar beneath. Tap a hand sledge against 2 × 4 scrap to spread the jolt of the sledge. Working from

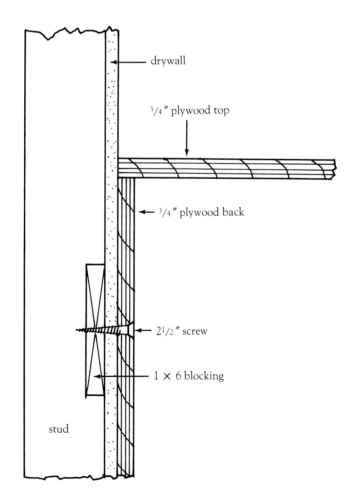

drywall

¾" plywood top

¾" plywood back

2½" screw

1 × 6 blocking

stud

4-31. A less common but very strong method of hanging cabinets involves backing them with plywood, in lieu of a mounting rail.

underneath is often the only way to save old wide-board floors. Once the floor is up, scrutinize boards with a magnet before reusing; remove any old nails that might be imbedded. A carbide-tipped blade in your circular saw would probably be able to cut through such nail fragments, but no blade is improved by striking metal. Wear goggles.

SIDING

Clapboards are rarely worth salvaging because they are thin and often deteriorated. On occasion, though, one needs a weathered clapboard to patch a facade—a friend of mine used old cedar siding to cover a bathroom wall. The final result looked good and shed water well, but he wasted 80 percent of the clapboards he tried to pry off the old barn.

The way to remove siding is fashion yourself a tool from an old truck leaf spring. Grind one end square and blunt, suitable for striking with a hammer; grind the other end as thin and sharp as you can. The spring has enough flex to slide into tight spaces and gently lift a flimsy board. If the board still will not lift, rap the tool so that the sharp edge cuts through obstinate nail shanks. (The steel of leaf springs, by the way, is quite good.)

The trend of using barnboard (weathered 1-inch boards) in interiors has mercifully subsided. The idea is not inherently flawed, but that gray, elemental look was, in my opinion, overworked for twenty years. Besides, such wood is often too weathered, decayed, and insect-ridden to use inside. Usually warped, it is terrible for fine work such as cabinets. But if you like the stuff, here are three tips: stain all newly cut ends so they will not be obtrusive; fumigate it before bringing it inside; and put black felt paper behind open knots so drywall (or whatever) will not glare through the darker surface of the wood.

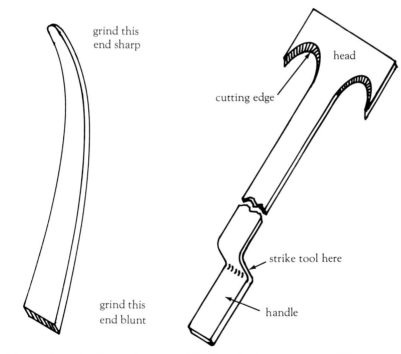

4-32. Grind down the ends of a truck leaf spring, one end blunt so it can be struck with a hammer and the other end sharp so it can fit easily under siding and such.

4-33. Slate hooks are commercially available from roofing suppliers. After sliding the cutting edges around nail shanks, strike the tool handle with a hammer to cut through.

Two carved hardwood finials from a horse-drawn hearse; the owner is still pondering a reuse.

Allen Brown

What to do with short sections of wood is one of *the* questions of salvaging. In this case the builder had milled fir and redwood left over from flooring. The design by the lamp was the first: proceeding from a 2-in.-thick, five-sided hunk of redwood, he built out until the figure was symmetrical, then placed the second 2-in.-thick "center." Pieces were toenailed through the tongues of the wood and held in place with a dab of mastic here and there.

Saint Orres Inn

Originally a trough for feeding stock, this sturdy log was given new life as a planter.

John Midyette III

Less than 8 ft. long, this bar may have stood in a private residence originally. To quote its present owner: "It was a complete mess, hacked and gouged, with more layers of varnish and grime than you'd believe." The base is new, as are the stand rail and the ball-and-claw feet beneath.

Saint Orres Inn, photo, Nicholas Wilson

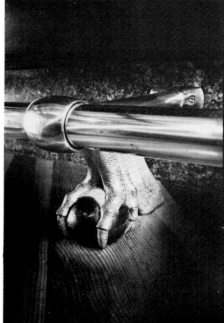

Topped with faces of wood gods, these highly carved legs probably supported the superstructure of a mantel, a large mirror, a hallseat, or some other Victorian built-in. Here they support a counter top and close in cabinetry beneath. The floor is old brick, coated with a clear, shiny finish, probably polyurethane.

Adolf deRoy Mark

Hardware

Safety Tips

- Goggles, gloves, and long-sleeved apparel are important if you will be working with caustic chemicals.
- Read the labels of all chemicals *before you start*.
- Do not try to strip plating yourself; hydrochloric acid, commonly used for the job, is extremely dangerous. Instead, have items stripped by a professional outfit.
- When disposing of chemical solutions, dilute them well and pour them down an exterior drain; flush the drain well with water afterwards. Debris from stripping such as fouled newspapers should be cleaned up at the end of each day (at least) and disposed of where they will not cause fires.
- Because hardware is usually small, secure it before drilling or stripping it with power tools.

Tools

- Cloth-covered rubber gloves last longer around caustic chemicals than solid-rubber ones. Goggles are also a must.
- Use natural-bristle brushes or some other type unlikely to be dissolved by stripping chemicals.
- A wire-brush wheel for your power drill is handy for stripping ornate hardware; use C-clamps to hold such pieces down.

Turn-of-the-century doorknobs, all made in America. Upper right (2), cast brass; knobs on spindle, brass plate; hexagonal, wrought iron.

Caked with paint, tarnished with age, missing screws or odd pieces, hardware is one of the salvager's delights, for small costs and modest efforts yield gleaming treasures. Much old hardware, even some of the more garish handles and doorknobs, was mass-produced by Sears and other big mail-order houses around the turn of the century, but mass-produced in those days did not mean scrimping on materials. True, some of the pieces are a bit overdesigned, but like lighting fixtures, gaudy hardware can complement ornate Victorian decor or contrast with stark modern ones.

ASSESSING PIECES

Most of the information that follows is about door hardware, with a few other miscellaneous pieces; installing hinges, however, is covered in chapter 3. Discussion of larger and exterior metalwork may be found in chapter 8.

Doorknob assemblies vary somewhat, but the basic elements are *knobs* or *handles*; *spindles*, often machined, which run from knob to knob, through the door; *escutcheons* or *roses*, plates which cover the holes cut into the door, to create a nice finish effect; *set screws*, which hold handles or knobs to spindles; *lock mechanisms*, often mortised into the edge of the door; *keyhole escutcheons*, separate from escutcheons around the doorknobs; *keys* to operate lock mechanisms; *face plates* and *strike plates*, which guide the latch bolt of the mechanism; and miscellaneous wood screws or machine bolts, sometimes plated, that hold various pieces to the door.

Your first concern is that all the parts be there. If the assembly is still on a door and it is operable, chances are that all are present. If you are looking at a pile of disassembled parts in a salvage yard, put pieces together as best you can. It is a good idea to take a screwdriver with you. Remember to look for the small screws that hold knobs to spindles and escutcheons to doors. When you have assembled all pieces, put them in a plastic bag so that none get lost, or wire them together.

Since spindles are more or less uniform in cross section, approximately 5/16 by 5/16 inch, replacing an old lock mechanism with a newer one is easy. Key cylinders—which fit into a housing—on the other hand, may not be possible to change, because they are often set into the escutcheon of older locks. Take such assemblies to a locksmith and see if a newer cylinder will fit in the space of the old one.

To see if knob-and-spindle assembly will fit the door you want to refurbish, thread knobs onto their spindles and measure; be sure to include the thickness of escutcheons. Most spindles allow several settings for knobs, either by screw holes *in* or machine-threading *along* the spindle. Appropos the last point, if the inside of the doorknobs are threaded, the spindle must be machined to fit the threading inside those knobs.

Older lock mechanisms are probably operable if their casing is still intact. If the lock fails to operate, it may be that one of its parts, as shown in figure 5–1, has dislodged. By unscrewing the bolts that hold the sides of the lock case together, you can examine the insides. It may be that parts are frozen with rust, a reversible situation if you want to take the time. If rusted

springs are within, however, make sure you can get replacements before buying; chances are that you cannot.

A dull, brownish finish on the knobs and escutcheons may just need polishing; some polishes can even remove minor rust. Apply a magnet to see what kind of metal you might have. Any badly pitted or tarnished steel or iron will probably need replating. Solid brass can be polished up, and nickel- or chrome-plating over brass can be stripped with acid to get back to pure brass. For most brightwork, however, replating is the probable course.

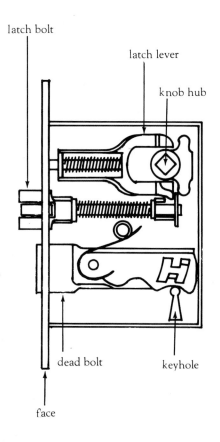

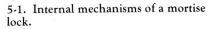

5-1. Internal mechanisms of a mortise lock.

The Josiah B. Durkee House. Originally built in Brookfield, Vermont, in about 1836, this populist Greek revival beauty was found by restorationist Gregory Schipa, who disassembled, moved, and fully restored it on a hilltop in Waitsfield, Vermont. It is only one of several restored houses in the Bent Hill Settlement.

What was a nondescript backyard of a town house in Philadelphia became a stunning composition of cobblestone, water, and wall-clinging foliage. Just visible in the top, center part of the photo is the window shown in the photo below. Center left, obscured by greenery, is the stone ram's head shown at the close of chapter 9.
Adolf deRoy Mark

A neoclassical semiround window reframed and reglazed to admit more light to an upstairs bath.
Adolf deRoy Mark

We are so accustomed to covering up pipes that we forget how finely cast they are, how strong and clean their lines. Here, the homeowner added a bit of whimsy to the architect's decision to leave cast-iron drains exposed.
Adolf deRoy Mark

Rising a story and a half, this glassed-in eating nook overlooks a yard riotous with flowers, plants, and bits of statuary. Atop the smooth plaster columns, where the brick arches come to rest, are recycled capitals.
Adolf deRoy Mark

Solid brass wall fixture with hallophane shade.
JO–EL Shop

This beige enamel cook stove sits in a fieldstone niche,
part of Allen Brown's castle. The floor is recycled brick.

Neoclassical semiround stained glass, circa 1900, with frosted colored petals and
jeweled insets.
"Reflections" Antique Stained Glass

Downstairs sitting room of Saint Orres Inn, Gualala, California. The motif of the doors
echoes the shape of the onion domes and recurs throughout the building.

Ornamental fretwork, stained oak, 10 in. × 30 in.; the curly pieces were probably steam-bent.
Architectural Antiques Exchange

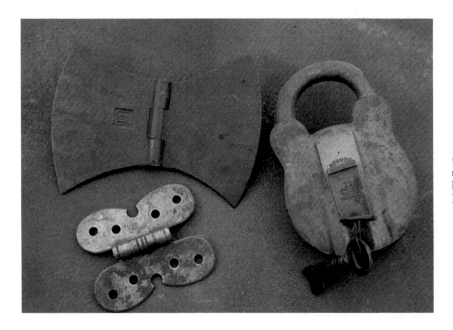

Miscellaneous hardware, updated. The hinge at upper left, wrought iron, is as yet undrilled for screws; lower left, a delicate steel butterfly; the lock at left has a brass inset.
Eric Bauer

English art nouveau brass fixture, 1900–1910; shades, signed *Nu Art*, carnival glass added later; reconstructed by Lennart Sandin.
Nowell's, Inc.

Cast-bronze demon door knocker, mid–nineteenth century, Mexican.
Architectural Antiques, Ltd.

Painted Mexican doors, oil on pine, from an old estate outside Magdalena; nineteenth century, although the wood may be a century older.
John Midyette III

Mexican candelabra of mesquite wood, circa late eighteenth century, wired for electricity.
John Midyette III

Handcarved mesquite panel doors, early eighteenth-century Mexican; 90 in. × 40 in.
John Midyette III

Exterior balusters reused as supports for a hearth seat in a
1682 Connecticut house. By building up the base and top
with successively larger boards and trim, the unit is
decorative yet strong.
Thanks to the Robert Webster family

Ethereal shades and playful ornament grace this art
nouveau fixture, a signed Muller Freres (1870–1914) piece.
Nowell's, Inc.

Cast-iron and enameled mantel, circa 1910, possibly
Belgian; outer dimensions 43 in. × 37 in. high. Log basket
not original.
Gargoyles, Ltd.

An early nineteenth-century half-log house, salvaged, comprises the main section of
this home in the hills of northern Virginia. Its back, south-facing side has a greenhouse
and a fieldstone Trombe wall.
Morton Riddle IV

A barrelful of refitted, repolished
brass-and-porcelain bath spigots.
Great American Salvage

Two bronze Victorian wall hooks, each about 14 in. high.
Great American Salvage

A festive barn, showing some Pennsylvania Dutch influence, in the Cumberland region of Maryland. Because of the blight at the turn of the century, a spate of barns such as this one were framed in chestnut.
Alex Grabenstein, Vintage Lumber and Construction Company

Strength and grace combine in this copper tub, its top edged with oak, its body reinforced with ornamental cast-iron straps that evolve into feet. The outside of the tub body, unfinished here, could be painted to match the decor of a room.
Great American Salvage

Probably a century old, this bidet is in remarkable working order. Although its cast-iron flushing mechanisms are crude by today's standards, they are nicely appointed with a brass trip lever. The edges and insides of the porcelain are festooned with blue flowers, a pleasing effect, rather like a fountain.
Gargoyles, Ltd.

A small corner where beauty lurks: streak-textured clear glass, cobalt blue petals, clear faceted center.
Architectural Antiques Exchange

Simple materials—an adobe wall, a salvaged window casing, hot peppers drying on a string, a blue sky—and a painter's eye.
Nat Kaplan

A colonnade of hand-carved spiral oak from Mexico flanks a modern window green-house in the Southwest.
John Midyette III

REMOVING HARDWARE

Paint is the bane of removing hardware, for it obscures screw heads and prevents them from turning out easily. After locating screws covered with paint, score around the head with a utility knife to break the seal, and clean out the screw slot with the knife or the point of a screwdriver. If the screw slot is somewhat stripped, redefine it. Wearing goggles, strike it with a screwdriver (hit its handle with a hammer), an old wood chisel, or in extreme cases, an impact driver with a screwdriver bit.

To take out a lock assembly, first unscrew the set screws holding the knobs to the spindle; pull off or unscrew the knobs. Unscrew escutcheons and remove them, first breaking paint seals around their edges with a utility knife if they are painted over. Two screws hold the lock mechanism to the edge of the door; after removing them, the lock should slide out easily. If not, reinsert the spindle and tug slightly toward the door edge to dislodge the mechanism. Remember to remove the strike plate that is mortised into the adjacent door frame.

Some callous souls remove locks by simply cutting out the unit, still in the wood, from the door stile; there is no need to waste a door in this manner, unless it is already beyond saving.

Those are the details, mostly a case of removing a few screws. Drawer pulls or cabinet knobs may be attached by a washered bolt whose head is on the inside of the drawer or door; match bolts with individual knobs, because bolts added later may have enlarged the hole in the back side of some knobs. If you remove more than one lock assembly, put each in a separate plastic bag.

RECONDITIONING HARDWARE

Most reconditioning is cosmetic—removing paint or shining a finish. A few tips about replacing missing parts are included as well.

STRIPPING PAINT

Paint can be successfully removed at home by using a commercial stripper. If you have too many pieces to do yourself, send assemblies out to a dip stripper. If you strip the pieces, wear cloth-coated rubber gloves and use a pan, such as enameled steel or heavy-grade plastic, which will not be affected by the stripper. Apply the stripper with a natural-bristle brush, as the solvent may dissolve nylon or other synthetics. Always brush away from yourself, being careful not to splatter stripper by applying it carelessly.

Allow the stripper ten or fifteen minutes to work and then scrape off the dissolved paint with coarse steel wool. A flat-bladed scraper will work if the escutcheon is flat, but you may scratch the finish. Use a toothbrush or any fine-pointed tool for fine work. If the piece is cast or otherwise sturdy, you may use a wire brush in an electric drill to remove paint from intricate designs. If the piece is not solid brass, however, this may remove its plating; replate the piece in most cases. (Professional replaters will also strip the piece beforehand.)

UNPAINTED BRIGHTWORK

Brightwork is a catchall term denoting any hardware, especially that

5-2. Apply paint stripper to the piece, allowing the chemical ten or fifteen minutes to dissolve paint.

5-3. If the hardware is at all ornate, use a rotary brush in a drill bit for cleaning.

5-4. French classical-style doorknob, 1894, solid brass with separate keyhole escutcheon.

5-5. American art nouveau–style knob, commercially manufactured, 1910, brass plate.

which has never been painted or lacquered. Solvol Autosol Metal Polish, an English product available in the States through Conservation Materials, Ltd. (see Sources of Supply), is highly regarded by conservators for restoring brightwork. To be sure, many other solvents are available, but Solvol also removes rust and corrosion from aluminum, stainless steel, brass, copper, and nickel without scarring them; the vehicle for this polish is a fine abrasive in solution.

This cleaner can be applied with cotton swabs to detailed brightwork areas and scrubbed in with a wooden toothpick, so effective is its solvent.

REMOVING PLATING

Nickel- or chrome-plating over brass can be stripped, leaving you with a solid brass piece that needs only polishing to look good. Removing plating is an unpleasant and potentially dangerous activity because it involves the use of potent acids. Most people will be better off sending the hardware out to be stripped professionally.

MISSING PARTS

As noted earlier, if the missing or damaged part is a lock mechanism, chances are that the old spindle will fit into a new lock-box, allowing you to use the old handles (or knobs) and escutcheon. If that escutcheon covers the keyhole of the new mechanism, however, you are out of luck. Either locate other old escutcheons of the same era or look elsewhere for another assembly. If you have one—and only one—doorknob that you want to use, use it on the outside of a closet door; a nondescript knob can be used inside a closet.

It sometimes happens that smaller pieces such as cabinet knobs get lost, so that an incomplete set remains. If that is your problem, you may have new ones cast from one of the originals. Having a forge do the casting will cost plenty, but there is a relatively low-cost alternative: making your own casting with special epoxy compounds. These compounds have pulverized metal in their mix, so that the finished product will look like metal and have the same approximate heft. A number of manufacturers produce these compounds, the Monzini line being the best known (available from Adhesive Products Corporation; see Sources of Supply).

One must first make a mold, described at length in chapter 8. The mold for the Monzini compounds should be flexible if the casting is small, though virtually any molding agent will work. For fineness of detail, moulage (used for death masks) is best; RTV molding rubber is probably the best all-around molding material and far easier to work with. As indicated by the manufacturer of the molding material, cover the original hardware piece with a mold-release agent so the mold will come off easily. After the mold has dried, remove the original; you are ready to cast replacement parts with the epoxy compound.

Mix the epoxy according to manufacturer's specs; Monzini recommends adding 1 percent Monzini hardener by weight to 100 parts of Monzini and stirring thoroughly. Once the parts are mixed, the epoxy will set up in about a half hour; the process can be speeded up by putting the casting in a warm oven or by holding a flameless heat-gun over it. When the compound is completely dry, remove the object and recoat the mold with a release agent so that the next item can be cast.

Monzini looks great and can be drilled, sanded, and so on; should any imperfections appear in the casting, holes can easily be filled by hand-applying fresh compound. Although the compound can be drilled and tapped, save work on cabinet knobs (which receive a bolt) by inserting a bolt (coated with release agent) into the end of the mold before you pour in the compound. When the compound has dried, turn the bolt out with a screwdriver, and then peel off the mold. In this way you will have a perfectly threaded replacement part.

Also available are low-melt metals (Cerro Alloys, Kindt-Collins Company) that you can heat up in a saucepan—make it a pan that you do not plan to use for cooking. The best mold to use for low-melts is RTV silicone rubber, which will withstand the heats involved. Follow manufacturer's directions to the letter; use powdered graphite to coat the mold so the metal will pop out easily.

REUSING HARDWARE

There are few absolutes in positioning hardware. To please the eye, handles and such should be set at the same height as other nearby hardware. Doorknobs are roughly centered along the door stile and placed 36 inches above the finish floor. Cabinet drawer pulls should be centered from side to side on the drawer face, slightly above the center of the height of the drawer. If a drawer has two pulls, space them equidistantly from each end. Center the window sash fasteners. In all cases use screws that will secure the piece to the wood behind, but avoid screws or bolts that are too big; they may split or otherwise weaken wooden elements. Pay attention to

the heads of the screws or bolts you use: they should have the same finish as the hardware itself.

SETTING A MORTISE LOCK

There are several types of door locks, mortise locks being by far the most common types of older hardware. Mortise locks are so named because their bodies are cut, or mortised, into door stiles.

The first steps of the operation are truing the edge of the door and hanging it, as described in chapter 3. Pull the hinge pins of a door to remove it. Because a door must be held rigid while you work on it, lay it across two sawhorses so it will be at a comfortable working height. You can mortise a lock into a door while it is still hanging, but that requires extra, unnecessary effort and makes no sense.

Locate the holes you must drill. New mortise locks come with a paper template to aid positioning. The middle of the doorknob, as noted above, is 36 inches above the finish floor. Measure up accordingly from the bottom of the door stile and draw a line across the stile, using a try square. Where you drill the spindle hole in the stile is deter-

mined by the center of the spindle hub of the lock, the hole through which the spindle passes. Measure from the edge of the lock mechanism to the center of the hub. Transfer that measurement to the door stile, and mark the line you drew with the try square.

Holding a ⅝-inch drill bit perfectly perpendicular to the face of the door stile, drill all the way

5-7. Keep the drill bit perfectly perpendicular to the surface being drilled. (The line of small holes in the foreground is for the key.)

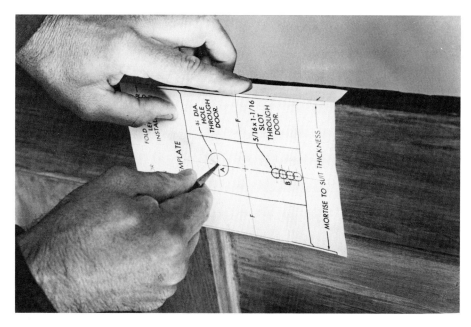

5-6. A new lock will come with a paper template indicating the locations of the holes to be drilled. Here, the center hole for the spindle is marked onto the face of the stile.

through. To prevent wood from splintering, stop the drill just as its auger point emerges through the other side; finish drilling from that other side.

With the spindle hole drilled, locate the body of the lock along the door edge. With the door on edge, hold the lock mechanism on edge above it, the spindle hub of the lock aligned to the line you drew earlier (on the stile) with the try square. Mark where the main body of the lock will hit the door edge. Set the lock aside and, with the try square, mark across the edge of the door to indicate the upper and lower limits of the lock mechanism. Next measure and draw a line exactly down the middle of the door edge, between the upper and lower lines you just drew. The drill bit must be centered along this middle line so that the lock body will be exactly centered in the edge of the door.

Use a drill bit whose diameter is just slightly wider than the main body of the lock mechanism; again, a ⅝-inch drill bit is most commonly used. So that you go no deeper than necessary, measure the exact width of the lock body and put a piece of masking tape on the bit to that depth. Drill holes along the middle line in the door edge until you reach the upper and lower limits of the lock body, as represented by the two lines. (Five holes are commonly drilled.)

Square up the sides of the hole with a chisel. Do not use a hammer or mallet for the chiseling operation. You will have better control guiding the tool by hand alone, and you will greatly reduce the chance of splits. Hold the bevel of the tool toward the inside of the hole. As you chisel, test-fit the lock body into the hole to prevent chiseling away any more than necessary. When the main body of the lock fits in the hole, trace around the edge of the lock face; chisel out that small area

until the face of the lock is flush with the edge of the door.

Test the doorknob spindles again and make sure they turn freely, without hitting any part of the wood, which might cause bind-

ing. Screw the face of the lock to the edge of the door and then slide the escutcheons over the spindle so those plates can be screwed down. Screw the knobs onto the spindle.

To set the strike plate, shut the

5-8. It is imperative that the door be adequately braced on edge so that it does not move when being drilled. To ensure further that the door does not move, straddle it.

5-9. Pare out the inside of the hole with a hand chisel; hold the bevel of the tool toward the inside of the hole.

5-10. So that you remove no more than necessary, periodically test-fit the lock mechanism.

5-11. When the body of the lock fits into the hole, trace the perimeter of its face plate.

5-12. Using a try square to make sure that the escutcheon is parallel to the edge of the door, mark the escutcheon and screw it down.

5-13. Slide the spindle through the escutcheon and screw (or slide) the handles or knobs onto the spindle; tighten the machine screws that hold the knobs to the spindle.

door and mark where the latch bolt strikes the door frame. An easy way to do this is to smear a bit of lipstick on the end of the bolt, turn the knob so the bolt retracts, and when the door is shut, release the knob. The spring-loaded bolt will shoot a lipstick mark onto the frame; center the strike plate around the bolt mark, so that the door closes without rattling when the bolt is in its strike plate.

SECURITY

No door lock is stronger than the door stile into which it is mortised and the door frame into which the strike plate is set. Most solid panel doors of years past are, happily, solid enough to hold a lock when a forced entry is being attempted; most hollow-core doors are not. The door frame of either type, however, is usually a problem; here are two things you can do to improve security.

Upgrade the strike plate, using one similar to that shown in figure 5-14. This plate is so deep that its mortise extends into the studs behind the frame, making it very difficult to dislodge.

Add a dead bolt. The weak point of the whole lock assembly may be the latch bolt, usually protruding only ½ inch beyond the edge of the door—simply not enough. If there is also a dead bolt that protrudes an inch or more, a reinforced strike plate should cover your security needs. If the lock has no dead bolt, buy a separate one, such as that shown in figure 5-15, to supplement your old lock. A latch bolt is controlled by a doorknob; a dead bolt is thrown by a separate key or trip key. A dead bolt is longer and its end is not beveled as that on a latch bolt.

THUMB LATCHES AND OTHERS

Thumb latches, which provide no security at all, are used only on interior doors; locate trip latches about 36 inches above the finished floor. Although such mechanisms are roughly centered in the width of the door stile, exact placement depends in part upon the length of the latch bar; if the bar is short, the body of the mechanism should be closer to the edge of the door.

Because thumb latches rest on the surface of the door, unlike a mortise lock, the only hole needed is for the thumb latch itself, which trips up the bar. Secure the handle with a screw or two, so that you can move the thumb latch without moving the handle; then position the latch bar so that it extends about ¼ inch beyond the edge of the frame jamb (side). Finally, position the catch so that the latch bar will rest in the catch when the latch is at rest. Mortise the catch into the face of the jamb so that it is flush. The latch may or may not have a restraining sleeve, which fits over the latch bar and prevents it from misaligning; screw on the sleeve last.

Doorstops, should you find any, can be mounted to the door or to the baseboard behind. Although the stop is frequently placed as far away from the hinges as possible, that is a mistake, because the door twists in the middle each time it hits a stop violently. Instead, the stop should be placed (on door or baseboard) only two-thirds of the door width from the hinge.

Finally, any mechanism will benefit from a little light machine oil shot into its innards; where there has been rust, use penetrating oil.

5-14. Because any lock is only as secure as the frame around it, the simplest way to improve security is to replace the existing strike plate with one that must be mortised well into the frame (indeed, into the framing behind the frame).

Schlage Lock Company

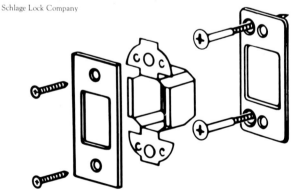
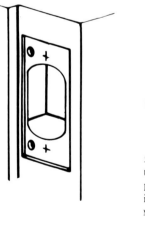

5-15. A separate dead bolt, which extends a full inch (or more) into the frame, provides security even if your regular lock is old-fashioned and less efficient.

Medeco Security Locks, Inc.

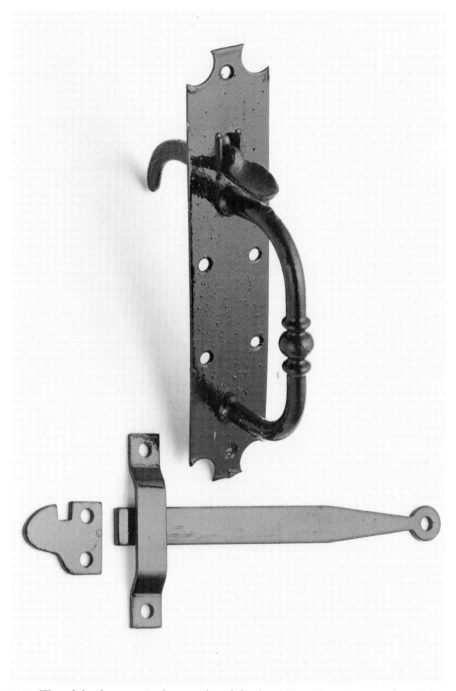

5-16. Thumb-latch parts. At the top, thumb latch and handle; at bottom, from left, strike plate, catch, and latch bar.

Hand-hammered thumb latch of bronze, early twentieth century.
John Midyette III

Wrought-iron hinge, holes probably stamped; late nineteenth century.
John Midyette III

A new piece, but so delightful we had to include it. A strong spring snaps the bird's beak down into the strike catch. A hefty, substantial piece, yet nicely fitted to the hand.

Eric Bauer

Wrought-iron door bands and ring handle, possibly early-nineteenth-century Mexican; difficult to date and place because it has been reused and modified several times. Note the band at left: it was cut into, perhaps to accommodate a surface lock box.

John Midyette, III

Lighting Fixtures

Safety Tips

Coming in contact with electrical current can be fatal, but because the repairs described below are done with the fixture disconnected, no hazard exists. When planning to remove or reinstall a fixture, however, read the entire chapter first—especially the section on disconnecting and connecting power–and proceed only if you understand the procedures described therein. Note the following safety tips as well.

- Disconnect electrical current at the service panel by flipping the appropriate circuit breaker(s) off or by removing (not merely unscrewing, but *removing*) the controlling fuse. Leave a sign at the service panel so that another member of the household does not inadvertently turn the power back on.
- After turning off the electricity to the outlet in question, test the outlet with a voltage tester (see figs. 4–1 to 4–3). Be careful that you do not touch the bared wire prongs of the tester; hold onto insulated parts. If the tester's bulb goes on, power is still present.
- Proceed only when you are sure no power remains at the outlet. If you have any doubt, consult additional sources, including reference works on electricity; a licensed electrician in your area; or the *National Electrical Code*, the standard of electrical safety.
- Use tools with insulated handles.
- When refurbishing a lighting fixture, take care not to gall the wire, especially when pulling it through the fixture; galled wires can mean short circuits later on. A continuity tester will enable you to test the wiring in a fixture; that tool can also "read" sockets, so that you will know if old ones are operable.
- When removing or reinstalling fixtures—especially heavy ceiling units—support them so that the wires themselves are never strained. In most cases a hanging chain or a threaded assembly (mounting bar) is attached to the outlet box (which is attached to the structure nearby). Have a helper support the fixture temporarily, if necessary.
- Wear goggles and gloves if you strip old lacquer or paint from a fixture. If the plating of the fixture needs replacement, send the piece out to a commercial replating company; the acids needed to strip plating are very dangerous.

A late-Victorian ceiling fixture, cast bronze with alabaster shades.

Architectural Antiques Exchange

Tools

- Use a voltage tester to make sure there is no electrical current in a circuit. Use a continuity tester, which has its own battery, to locate a short circuit in a socket or a length of fixture wiring.
- Buy good-quality tools with insulated handles. You can make most lighting repairs with a screwdriver, heavy-duty pliers with wire-cutting jaws, and needle-nose pliers for work in tight spaces.
- Wire strippers are much easier to use than a penknife and less likely to sever the individual strands in electrical cord. Calibrated settings on the wire cutters match differing wire gauges.
- Use a magnet to determine whether the lamp metal is ferrous or not.
- If you will be stripping paint or lacquer from an old fixture, wear goggles and gloves and ensure adequate ventilation.

Because most of us grew up in a world already electrified, we have little sense how ingenious electric lighting is or with what fascination it was regarded when new. The fixtures that have survived speak of those dead times through eccentric and lovely shapes, imparting that sense of wonder and, to a degree, the artistic intentions of their makers. Some pieces are almost menacing, with Gothic spikes and spidery metal webbing; whereas others reflect the lassitude of the *fin-de-siècle*, iridescent gloves of purple and green floating at the end of silvery tendrils. Later come the clean industry of Arts and Crafts design and the preachy utility of art deco. When we buy old fixtures and hang them, we see light in a new way, as if for the first time.

Because working with electrical parts can be hazardous, it is assumed that all work described is done with the *fixture disconnected* from electrical service, with the *power off*. For particulars of disconnecting from or hooking up to live power, see figures 4–1 to 4–3 and the last section of this chapter. Arguably, such information should come first, but most readers will buy their fixtures already disconnected or will have someone else do the actual installation. Readers intending to upgrade residential wiring should consult the Bibliography, especially the *National Electrical Code*, for the last word on correct procedures and safety.

Lighting fixtures may be seen as a series of mechanical connections, parts that join together. These parts vary to a degree, but the field tended to become standardized early on. As you examine any fixture, be

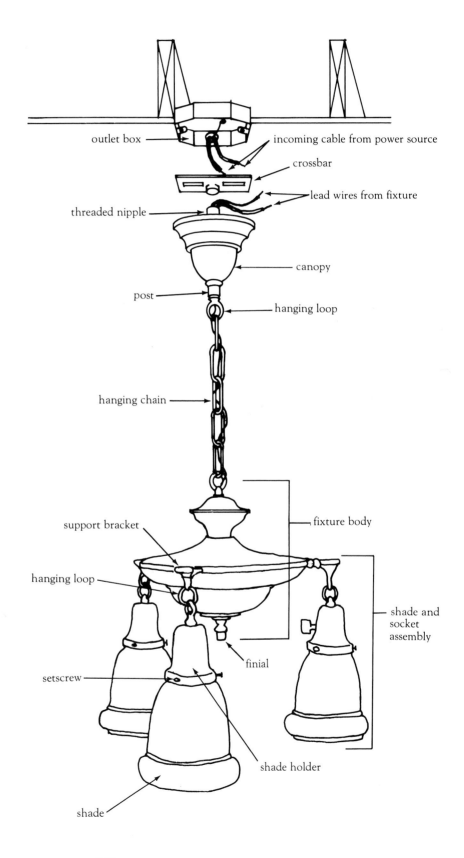

6-1. Lighting fixture terms.

outlet box

incoming cable from power source

crossbar

lead wires from fixture

threaded nipple

canopy

post

hanging loop

hanging chain

fixture body

support bracket

hanging loop

shade and socket assembly

finial

setscrew

shade holder

shade

125

on the lookout for pieces that are not original, for they should be replaced to restore a light correctly. Such replacement pieces may be of a different material, a different style, or simply may not fit tightly and operate freely.

For starters, there are *wall-mounted* and *ceiling-hung fixtures*, the former usually smaller and less complex, although either type may hold several light sockets. Because ceiling-hung types are more complex, we shall consider them most closely. Both fixtures attach mechanically (with machine screws) to an *outlet box*, which is itself attached to a structural member (stud or joist) behind the finish surface. Less often, an outlet box will mount to a finish surface only.

Most ceiling-hung fixtures hang from a hollow *post* (also called an *extension pipe* or *tube*) or, frequently, from a *chain*. Both the chain and the pipe must be firmly affixed to bear the considerable weight of the fixture: the chain usually hangs on a *swag hook* or *loop*; the post has a threaded end that screws into the *crossbar* of the outlet box. (Here again, there are variations: a swag hook may end in a wood screw that turns directly into a joist edge or may end in a machine thread that, like the end of the post, screws into an outlet box crosspiece.) Covering the end of chain or post is a bell-like piece, the *canopy*, which covers and protects electrical connections within the outlet box.

Fixture bodies—the main bodies of lamps—vary so greatly that generalizing about them is very difficult. The chain or post usually ends at the body, connecting to a *loop* or a threaded *nut* on the body. The parts of the body are usually held together by a threaded post assembly running inside the body. The body acts as a housing for electrical wires running from the outlet box to the individual light sockets. These generalizations hold for the fixture we dissect in figures 6–5 to 6–26.

Simpler lamps may lack a fixture body altogether: in them, wires run directly from outlet box to individual sockets.

The parts of the fixture body are: the top and bottom pieces (or plates) of the main body, held together with threaded pipe *nipples*; various locknuts that hold nipples fast; a *hickey*, a **C**-shaped female part that receives two nipple sections; and various hardware trappings such as brass *finials* that ornament the main body, and *loops* or *brackets* from which hang individual sockets.

Shade assemblies include *sockets*, which may be *pull-chain*, *push-through*, *turn-knob*, *key*, and so on; *shade holders*, which may slip over, screw, or clamp to sockets; *shades* themselves; *bulbs*, and so on. Gas lamps have a host of distinct parts with special fittings, including *chimney holders*, *chimneys*, *turnkeys*, and the like.

ASSESSING FOR PURCHASE

In this section we are most concerned with fixture parts, not with the wiring itself. Most lights, in fact, need to be completely rewired, so the condition of the wiring is not an important element of the assessment.

The composition and condition of the light fixture will strongly affect your decision to buy and your success in reclaiming. Of all the materials fixtures are made of, brass is by far the most preferred, for it is handsome and easy to clean. Other materials include steel with a brass plating (by far the most common), white metal, aluminum, and nickel over brass.

To tell what metal you have, apply a magnet to the piece. If the magnet sticks, the fixture is not brass; it may be plated brass (over steel), which will not clean up well if it is tarnished; replating is the only

6-2. Assume that you will have to replace all wires, for they often gall against metal edges.

6-3. Use a magnet to determine metal: a brass-colored piece that the magnet will stick to is probably steel plated with brass.

answer, and its expense may discourage you from buying. You can discern white metal and aluminum by looking at the back or inside of pieces; if fixtures of these metals have a tarnished brass coating, replating is again the only answer—you cannot polish what is not there. If you do not mind a nonbrass surface, strip the remaining plating.

These tests and observations are best performed surreptitiously if you hope to haggle a good price for the fixture. In some cases you may have to lightly scrape the back of the piece if you cannot determine the metal. Fixtures may also be made of a number of materials: even solid brass bodies will occasionally have a plated steel canopy, for example.

Look closely at the fixture: do all parts seem original or are some obvious replacements? Are any parts irreplaceably damaged? Shade holders are particularly tough to replace. Dents in the main body of a fixture may be gently hammered out from the inside if the metal is not badly creased.

Assume that you must replace all the wiring. Individual wires often fray or corrode, and besides, the insulation of newer wires is far superior to that on old ones. Likewise, chain can be replaced, although matching replacement chain to the general hue of the light may require digging through a few replacement-parts catalogs.

The guts of the fixture—the little nuts and bolts, hickeys, and threaded nipples—are easily replaced. Most can be purchased at a good hardware store.

Shade-and-socket assemblies, on the other hand, are critical and must be intact unless you have a stockpile of old parts from which you can cannibalize missing pieces. Are all shade holders the same? Do all holders have tiny setscrews that hold the shades in place? Are the sockets the same kind? There is a world of difference between an old

brass socket shell and a shiny new one made out of aluminum. If a fixture originally had pull-chain sockets, does it now have more than one type? Pull-chain sockets are notoriously delicate. Turnkey knobs are much easier for the amateur to obtain and replace.

Test sockets with a small continuity tester (fig. 6–21) to see if they work. Finally, carefully inspect sockets to see if each still has its insulative paper liner within. New liners will probably not fit old sockets and you *must* insulate the socket mechanism from its shell. If all parts of the socket are present—cap, shell, and paper liner— you can replace the switch mechanism of the socket. But the part of the mechanism that sticks out— whether knob, key, push-through rod, or pull-chain—may differ from existing parts already on the lamp. The alternative is replacing all the socket mechanisms of a fixture to make them the same. This is

perhaps a waste of time because new knobs, pull-chains, and the like, will lack the style of old ones.

Finally, are the shades in good shape? If one is broken, you may have a difficult time finding another shade to match those remaining. Replacing *all* shades, however, is less of a problem, for there are many sources of replacement shades, new and old.

A word about sources of supply. Most electrical wholesalers will not deal with retail trade; one must be a dealer to order from them. A lighting specialty store may have what you need; likewise a small outfit or an individual repairer may have surplus parts. If small suppliers ask a lot for one small screw or the like, do not complain: such parts are rare, small though they be. The last resort may be the old hardware store (the one that has been there forever) in your neighborhood, where elderly clerks offer same-day service.

6-4. Pay close attention to small parts, especially shade holders. This example has delightful flower-headed set screws, which would be impossible to replace if any were missing.

REHABILITATING AN OLD FIXTURE

You can operate on most types of lighting fixtures with a modest collection of tools, most of which are common.

You need two pairs of *pliers*, preferably one with locking jaws (such as Vise-Grip locking pliers); two *screwdrivers*, one straight head and one Phillips head; a very *small head screwdriver* if there are tiny screws to work; a *magnet*, for assessing fixture parts; *wire cutters*, preferably with a stripping jaw, which removes the insulation of wire without severing the wire itself; *needle-nose pliers* for working in tight places, although those pliers should not be used for strenuous gripping.

6-5. An old fixture, before repairs.

General-purpose tools include an *electric drill* with a rotary brush for cleaning up pieces, as well as any bits you need to drill out old wire and the like; a *plastic pan* in which you can clean up parts; a *natural-bristle brush*, which solvents will not dissolve; *cloth-covered rubber gloves*, which resist solvents better than those with rubber on the outside; and *goggles* or safety glasses to keep solvent out of your eyes.

A *voltage tester* is indispensable if you will be working around live circuits. A *continuity tester* is used to check if sockets and the like are working properly.

Note: Electrical tools should have insulated handles. Keep your fingers away from uninsulated parts while using such tools.

DISASSEMBLING

All work in this section is to be done when the fixture has been disconnected from the circuit feeding it; those readers facing a still-connected fixture must disconnect power at the entrance panel.

Disconnecting Metal

Because they are easily damaged, remove glass shades, which are held in place by small screws (or clips) in the shade holder. Set them aside before you start handling metal parts. Perhaps the easiest way to work on a lamp is to suspend it from a hook in the ceiling, as shown in this section, so that you can work at chest height, with both hands free.

If you are new to fixture repair, have a clear counter space on which you can lay pieces in the order you disassemble them. This will save a lot of head-scratching later about which piece goes where.

First, remove presently defective wire, which means, in most cases, completely rewiring the lamp.

Remove the canopy from the post or chain that it covers; usually, a single screw holds the canopy in place. Although most posts thread into the cross bar of an outlet box, there may be an antiquated crow's-foot mount such as that shown in figure 6-6; unscrew it as well. If the fixture hangs by a chain, spread apart links to disconnect.

To keep them from being damaged while you wrestle with the main body of the lamp, next remove individual socket assemblies. Snip any wires leading from the main body to individual sockets and very gently open chain links, if any, from which sockets hang. Because short sections of chain might break and may be difficult to replace exactly, you may wish to unscrew the small hardware brackets from which the sockets hang. You may need to open up the body of the fixture to get at the nuts restraining such bracket screws. When you have removed socket assemblies, set them aside so they will not get bent.

The main bodies of most lamps are held together by a threaded pipe running through the middle of the body, restrained on either end by washer-and-locknut assemblies or by ornamental nuts. The example shown was taken apart by gripping the ornamental nut on the bottom with pliers while inserting a screwdriver in a threaded loop at the top. When the screwdriver was turned counterclockwise, the assembly came apart. Care was taken not to break the loop at the top of the fixture. Once the main body has been opened, clip the junction of wires inside.

Should any piece resist your efforts to unscrew it, add a few drops of a penetrating oil such as WD-40 or Liquid Wrench. Allow the oil to soften any corrosion present and try again. Corrosion is not uncommon on steel pipes or where disparate metals join.

6-6. After disconnecting power to the fixture (if it is hooked up), unscrew the canopy, which covers the fixture base. (Note the old "crow's foot" base, peeping above the canopy.)

6-7. Separate chain sections with two pairs of pliers for leverage.

6-8. Snip the wires running to individual sockets.

6-9. Holding the ornamental finial nut fast with pliers, turn the hanging loop at the top (also a nut) counterclockwise. Be careful not to split that loop: if it does not turn easily, apply corrosion-dissolving fluid.

6-10. Support the bottom of the body when nuts are removed.

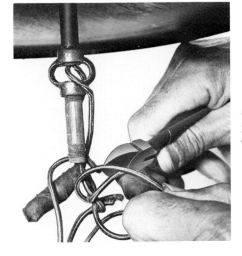

6-11. Snip wire connections. The metal piece from which the wires summon is called a hickey.

6-12. Slide sockets out of shade holders, being careful not to damage any parts of the socket such as the turnkey shown here.

6-13. Depress the sides of the socket body (or shell) from the cap and pull the switching mechanism out. Be especially careful not to damage the paper liner around the mechanism.

Removing Wire

Wires will be a bit of a problem to remove if the pipes carrying them have corroded or rusted. In our example removing the wire from the upper portion of the fixture was no problem. It was simply pulled through the hanging chain after being snipped at the top. Inside the main body of the fixture, however, the hickey was corroded badly, and the repairer elected to replace it altogether with a new hickey and new steel nipples. If you want to save the original nipples, it may be necessary to drill them out to remove old wires corroded within. Because pipe size has been standard for a long time (1/4-inch iron pipe and 1/8-inch iron pipe), it makes sense to replace hickey, nipples, and nuts.

Wires to the sockets connect to screw terminals on the sides (usually) of the inner switching mechanism. To get at those screws, disconnect the socket from its cap, usually by simply depressing the sides of the shell, although some older shells may be held in place with screws. *Exercise extreme caution* as you slide the inner mechanism out of the shell. Do not damage the insulative paper liner within. It is simply too difficult to replace, and new liners do not fit into old socket shells in many cases.

CLEANING THE FINISH

Our example was solid brass, with cast-brass fittings, which can be cleaned up nicely with a solvent. If yours is made of the other metals mentioned earlier, they may require replating.

Remove cast pieces by loosening the screws or nuts found inside the fixture body that hold these castings. Use corrosion solvent to loosen nuts if they do not turn off freely.

Be very careful when disconnecting socket holders. Never force little screws that resist you; apply corrosion-dissolving solvent and try again later. Be especially careful that you save all such screws.

Brass fixtures discolor from exposure to moisture, exposure to certain airborne chemicals, from varnish that has tarnished, and so on. Lacquer remover, preferably a nonflammable type such as Lac-Off, is a good all-purpose cleaner. Sponge-bathe the brass over a tub of solvent, then let pieces soak for the prescribed time (usually ten minutes). Gently scrub away residual lacquer with a plastic scrub pad or something not affected by the solvent. Rinse pieces with water and dry them well before proceeding.

Cast-brass pieces often have intricate textures that need more

vigorous treatment: wire-brush them. If your drill has a bench attachment such as that shown in figure 6–16, you will have both hands free to hold the casting.

As you work with the solvent, rinse your gloves often with water, thus prolonging their life and confining solvent to where it is wanted.

Some restorers relacquer brass lights. Others, as in our example, do not, reasoning that a light fixture is rarely touched and that lacquer discolors in time, turning brown and dull. Instead, the piece may be left unfinished or polished with brass polish. If you choose to refinish or polish parts, do so before reassembly, touching up small spots after all parts are reassembled.

REWIRING AND REASSEMBLING

Keep in mind that there are many types and colors of replacement hanging chain, fixture wire and the like. If any element is highly visible, choose it carefully so that it does not detract from the total aesthetic effect of the fixture. Cheap shiny chain, for example, can ruin the appearance of a classy old fixture.

Most fixtures are rewired with No. 18/2 cable, also called *lamp*

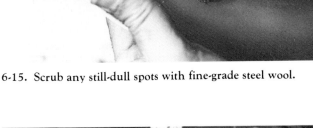

6-15. Scrub any still-dull spots with fine-grade steel wool.

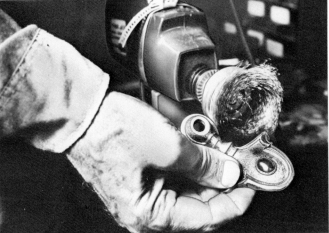

6-14. This fixture was dull from varnish that had turned, so solvent was brushed on.

6-16. Highly ornamented solid-brass pieces, such as this hanging bracket, may be scrubbed with a wire brush. Here, a hand drill in a stationary mount turns a rotary brush.

cord; plastic-covered wire is the most versatile and the least resistant to wear. The designation 18/2 indicates two wires, each 18 gauge in thickness. There is also 18/3 cord, which includes a ground wire, but the third wire is somewhat superfluous unless you are replacing all socket mechanisms with new ones equipped with a third terminal screw to which a ground wire can attach. In most cases 18/2 lamp cord is sufficient.

Before rewiring, replace threaded pipe nipples, nuts, and the hickey if they are corroded. The hickey, by the way, may act as a

sort of adapter, receiving ¼-inch iron-pipe in the top, and ⅛-inch iron-pipe in the bottom. In the example illustrated, an archaic crow's-foot mount was replaced with a nipple threaded into an outlet box crossbar (see fig. 6–24). Thus, the fixture could be suspended directly from an outlet box. The hickey was also replaced. As you install new parts, examine them closely. Not infrequently, you will find burrs on the ends of new nipples, which could puncture the insulation of wires passing through. Remove such burrs with a round file (also called a rat-tail file).

6-17. Old and new hickeys.

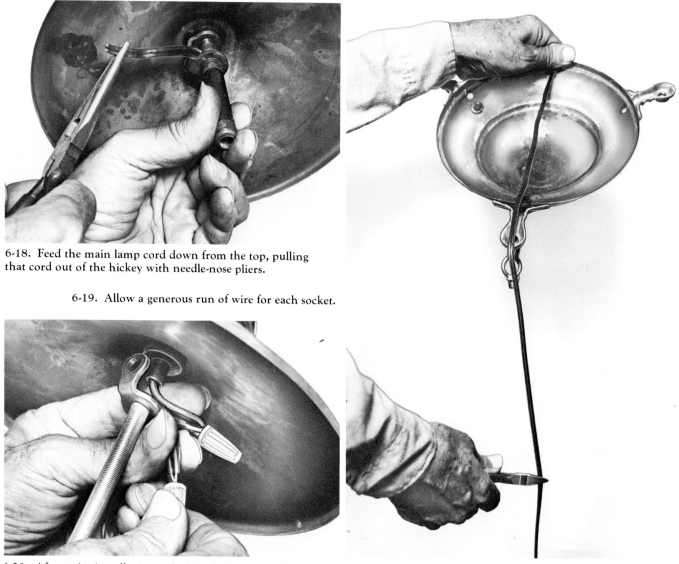

6-18. Feed the main lamp cord down from the top, pulling that cord out of the hickey with needle-nose pliers.

6-19. Allow a generous run of wire for each socket.

6-20. After stripping all wire ends, join the incoming lamp cord to individual socket wires; use wire nuts.

The Fixture Body

Feed lamp cord from above, down into the body of the fixture, leaving at least 1 foot extra inside the body for subsequent connection to individual socket wires. Lamp cord is usually stiff enough to feed down through ¼-inch pipe, but you may need to pull it out at the top of the hickey. Use needle-nose pliers to pull the wire through.

Branch wires running from individual sockets should also have enough extra wire for connection inside the main body of the fixture.

Inside the body of the lamp, group the wires running from individual sockets. Because each socket has (or should have) a silver-colored and gold-colored screw, group branch wires according to the screw to which they connect. Hence, you will have two groups of wires in the fixture body. The lamp cable that runs to the fixture—from the outlet box—has at least two individual wires within and may have a third (ground) wire. If the wires of the lamp cable are color-coded, attach the black wire to the group of gold-screw branch wires; attach the white

wire to the group of silver-screw branch wires. (In the outlet box, these two main lead wires attach to two wires from the power source.)

To join wire groups, strip off about 1 inch from each wire with a wire stripper or, carefully, a penknife. Twist the filaments of each wire clockwise (if the wire ends are facing toward you). Screw a wire nut over the ends of the assembled group. You may wish to tape groups of wire together so that the inside of the fixture is a little neater, but that is not strictly necessary.

132

Rewiring Sockets

Before rewiring old socket mechanisms, test them with a continuity tester. Because it has its own battery inside, a continuity tester should be used only on objects *not* connected to power. (Use a voltage tester, figs. 4-1 to 4-3, to test electrical current in a line.) First, test the socket to see if it is conducting. Clip the *spring-clip* of the tool to the silver terminal screw of the socket and touch the *probe* of the tool to the metal side of the socket. The tool should light; if it does not, the socket is defective. To see if the switch mechanism is working, clip to the brass or gold-colored terminal screw and touch the probe inside the socket, to the tab in the center. Turn the switch off and on: if the tester does not light at all, the switching mechanism is defective.

Use your continuity tester to check for shorts after rewiring too. Such trouble is usually caused by plastic insulation that gets scraped off wires as they are being pulled through the fixture. You will save a lot of work by checking with the continuity tester before you close up the fixture. Likewise, use the tester on the light fixture before you attach the unit to power lines, as described below.

Now attach individual sockets to the main body of the fixture and wire those sockets. Actually, you might have wired sockets first and then grouped branch wires—the order really does not matter. But the weight of a socket should never be supported by branch wires, because that weight could pull wire connections apart. Rather, socket assemblies should be supported by chain links, brackets, and the like.

At sockets, feed branch wires through socket caps. Strip wire ends back 1 inch, with a wire stripper. Twist individual wire filaments together and shape each wire around a terminal screw in the direction that the screw tightens down. Tighten screws. Carefully fit

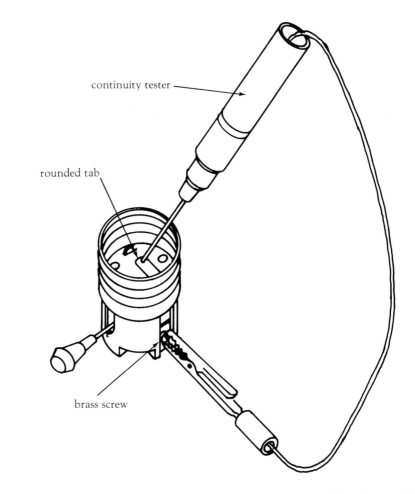

6-21. Use a continuity tester to test your socket before rewiring it. Touch tester clip and point to silver-colored screw and the side of the socket; and then touch clip and point to the gold-colored screw and the tab inside the socket.

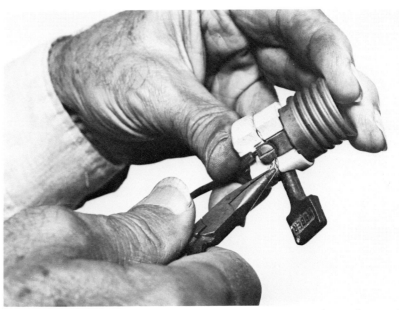

6-22. Strip individual wires about an inch, lightly twist strands together, and shape so that the wires turn the same way as the screw. Needle-nose pliers help tuck stray strands in place.

6-23. Slide the paper liner over the newly wired mechanism and then press the cap in place, so that it snaps solidly to the socket cover.

6-24. The old crow's-foot mount was replaced with a crossbar, which screws directly to the outlet box.

the paper socket liner and shell over the wired mechanism and snap (or screw) the shell to the cap. The cap attaches to the main body of the fixture and supports the weight of the assembly.

To close the main body of the fixture, hold the top and bottom of the body together, so that threaded nipples stick out (in most cases) top and bottom. The top nipple receives, in chain assemblies, a hanging loop; the bottom nipple, a decorative cap or finial. With the hanging apparatus thus affixed and the two lead wires sticking out of the top, the fixture is now ready to mount and connect to the outlet box above, as described in the section on disconnecting and connecting power that follows.

Other Attachments

The electrical connections of most ceiling fixtures take place within an existing outlet box, whose power is usually controlled by a wall switch. In some cases fitting the cord of the fixture with a *plug*, to plug into an existing wall receptacle, is easier. A further variation is to put a *cord switch* along the cord, so that power can be turned off and on close at hand.

6-25. Most wall fixtures also use crossbars; alternatively, an offset tab enables you to hang the fixture on a nail when the fixture cord runs to a separate outlet.

6-26. The restored fixture.

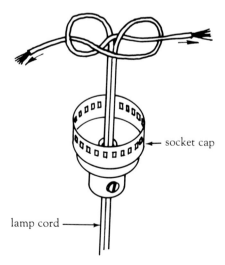

socket cap

lamp cord

6-27. An underwriter's knot.

DISCONNECTING AND CONNECTING POWER

Electrical current runs through insulated *cables*, from a *service panel* to various electricity users, or *outlets*, around the house. Each distinct run of cable, controlled by a breaker or fuse in the service panel, is called a *circuit*. Because not all outlets use the same amount of current, circuits are rated according to the loads they carry. Breakers (or fuses) and cable sizes are carefully matched to loads. We are, of course, most concerned with lighting circuits, which are generally rated for 15-amp loads; a typical lighting circuit is thus controlled by a 15-amp breaker, with current running on No. 14/2 wire. (Lighting circuits are occasionally No. 12/2 wire, which is heavier and gives the homeowner more options for future use.)

Circuits run to various types of outlets, where cable enters individual *outlet boxes*, usually mounted to a structural member such as a stud or joist. As the cable passes through openings in the box, clamps inside tighten to hold the cable fast, so that it cannot be pulled loose. Such mechanical connections are important because they protect the integrity of all electrical connections inside the outlet box.

After pulling cable into a box, strip back the outermost layer of insulative sheathing, without, however, cutting into or disturbing insulative coverings of the individual wires within. No. 14/2 cable denotes cable that has two insulated, 14-gauge wires within; No. 14/2 w/grd., two insulated wires plus a third, uninsulated, wire that acts as a ground. The insulative (usually plastic) sheathing of the wires is color-coded, black being the hot wire; white, the neutral wire. *Note that hot and neutral wires are never connected to each other.*

To oversimplify the explanation somewhat, the hot wire carries

6-28. A wonderfully silly piece, turn-of-the century French, labeled "Muse des Bois." The lady and stand are pewter, as are the tendrils; the socket flowers and acorns, brass.

Gargoyles, Ltd.

Plug attachment varies somewhat. The easiest to attach are *snap-on* or *automatic* plugs that just snap onto the end of the cord. No wire stripping is necessary. A more traditional plug requires that you separate the two wires of the cord about 3 to 4 inches and tie an *underwriter's knot*, as shown in figure 6-27. The knot tied, strip each wire end 1 inch, twist wires, and attach them to terminal screws. Replace the insulative paper liner over the connections.

Several types of cord switches require that you sever one of the wires, strip its ends and screw down those ends to terminals within the switch body. The other wire, whether snipped or not, is not interrupted by the switch. Better cord switches have cord clamps within, to keep wires from pulling free; screw together the halves of the switch to cover and insulate connections. Newer cord switches may require no stripping at all.

135

voltage-charged current towards the outlet, the white wire carries voltage-spent current away from the outlet. Both wires are needed if electricity is to flow through the cables. The ground wire, on the other hand, carries current only in an emergency, when current is escaping or leaking from its intended path, say, when a hot wire comes loose from a screw and touches the side of the box. Older houses may not have cable with ground wire.

Where a ground wire is present, it should be bonded with a screw or grounding clip to the outlet box, thereby providing an emergency route back to the grounding rod of the service panel. Where there is a grounding screw (usually green) on a fixture, wire-nut a short, jumper wire to the base of the fixture itself. But because many old fixtures are metal and their bases are mounted to outlet boxes with machine screws, these fixtures are automatically grounded to a metal box.

DISCONNECTING A FIXTURE

Electrical procedures have become standardized over the years so that hookups would be safe and, to those working on the electrical system, predictable. But, after turning off the electrical current to an outlet, *always test with a voltage tester,* as described below, before handling wire and the like. The procedure is similar to that shown in figures 4–1 to 4–3. Test incoming wires and then wires *and* the box itself. Especially if yours is an older home, you can never be certain that it has been wired in a thoroughly standard (and predictable) manner. Only by testing with a voltage tester can you be sure that current is off. To be doubly sure, check your voltage tester itself, plugging it first into an outlet that you know is live. Do this *before* plugging the tester into the outlet you will be working on. If the

tester does not light in the live outlet, the tester is defective.

To reiterate safety precautions:

1. Determine which switch, if any, controls the fixture; turn it to an "on" position. If switches on the fixture or its cord control the power, turn them on.
2. Have a helper at the service panel pull breakers until the one controlling the fixture is found—the light will go out. Flip that breaker off and tape it down and label it so that another person does not inadvertently turn it back on. If the panel has fuses, completely unscrew the governing fuse.
3. After unscrewing the fixture from its outlet box, proceed gingerly until you can apply a voltage tester to wire ends, after carefully removing wire nuts or electrical tape. This last step is probably superfluous, but it may be the only way to know for sure that current is off if switching mechanisms are somehow defective.

Uncovering the Outlet Box

Turn off electricity to the outlet.

The outlet box is covered by the base of the fixture. Most multilight fixtures such as the one shown in the preceding sections have a small canopy that covers the box. The canopy is held in place with a single screw; loosen that screw and the canopy slides down, revealing the outlet box. Wall-hung fixtures and some ceiling-mounted models may have two machine screws that screw directly to the box; remove those screws to gain access to the box.

Where the fixture also has a crossbar, such as that shown in figure 6–24, you can either loosen the nut holding the threaded nipple to the crossbar or unscrew the screws holding the crossbar to the outlet box. Whatever the case, be ready to support the weight of the

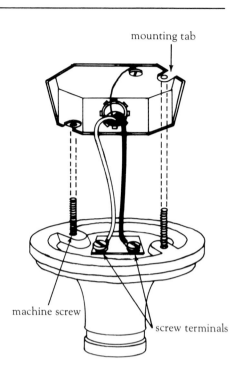

6-29. Wires may attach directly to terminal screws on the base of the fixture, black wire to gold-colored screw, white wire to silver-colored screw. Bare copper wire (ground) screws directly to the metal outlet box, unless there is a green grounding screw on the base of the fixture.

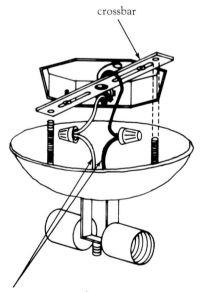

6-30. Wire-nut connections allow you to run short "jumper" sections to fixture terminals, here, two lead wires.

fixture when it is detached from its mountings.

Several groups of wires nest inside the box. Pull the fixture away from the box slightly and you will pull the wires out as well, making them more accessible. In most cases no bare wire ends will be exposed; connections will be covered with electrical tape or, in more recent installations, with wire nuts. Being careful not to touch *any* wire ends, twist off wire nuts or snip away tape to expose the ends of grouped wires. Use only tools with insulated handles for this operation. Finally, touch the prongs of the voltage tester to the ends of each wire group and to the box itself. If the tester light does not go on, you can safely handle the wires.

Using a Voltage Tester

With the wire ends exposed, touch one prong of the tester to a group of hot (usually black) wires and the other prong to the side of the metal outlet box. Then touch one prong to the group of hot wires and one prong to the group of neutral wires (usually white). Finally, touch one prong of the tester to the neutral group and the other prong to the side of the box. This last test is an extra precaution in case the installer crossed the colors.

Once this test is complete and your tester does not light, snip the two lead wires from the fixture and remove the fixture. Should you need to turn the power back on, wire-nut the snipped wire ends and push them back into the outlet box. Ideally, the outlet box should be covered; covers are available for that purpose.

While on the subject of voltage testers, here is how to test a switch. Remove the cover plate. Using a screwdriver with an insulated handle, unscrew the two screws holding the switch body to its box. Without touching the sides of the switch or the box, pull the switch out. Touch

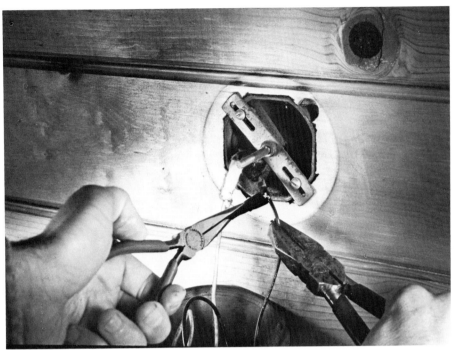

6-31. Test wire ends with a voltage tester before handling wires. If wire ends are wrapped with tape, pull off the tape using pliers with insulated handles. Touch prongs to black and white groups of wires.

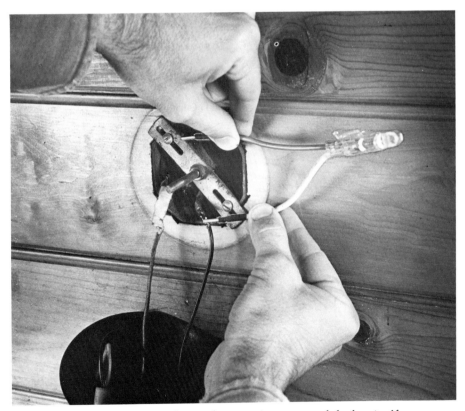

6-32. Also use a voltage tester alternately on a wire group and the box itself.

the two prongs of the tester to both screw terminals on the switch body, with the toggle in both up and down positions. Then touch, alternately, each screw and the metal outlet box, again, with the toggle in both positions. If the tester does not light at all, you can be very sure there is no power at that point. If you get a reading at any of the positions, you will know which is the incoming hot wire.

During any tests, *do not touch your fingers to the bare metal of the tester prongs*; hold only insulated parts.

CONNECTING A FIXTURE

Before starting, read the preceding section about using a voltage tester.

Disconnect power to the outlet box and pull the groups of wires out so that you can work with them easily. Never disturb existing connections more than you must. If there are jumpers or pigtails—short pieces of wire protruding from each wire group—connect the lead wires of your fixture to those pigtails. You do not need to undo wires already grouped together unless that is the easiest way to connect to them.

The best way to connect wires is to use wire nuts. Where wires are of similar diameters, group them, hold them close together with a pair of pliers, and with a second set of pliers, twist their bared ends clockwise so they will stay together. Then twist on a correctly sized wire nut. So joined, the bared ends of wire will not come loose and, as importantly, will be covered by the insulative plastic of the nut.

Where wires are markedly different in size—such as No. 18 or No. 20 wire leads from the fixture and No. 14 wire from incoming service cable—strip the smaller wires about 1½ inches, the larger wires about 1 inch. Wrap the smaller wire around the larger one, clockwise,

shown in figure 6–33. Bend the larger wire over the smaller for a better mechanical connection and apply the wire nut.

The simplest wiring situation you will encounter is a single incoming service cable—containing two insulated wires and perhaps a third uninsulated wire—in the outlet box. If the screws on the bottom of the fixture are not differentiated (one brass, one silver) or the lead wires from the fixture are not color coded (black for hot, white for neutral), it does not matter which incoming wire you hook up to which fixture terminal. If such differentiation or color coding exists, attach the black wire to the brass (or gold) screw and the white wire to the silver screw. Likewise, if there are wire leads instead of screws, connect black wire to black wire, white to white.

If the fixture also has a receptacle in its base, hook up hot and neutral leads as indicated. If you find a ground screw (usually green) on the base of the fixture, run a pigtail from the ground wire bunch to that screw; the ground wire bunch should also be screwed or clipped to metal outlet boxes.

After twisting wire nuts onto wire ends, gently push wire groups back into the outlet box, making sure that no bare wire peeks out from any of the wire nuts; it could short against the metal outlet box. Fit the canopy of the fixture (or the base of the fixture itself, depending upon the detail of your lamp) over the outlet box and tighten the machine screws holding the fixture to the outlet box. When the power is turned back on, the light should work.

When tightening, do not overtighten any parts while working on a fixture. Especially if the metal is thin, screws threaded into the fixture body of a shade holder may pull free. At that point you will have a mess on your hands and may have to get a new threading. When tightening the screws that hold

shades in place, tighten just so the shades will not fall out. You should be just able to turn the shades; if the screws are so tight that you cannot turn shades by hand, the glass may crack from thermal expansion once the light bulbs heat up.

Fixtures can be enhanced by installing a rheostat in place of an existing switch. Rheostats allow you to dim the lights. Installation is easy, but the unit may have white and black lead wires rather than the brass screws of most switches; again, use wire nuts for the connection. Remember that any switch interrupts the hot line only; neutral wires are always continuous. Buy an expensive rheostat—cheaper ones wear out and may produce electrical interference that your stereo receiver may pick up. Also, make sure that the bulbs in your fixture are suited to rheostatic control. Some will burn out more quickly if they do not get a full 110-volt current.

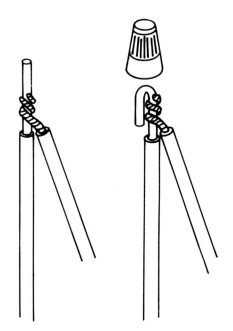

6-33. To join wires of disparate size, wrap the smaller around the larger, in the direction that the wire nut will turn. Bend the larger wire over and twist on the wire nut.

A 1900 gas-and-electric combination, solid brass with pressed-glass shades. This piece was manufactured to use both electricity and gas.
JO-EL Shop

Porcelain art deco fixture, with brass cap screw and brass pull-chain; clear filament bulb, circa 1930.
JO-EL Shop

Cast-iron exterior fixture with frosted shade, circa 1910.
JO-EL Shop

Victorian etched glass shades.
Great American Salvage

Facing page: Not an old piece, but an ex-
quisite one, largely in pastel blue, royal
blue, and off-white.

Seen in Nowell's, Inc.; shade by Silk Degrees, Santa Cruz,
California.

A hallophane shade, much in demand
these days; with antique clear filament
bulb, about 11 in. across.

JO-EL Shop

CHAPTER SEVEN

Plumbing Fixtures

Safety Tips

- Removing and installing plumbing fixtures does not usually require disturbing finish surfaces, but should you need to do so, use a voltage tester to ascertain that current is indeed off in the outlets close by. Likewise, shut off water supply to any pipes to be cut into.
- When cutting through pipes and the like, do not use power tools, because the electrical systems of many houses are grounded through cold water mains. The chances of being shocked in this manner are slight, but use hand tools to be completely safe.
- Whenever you disconnect waste pipes, cover the section leading to the septic system; sewer gases can be unhealthful. A wad of newspaper stuffed into a plastic bag is an easy plug.
- Adequately support bathroom fixtures during removal and installation; many are heavy. For tubs this may mean reinforcing joists beneath; for sinks, possibly adding supporting boards between studs.
- Take care handling heavy objects; read the section on moving tubs for more information.
- Do not overstrain tools if a connection will not budge; a tool could break or a pipe collapse. Instead, apply rust-dissolving chemicals, heat, and the like.
- Wear goggles for all chiseling work.

This wall-hung unit was made more water conservative when it was reused. By elevating it an additional 3 feet (it was originally just above the base) and replacing an antiquated flushing mechanism with a Fluidmaster ballcock, the owners report using only two gallons of water per flush.

Saint Orres Inn

Tools

- A basic collection of plumbing tools includes a pipe cutter, which ensures square cuts and is easy to use; pipe wrenches, for larger couplings or those requiring some force to loosen; crescent wrenches, for smaller nuts; and a hacksaw, for miscellaneous cutting.
- A basin wrench enables you to tighten or loosen the water nuts at the top of basin supply pipes.
- A torch for soldering connections should be capable of heating the joint within a half minute; back such solderings with a fire-resistent surface when soldering near structure.
- A cold chisel and a ball peen hammer can cut through bolts and other elements that are corroded together. Wear goggles for all chiseling work.
- A spud wrench, whose jaws are quite wide, is necessary to tighten the slip-nut couplings of wall-hung toilets.
- A seat-grinding tool is necessary if new washers do not correct that leaky faucet.

Older plumbing fixtures are for the most part heavier, more commodious, and lovelier than modern pieces. Nor can those who favor old trappings be accused of a cranky nostalgia: contemporary lavatories, for example, simply do not confine one's joyous morning splashing; much of the water makes sodden the soap or ends up on the floor. Latter-day tubs commit the same sin. Longing for a resurrective soak at the end of the day, you can rarely stretch out and be totally immersed; alternately, your knees or your shoulders must be above the water, frigid isles of discontent. Oh, for the tub that President Taft owned, in which three smiling plumbers could sit! As for the *look* of modernity, since the 1950s there have come only overdesigned horrors of the bath—octagonal, square-shouldered porcelain lumps and plastic spigots that mimic cut crystal most unconvincingly. No thanks.

Because this is not a book about plumbing, we will limit our inquiries to removing, reconditioning, and reinstalling fixtures. Those interested in, say, extending present supply pipes should consult the Bibliography. A plumber familiar with old plumbing setups will be a valuable source of information and, often, of parts. Upgrading fixtures usually does not fall under the purview of building codes, but do check with those authorities before beginning *any* plumbing work. At the very least, you may need a permit and an inspection or two to see that you have done the work right.

Plumbing-supply stores are notoriously rude places for those who do not know the lingo; study illustrations in this chapter before forays to buy parts.

Plumbing is an intake-outtake system much like our own bodies.

Water comes in via *supply or delivery* pipes, is used in a vessel or *fixture* (for example, lavatory, tub, toilet), and exits down a *waste or drain* pipe. Thus there is a *supply system* with various *valves, spigots,* and *faucets* that control and confine the flow of potable water; and a *DWV* (drainage-waste-vent) *system* of larger-diameter pipes, which allows wastes to escape, largely by the effect of gravity, downward.

Through years of experimentation, plumbing specialists have standardized materials, their sizes, and the *fittings* (connectors) that tie the parts together. Plumbing parts are so standardized, in fact, that the amateur plumber has a relatively easy time of it. Likewise, the positions of fixtures have become standardized over the years, as shown in figure 7-1. (The height of a lavatory is the most variable of the dimensions shown, but minimum distances from the wall of toilets and tubs are relatively fixed.)

Salvagers, take note! When buying old plumbing fixtures, you may run afoul of this standardization. The problem is not the size of the fixtures themselves, but rather the pipes that service them. The threaded supply stems of older faucets are notoriously tough to match with nuts, which vary in diameter and threading interval. Therefore, when buying old fixtures, be sure that their supply stems have *water nuts* screwed on (see fig. 7-14). You might be able to find *adapters* (fittings that adapt different-sized pipes) if the fixture lacks water nuts, but do not count on it.

Drainpipes cause less of a problem, but they too are occasionally

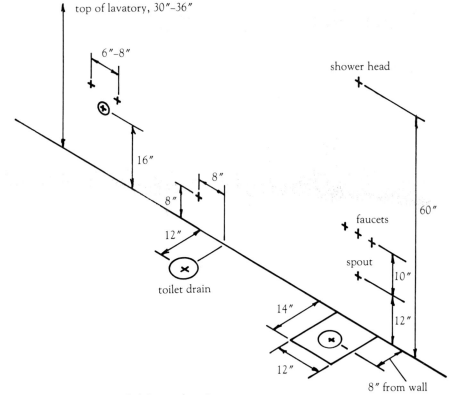

7-1. Recommended fixture locations.

top of lavatory, 30″–36″

6″–8″

shower head

16″

8″

8″

12″

toilet drain

60″

faucets

spout

14″

10″

12″

12″

8″ from wall

odd. Lavs, for example, once had 1⅛-inch drainpipes, which are no longer made. Although solutions to this problem do exist, it is a situation that is best avoided. Finally, if you want to match disparate hardware and fixtures, measure all parts carefully and take notes of your readings. Faucet units, for example, have stem spacing that may not match the holes in a lavatory.

Plumbing materials vary, but mixing them is almost never a problem. Supply pipes are usually copper, sometimes brass or galvanized steel, rarely lead (if they are, remove them!). DWV pipes are increasingly plastic—acrylo-mitrile butadiene-styrene (ABS) or polyvinyl chloride (PVC)—as building codes change; in the old days, cast iron was common (and is still required by many stringent codes), as was copper and brass. Note that PVC is wholly acceptable as DWV pipe, but its use as supply pipe is now suspect. Lawsuits against its use allege that it will release chloroform, carbon tetrachloride, and DEHP into potable water.

Whatever the materials you choose for supply and waste pipes, those pipes must be fitted together in airtight joints. *Fittings* are, basically, mechanical connectors of a joint. Additionally, fittings may change direction, accommodate differences in pipe size, and so on. Fittings that allow you to connect disparate parts are called *adapters*.

Determining which adapter you need—or what a given adapter does—is a deductive task. The ½-inch female copper-to-threaded adapter shown in figure 7–3, for example, has a threaded female end which receives the threaded male end of a ½-inch galvanized pipe; other end of the adapter is a straight female coupling into which ½-inch copper pipe can be sweated (soldered). This adapter is fairly simple. Single adapters can also turn (*elbow* or *tee*); reduce or increase size (*reducer* or *enlarger*); be male, female, or both; change materials (for example, copper to PVC plastic); and so on. So, think things through before choosing your adapters: what sizes are the pipes you must connect and how do you get from one to the other with the least fuss?

LAVATORIES

Lavatories consist of a *lavatory bowl*, or *basin*, usually porcelain over cast iron; *faucet assemblies*, which consist of a single unit called a *deck faucet* or of individual faucets; and a *drain-*

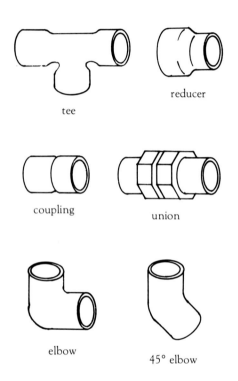

7-2. Typical fittings. Left to right, top to bottom: tee, reducer, coupling, union, elbow, 45-degree elbow.

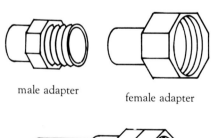

7-3. Adapters. Left to right, top to bottom: male adapter, female adapter, 1/2-in. female copper-to-threaded adapter.

7-4. Marble lavatory with nickel faucets.

pipe assembly, which may be a simple pipe or may have a pop-up waste drain that controls the flow of waste water. Plumbing configurations vary, including their shapes and sizes, but their working mechanisms are generally similar.

ASSESSING FOR PURCHASE

Little that goes wrong with a lavatory will preclude its purchase; most repairs are relatively minor, and acceptable replacements are easily procured and installed.

Most salvageable lavatories will have been removed and stored, but if the unit is still in operation, by all means try it. If, when turning faucets off and on, you notice water leaking from beneath handles or the faucet continues to dribble after it has been shut off, the problem may be no more than a worn-out washer; at worst a *faucet seat* needs refacing, not a big job (fig. 7–12).

Fill the sink and observe beneath it to see if it leaks. If so, the drain seals are worn out or pipe has corroded. Such leakage is not common and will be accompanied by rubber gaskets that have worn out or plumber's putty that has dried. To check if this has happened, look closely where the drain flange seats in the bottom of the basin and where, on the underside, the pipe tailpiece exits. Replacing the gaskets and putty seal is somewhat tedious but is not conceptually difficult.

Chipped or discolored porcelain can be replaced by a professional refurbisher; check the Yellow Pages under "Appliances, Household Refinishing," or get a reference from a plumbing-supply outfit. Although some refurbishers still reenamel pieces, many recoat with an acrylic, which looks good and, unlike porcelain enamel, can be spot-touched later on. Whink Rust Stain Remover (Whink Products Company) and Mequiar's Marble Polish (Mirror Bright Polish Company),

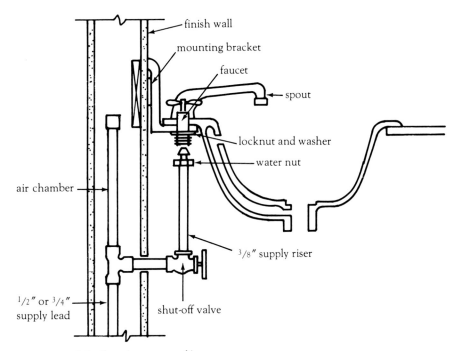

7-5. Supply system of lavatory.

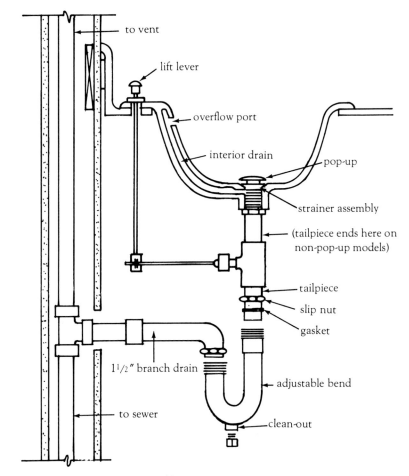

7-6. Drain (DWV) system of lavatory.

both listed in the Sources of Supply section, may remove stains from your fixtures.

Touch-up paints for porcelain are available, but they are rarely satisfactory: matching the color of an old enamel is all but impossible, and the paint may not adhere properly. A badly stained sink should come clean with a lot of elbow grease, chlorinated cleanser, and a scrub brush. If that does not work, allowing some bleach to stand in the bowl may do the trick. (Bleach, however, is very hard on rubber and may require that you replace the washers around the drainpipe.) If stains resist those efforts, have the piece refinished.

Lavs are mounted in roughly three ways: hung from a mounting bar on the wall, supported by a counter, or bolstered by legs or a pedestal of some kind. If you intend to support the piece on a counter, the details of its previous mounting do affect you. If the legs or pedestal of a unit have disappeared, they may be difficult to replace; it is best not to buy such a unit.

If the sink was hung from a wall—by far the most common method in the old days—carefully examine the back side of the lavatory to be sure that both its mounting tabs are intact. Although unlikely, a tab may have been broken: you will see an obvious metal shear with jagged edges. Such a sink cannot be mounted safely. Useful to buy at the same time as the lavatory is its mounting bar, which screws to the wall in your bathroom; salvage yards usually have a few lying about. Test the fit of the mounting bar to the tabs on the back of the sink—do they match? Mounting bars are usually a standard width and so fit almost all sinks, but yours may be an odd one. If the bars around the yard do not fit the lav you like, inquire elsewhere and test other mounting bars. It seems a silly reason for not buying an otherwise nice sink, but if

you cannot find a bar that matches the mounting tabs of the lavatory, you cannot hang the fixture.

Lavatory pedestals are frequently damaged when removed. Do not accept any that have cracks all the way through, no matter how strenuous the assurances of the seller. Loaded with water, a lav weighs quite a bit, and those cracks will spread.

Make sure that all parts of a faucet are there, even down to the little enamel *H* and *C* insets on the top of the spigots. And, most important, make sure that water nuts are on the threaded stems projecting from the underside of the lavatory.

Finally, if you intend to match faucets to a lavatory, measure the spacing of holes in the lav and the threaded stems of any deck faucets. These days, faucet stems and lav hole positions are standardized at 4, 6, and 8 inches from center to center, but do not assume that for old fixtures.

REMOVING OLD LAVATORIES

How you remove an old lav depends upon how it is supported; there are a few preparatory steps before lift-off.

First disconnect the supply pipes servicing the lavatory if it is hooked up. Shut-off valves will be at the base of the fixture or on the floor just beneath; if there are no individual shut-offs, follow the water pipes back toward their source until you find a main shut-off valve. After turning the shut-off closed (turn

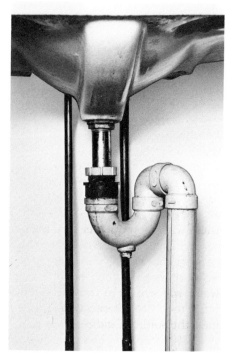

7-7. This wall-mounted lavatory is typical in that its plumber used a hodgepodge of parts. Running down from the lav drain is a shiny tailpiece, which disappears into a slip-nut coupling at the top of a 1 1/2-in. branch drain. The whole drainpipe assembly is white plastic (PVC), except for a small black plastic fitting (ABS) right below the slip nut. The bend in the drain has a clean-out nut at its low point. On either side of the drain are 1/2-in. copper supply pipes (risers) that run up to threaded faucet stems (not shown) sticking out of the underside of the lav. The preferred way to hook up risers is to use 3/8-in. pipe, but this hookup is serviceable. At the top of each riser the plumber soldered on 1/2-in. female adapters, which are screwed onto the faucet stems.

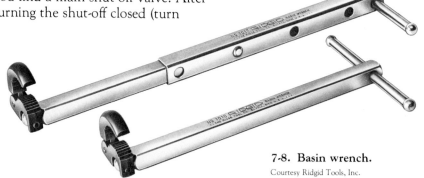

7-8. Basin wrench.
Courtesy Ridgid Tools, Inc.

clockwise), open faucet handles so that any water in the pipes flows out.

You can disconnect the faucets from the supply pipes, or risers, beneath the sink in two ways. If someone wants to reuse those risers, you will need a *basin wrench*, a long-handled tool that enables you to reach up and loosen the water nuts at the top of the risers, while the sink is still in place. The second way to disconnect, if you do not care about the risers, is to cut through them with a pipe cutter or a hacksaw. A third way, unsoldering the nearest joints along the risers, is a waste of time, difficult because some water will still be in the risers, making it tough to get enough heat to melt the solder. *Caution:* Any time you apply heat to pipes already connected, they must be drained and their *faucets must be open* to prevent an explosion caused by built-up heat within pipes. Have some rags ready when you finally do disconnect the risers, as they will have some water in them.

Before disconnecting the drainpipe, have something handy to wad into the pipe, thus preventing sewer gases from entering living space. A piece of newspaper crumpled into a plastic bag makes a good wad.

Most lavs have a short tailpiece that feeds into the drainpipe. At the top of the drainpipe is most often a washered slip-coupling that can be loosened with a pipe wrench. Loosen that coupling, lift the lav up, and the tailpiece will slip free. If the hookup is really archaic and you cannot easily loosen any couplings, simply cut through the drainpipe, but not through the tailpiece.

With the drain and supply pipes severed, lift up the lavatory, preferably with the help of a friend if the lav is oversized. If the unit is wall mounted, you need only lift straight up, unless additional screws hold the back to the wall. Lift the basin just high enough for its tailpiece to clear the drainpipe.

If the sink is also supported by tubular metal legs, they will probably fall free as you take weight off them. If the lav is supported by a counter, chances are that clips on the underside of the counter must be unscrewed first. Save those clips. Additionally, counter-mounted lavs may have been bedded in plumber's putty or some such caulking; rock the units slightly to break the putty seal or, after scraping with a knife under the lip of the lavatory, carefully slip a flat bar beneath and pry up.

Pedestal sinks are often bolted to their pedestal and may also be bedded in putty; frequently a bed of plaster lies beneath the pedestal base. To keep from harming the base of the pedestal, chop away the floor (usually tile) with a mason's chisel if that is practical. Go all around the base, getting as close as you can to it. Then, drive your chisel *between* the tile and the subfloor beneath, working slowly as a helper holds the base to prevent it from tipping. Once you have freed the pedestal, you can invert it and gently chisel off the plaster and tiles still stuck to it—much easier and safer then trying to separate plaster and pedestal while the base is still standing.

Before transporting such items, wrap them in an old blanket so the enamel does not get damaged in transport. If you will be traveling any distance, remove the hardware as shown in the following sections; protruding faucet stems are particularly vulnerable.

FAUCET REPAIR

This section is pertinent to both lavatory and tub faucets, their innards being basically the same.

Curing Leaks

If water continues to run after you have shut the faucet, chances are

that a washer is worn out. If that repair does not suffice, the seat of the valve may be worn. If water is seeping from the body of the faucet, the problem is probably a packing washer that is worn.

To get to the faucet washer, the part that wears out most often, unscrew the packing nut and turn the whole faucet-stem assembly out, counterclockwise. At the bottom of

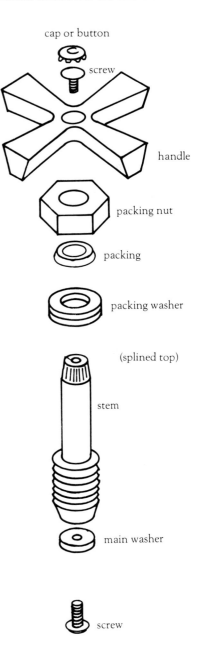

7-9. **Exploded view of a faucet-stem assembly.**

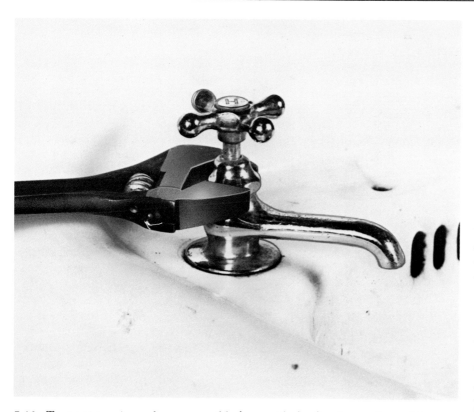

the stem is a small screw that holds on the washer in question. Unscrew the screw, replace the washer, and reassemble the pieces.

If that remedy does not stop the flow of water, the seat is probably worn. Again unscrew the cap nut and turn out the stem assembly, but this time fit a *seat reamer* (also called a *valve seat grinding tool*) down into the body of the faucet. Seat reamers vary somewhat, but most have a little guide halfway up the stem of the tool, which keeps the grinding edge in proper position. Remove the faucet assembly, turn the tool into the seat as directed on its operating instructions, wash out any grindings, and replace the faucet-stem assembly (which now has a new washer, of course).

If water is leaking out of the body of the faucet, the packing of the stem—usually rubber O-rings— has worn out. To get at those rings, pry out the *H* or *C* cap on top of

7-10. To get at a main washer, responsible for most leaks, first loosen the packing nut.

7-11. The faucet washer is at the end of the faucet stem and can be replaced after removing the small screw at the very end.

7-12. Ream the faucet valve seat (in the body of the faucet) with the tool shown. The small nut halfway up the tool shaft keeps the tool in place so that the grinding surface is flat.

7-13. To get at faucet packing, you will have to remove the handle in most cases. Pry out the button atop the handle to get at the holding screw.

the faucet and screw out the screw underneath. Remove the handle, which usually sits on a splined shaft, and (if your assembly has it) turn the small nut above the packing nut to get at the packing ring. Replace and reassemble parts. To grip the nuts, you will need two wrenches if your assembly has the small nut; if it lacks the nut, a wrench and a pair of pliers with serrated jaws to grip the stem will do the trick.

Faucet assemblies vary, so do not be surprised if your disassembly varies somewhat. In some faucets, for example, you might have to pry off the ornamental caps and turn out the screw beneath to remove the stem; on most units you need only to loosen the packing nut.

Replacing Faucets

With the lavatory taken down from the wall, you can easily remove faucets with an ordinary wrench. If the fixture is still hung from the wall, you will need a basin wrench for the job.

On the underside of the lavatory, where a faucet stem emerges, is a washer and a locknut. The water nut, something else, is at the very end of the faucet stem; see figure 7–14. Unscrew the water nut and remove it; unscrew the locknut; the washer simply slides off. Pull up the faucet, which should come out easily, though if it is seated in plumber's putty that has hardened, you may have to rock the faucet first to break the seal.

Installing a new faucet is just as straightforward, though you should first clean up any residue from the old unit(s). If you intend to have the basin resurfaced, do so before adding new hardware. Otherwise, scrape free any old putty with a putty knife and scrub the area well with a plastic scrub pad—metal pads may scratch and dull the surface. On the underside of the lav, wire-brush away any rust and, before replacing them, wipe the outside of

locknuts and faucet stems with an oily rag to forestall future rust.

The new faucet should have a layer of plumber's putty between its flange and the top of the lav, although some units have a gasket

7-14. Because the unit here is down from the wall, we could use an ordinary crescent wrench for disconnections. At the end of the threaded faucet stem is the water nut, with a broken-off remnant of a riser visible. The wrench grips the locknut, which holds the faucets fast to the lav; below the locknut is a starred washer.

instead. If you are installing a deck faucet (two faucets on one base), the faucet stems must match the holes in the lav. Slide on the washers and tighten locknuts until the unit is secured, ready for connection to the supply risers.

If your lavatory is presently unmounted, subsequent attachments will be easier if you attach the *supply risers* (which are available as separate 3/8-inch-diameter by 12-inch-long pieces) before remounting the lav. Supply risers should be a smaller diameter than the supply pipe from which they depart. This smaller size (such as 3/8 inch) delivers the water at a greater pressure and makes delivery pressure less susceptible to other water uses on the line, such as flushing a toilet. The reduction in pipe diameter can occur with a reducing tee (for example 1/2 by 3/8 by 1/2 inch), straight reducing coupling (1/2 by 3/8 inch), or with a shut-off valve whose outtake is smaller than the intake (1/2 by 3/8 inch).

7-15. With the locknut removed, simply lift out the faucet.

LAVATORY DRAINPIPES

The drainpipe that emerges from the bottom of a lavatory is actually several elements: the pipe itself, or *tailpiece*, usually flanged (flared) at the top; a layer of putty between that flange and the lavatory basin; and, from beneath, a *Mack washer* and a *locknut* that screws to the threaded section of the tailpiece (see fig. 7–6). An internal drain (within the body of the lavatory) runs from an overflow port to holes in the top of the drainpipe, where it passes through the lav body. As noted earlier, the tailpiece fits down into the branch drainpipe servicing the fixture, the connection made airtight with a slip-nut coupling.

Drainpipe construction often varies, but the above basics will see you through most repairs. The fixture may also have a pop-up assembly, with a linkage between a lift rod and a ball-rod assembly that runs into the lower part of the tailpiece. In other constructions the tailpiece itself may be several pieces, with a separate flange that screws onto the top of the tailpiece. But those particulars are of little importance overall; just note them when you consider buying the unit, being sure to record the diameter of the tailpiece.

Removing Tailpiece Assemblies

Most often, it is not necessary to upgrade the tailpiece of a lavatory at all if the sink does not leak and the tailpiece is in good shape. Time was that an irregular-sized tailpiece meant a troublesome fit to the upcoming branch drain, but present-day slip-nut couplings can accommodate variations of at least ¼ inch. (Branch drains for lavatories should be at least 1¼ inches in diameter, preferably 1½ inches; kitchen or work sinks should have 2-inch branch drains.)

The main problem with a lav tailpiece occurs when: the part is badly corroded or has become bent; only a threaded section of the tailpiece remains, with threads that are difficult to match (see fig. 7–19); or you must replace putty or washers to correct a leak. In these cases remove the old drain tailpiece assembly.

Try the easiest cure first. If yours is a two-piece assembly in which the flange screws to a longer pipe, you may be able to release the parts by turning the strainer counterclockwise, as shown in figure 7–16. Chances are, however, that this method will not work. The putty holding the strainer has probably hardened or the crosspieces in the strainer are only lightweight and will tear out. If so, go on to the next step.

Try to unscrew the tailpiece from the underside of the lav, as shown in figure 7–17. There is usually a nut or a knurled lip that your pipe wrench can grip. If nothing happens, squirt in some Liquid Wrench or any similar corrosion dissolver. If, as happened in our example, the tailpiece does turn off, it may reveal a threaded stem within, which you must then try to turn out with a pipe wrench.

The more corrosion dissolver you apply, the easier your task will be if rust is freezing the parts together. Not infrequently, however, a rubber Mack washer will lie between the bottom of the lav and the threaded parts you are trying to free. In that event use a utility knife to cut away the Mack washer; it may take about fifteen minutes of assiduous digging to get it out, as most of the washer will be protected by the flange of the nut. But once the washer is removed, you should be able to turn the tailpiece off. (The example shown has a two-piece tail assembly.)

In our example a threaded stem remained that resisted all gentle efforts to dislodge it; the putty was simply too hard. That stem had to be dislodged with a cold chisel. Wear goggles and take care not to hit the sink itself. Lav drain holes are usually not threaded, because tailpieces are somewhat smaller and merely fit through, seated in beds of putty. Once a threaded stem and its flanged top is out, chip away the old putty.

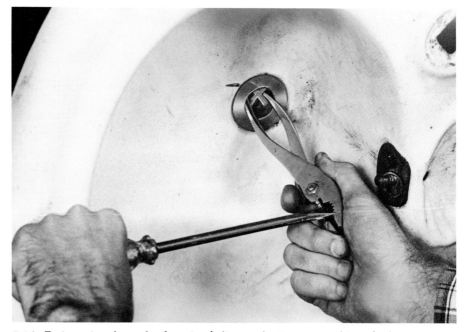

7-16. By inserting the ends of a pair of pliers and using a screwdriver for leverage, you may be able to turn out the strainer, which threads into the end of the tailpiece.

7-17. If pliers and screwdriver fail, invert the lav and try turning off the tailpiece with a pipe wrench; turn counterclockwise.

7-18. In this example the rubber Mack washer (between the bottom of the basin and the flange of the tailpiece) had seized, making it impossible to run off the tailpiece with a wrench. It was necessary to whittle out the washer with a utility knife.

7-20. Fruits of victory. On the right, a new tailpiece, with Mack washer and locknut; on the left, what was left of the old tailpiece assembly.

7-19. The tailpiece screwed off, the threaded stem of the strainer remained. The strainer was bedded in putty so ancient and tough that there was nothing else to do but chisel the stem out with a cold chisel.
Safety note: Although I did wear goggles to prevent fragments from harming my eyes, I used the wrong hammer; use a ball peen (machinist's) hammer instead. A framing hammer is more likely to fragment, ruining its face.

153

7-21. Before replacing lav hardware, clean off any loose paint or rust with a wire brush.

7-23. Slip the rubber Mack washer onto the tailpiece and turn the locknut down tight.

Installing a New Tailpiece

Before inserting a new tailpiece assembly, clean up the bottom of the basin. Scrape away any old putty or washer remnants with a penknife. If the enamel is damaged, have it refinished now. If the enamel is acceptable but the underside of

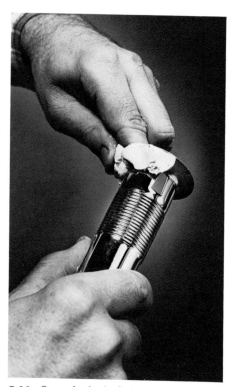

7-22. Spread a bed of plumber's putty on the underside of the tailpiece flange so that the joint will be watertight; you can scrape off any excess afterwards.

the lav is rusty or scaly, clean it up with a wire-brush attachment in a drill. Spraying with a rust-inhibitive paint is acceptable if you brush all irregularities away or if the bottom of the sink will not be visible.

New assemblies vary, although their sizes are more uniform than old tailpieces. Our example had a single-piece threaded stem beneath to receive the locknut; it was much lighter than that which we cut out, but sufficient. Apply plumber's putty to the underside of the flange as shown in figure 7-22. Insert the pipe into the drain hole in the lav and, after feeding the rubber Mack washer onto the tailpiece, tighten the locknut. *Important:* As you look into the drain hole of a lavatory, you will notice smaller holes around the inside lip of the drain hole; these holes are exits for water running down from the overflow ports in the top of the lav. Align the holes in the top of the tailpiece to those inside the drain lip.

At this point you are ready to remount the lavatory. All of the preceding work was done with the lav off the wall, because the hammering and chiseling necessary to remove the old drain is jarring work. Were such work attempted while the lav was still mounted, you would probably knock the fixture right off the wall.

REMOUNTING DETAILS

The mounting detail you need depends upon whether your lav is wall hung, supported by legs or a pedestal, or cabinet enclosed. For each of these mountings, the loads involved must be adequately supported: an average-sized lav, filled, approaches seventy or eighty pounds. But first, a word about hooking up pipes.

Attaching to the Branch Drain

A common fear of amateur plumbers is that they will not be able to exactly align the tailpiece of a fixture to the branch drainpipe. Relax—someone has already thought of a solution. Most drain traps have adjustable bends with slip couplings. Fit the tailpiece to the lav, mount the lav, and then connect the trap to both ends. It may be necessary to add a jog of drainpipe to get close enough to the fixture or to trim the length of the tailpiece with a pipe cutter, but you can swivel the bend into final position, as shown in figure 7-24. Bends should have cleanouts at the lowest point, so that you can recover dropped rings, spoons, and the like.

Counter-mounted Lavatories

Most lavatories that mount to counters have a lip that rests on top of the finish surface. You can mount the sink or lavatory first and then run tiles up to the edge of the lav, but that method may allow water to seep under the lav lip. Besides, the lip of the lav may cover the rough edges of tiles cut to fit. Whatever detail you choose, bed the lip of the sink in a generous amount of plumber's putty. Some authorities recommend that you bed the lav in silicone caulk, but should you want to remove the lav for any reason, silicone is extremely tenacious stuff and would have to be scraped away before any new sealer can be put down. Putty is better.

Most lavs and sinks have clips that draw the lip tightly to the top of the counter, thereby preventing movement. These clips vary

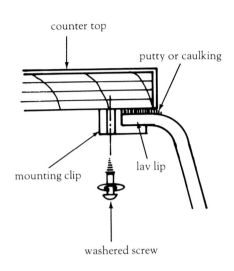

7-25. Lav mounted beneath the counter; caulking is critically important.

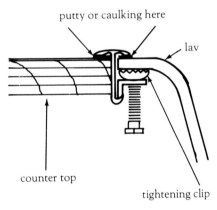

7-26. Lav mounted flush with counter; clips will vary.

markedly from supplier to supplier, but a few of the more common types are shown in figures 7–25 to 7–27. If yours is an under-the-counter sink, put a bead of silicone or plaster on *top* of the sink lip; this layer will prevent water splashing behind and will fill any irregularities between counter and the basin lip. Trim such caulking after you have tightened the clips but before it dries entirely.

The standard height for a bathroom lav is about 30 inches, but why not raise it 6 inches if you must stoop when using most lavs? The countertop should be at least ¾ inch thick; flexion from too light a top could be disastrous to any waterproof seal around the lav. Particleboard is touted for use beneath plastic laminate surfaces, but for a deluxe job, use ¾-inch exterior-grade plywood; it will be trouble-free and is much stronger.

Pedestal- and Leg-supported Units

Little can be said about such units, really. They should be mounted on a finished bathroom floor, with a healthy layer of plumber's putty spread beneath the pedestal to take up irregularities and prevent rocking. The subfloor must be sturdy, preferably at least ⅝-inch plywood if your joists are 16 inches on center. Level the top of the sink.

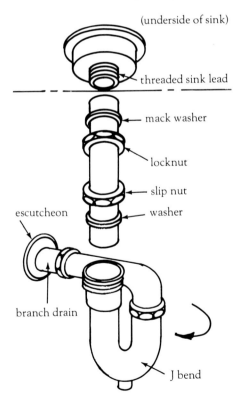

7-24. The final alignment of tailpiece to branch drain is facilitated by an adjustable trap, such as that shown beneath a kitchen sink. The bend swivels until its slip nuts are tightened down.

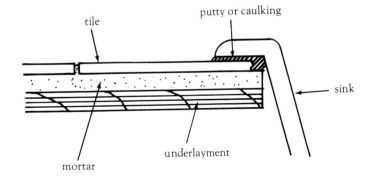

7-27. Lav mounted above the counter. The lav or sink lip covers the edge of the tile. Caulk well.

155

Wall-mounted Lavs

The most important detail for a wall-mounted lav is reinforcing the wall behind the lav. If your lav will be about 30 inches high, set a 1 × 6 board into the studs behind the wall. This means, of course, that you must tear off the finish wall surface, if any. The 1 × 6 need only attach to two studs, so make it only 18 or 19 inches long. If you must remove a finish wall surface, cut it back only to the centers of the two studs, so that you can nail the edges of the replacement Sheetrock onto the exposed studs. To avoid getting shocks, cut all power to the bathroom—before cutting into the finish wall. This is also a good time to upgrade electrical service, such as additional outlets or GFI (ground-fault interceptor) outlets.

The 1 × 6 should be *let into* studs: hold the board level across two studs, mark its width, and cut into those studs to the depth of the board; clean out the slot with a chisel. Nail the 1 × 6 into the slot with three 10d nails at each stud. Cover the area with new Sheetrock or plaster (whatever is there now). Level and screw the mounting bracket to the 1 × 6, as shown in figure 7–28. Now you are ready to hang the lav onto the bracket.

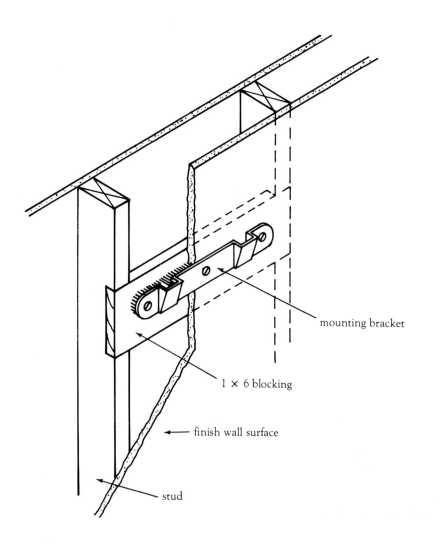

mounting bracket

1 × 6 blocking

finish wall surface

stud

7-28. Support for a wall-hung lav.

BATHTUBS

Bathtubs are footed and nonfooted, the former being much favored by salvagers, because footed ones are older, quainter, and generally much easier to install. Cast iron is the favored material—except by those called upon to move it—weighty, yes, but also durable and heat retentive. Enameled steel tubs are "poor cousins," and fiberglass units are so flimsy that they rarely survive a removal.

ASSESSING TUBS

The two most important requisites of a tub are that its parts be largely intact and that its surface be sufficiently unblemished to obviate re-enameling. Money qualifies either of these statements: if you have a hundred dollars or so to spare, you can get a tub reenameled. Acrylic refinishing, an acceptable alternative, costs about half that and can be touched up if it is nicked; baked enamel cannot be touched up successfully.

Legs are not widely interchangeable among tubs because of peculiarities of attachment: some merely slide into a slotted nub, whereas others require machine screws or bolts. If you have one original leg, you can use it as a template to have others cast, but depending where you live, legs will cost twenty to sixty dollars (or more) apiece. You can forgo legs entirely if you want to box in the tub, but this requires moderately strong carpentry skills. Faucets are useful only if they have their original water nuts (fig. 7–14), but a wide range of reproduction faucets make replacement easy. Drain-and-overflow assemblies usually are replaced; preassembled kits are available from many sources.

Most stains on porcelain are

brown or green, the former caused by iron and other minerals, the later by fluoridated water. Soaking either stain in bleach for a half hour, rinsing, and then vigorously scrubbing with a scrub brush (and chlorinated cleanser) should do the trick. If possible, ask the owner if you can try to remove stains before you buy the tub; a seller should

have little reason, save perverseness, to object to your scrubbing up a tub. Whink Stain Remover can also be used to clean up a piece (see Sources of Supply).

Finally, if you intend to match old parts, say, when adding new faucets, measure the tub holes, center to center, to be sure the match will be a success.

REMOVING AND MOVING TUBS

Turn off and disconnect supply and waste pipes, as described earlier. If the tub is an old legged model, the pipes should be quite accessible. Remember to wad a plastic bag into the drain, once disconnected, to keep septic smells at bay.

If the tub surface is in good condition, keep it that way by applying papier-mâché to its inside before you commence work. You can make an acceptable papier-mâché just by wetting five or six layers of paper spread inside the tub; let them dry for a day. This almost always adheres to the contour of the tub; if it does not, add just a little flour to the hot water. Even the most careful worker drops a tool occasionally, which could cost you a reenameling job without the papier-mâché; moreover, many tasks are easier if you can stand in the tub while working.

If the tub is an old one with legs, have three or four friends lift it free of pipe connections and carry it to the middle of the room. At this point you should remove all legs for safekeeping; they are easy to break if the tub rests on them during transit. Remove the drain assembly as discussed below; unless it is particularly sound or lovely, just destroy it and install a new one. The reason for removing the assembly is to prevent gouging the floor as you drag the tub or, less likely, chipping the enamel around the drain flange if the drainpipe suddenly snaps off. Finally, take off any faucets, keeping all nuts and washers together.

If the tub is not free-standing but is sturdy enough to be worth taking, you will have to cut into the surrounding walls to free it. Turn off electricity running through the walls and, at the same time, turn off any water to the tub. To cut through the finish surfaces around the tub, start about 6 inches above tub shoulders. Wearing goggles, use either a utility bar struck by a ham-

7-29. A particularly nice master bath. Barn timbers and boards, Mexican terra-cotta tiles, and a window overlooking the trees complement the stark white of the tub.

Mike Greenberg

157

mer or a cold chisel to break through tiles. If the wall surface is a plastic laminate, punch through a bay between studs with a cold chisel and then finish cutting away with a reciprocating saw with a Carborundum blade. Once you have an idea where all the studs are, you can pry off finish surfaces with a wrecking bar.

Important: If you do use power tools to cut through the finish walls, do not use such tools to cut through water pipe. Many electrical systems are grounded on a main water pipe and you may circumvent the grounding system by cutting into metal pipes with power tools. *Use hand tools only.*

Once the perimeter of the tub is exposed, look closely for holding nails in the tub lip. Avoid damaging the enamel of the tub as you pull out these nails; if you use something like a cat's paw, slide a piece of cardboard or shingle between the tub and the tool. The tub should slide out after you pull those nails. If its removal is difficult, tear out one of the end walls around the tub; such walls were often built after the tub was in place.

Get plenty of help when moving a tub. Never lift a tub when you can drag it. A sturdy canvas drop cloth is invaluable for dragging; rent or borrow one.

If you must move the tub over stairs, check for sturdiness where the tops and bottoms of stairs attach; if these look safe, test the stairs by jumping on them (be careful!). Station two workers up and two down, the upper pair holding onto a stout rope passing through the overflow hole at the end of the tub. The two workers at the top can thus lower the tub without bending over it; the people at the bottom merely restrain the tub from picking up speed as it slides down the steps. If you are shorthanded, move a tub down stairs with one person at the top holding the rope and the other end

of the rope wrapped around a newel post or some such sturdy member.

To raise a tub into a truck bed, use concrete blocks or cribbing (lengths of 4 × 4 or 6 × 6 lumber) to raise the tub one end at a time, adding blocks or cribs at alternate ends until you reach the level of the truck bed.

REPAIRING AND REPLACING TUB HARDWARE

Tubs, like lavatories, have two supply pipes and a drain assembly. Although their supply hookups are similar, their waste pipes are markedly different.

Faucets

The primary difference between lav and tub faucets is ninety degrees: that is, whereas lav faucet stems run straight down, tub stems go straight back into a wall or into the side of a tub.

As with lav spigots, make sure that there are water nuts on the back of the faucet stems before buying. The example shown in figure 7-30 had only one, but as we replaced the faucets, the missing water nut did not matter. Water nuts connect the faucets to supply risers, which usually come up from the

7-30. The back of this tub shows the large overflow pipe and two faucet stems, one of which has a water nut and a threaded elbow.

floor. Coming off the back of the tub, water pipes must make a 90-degree turn down to the floor. This turn is easily handled by a threaded elbow such as that shown in figure 7-30; you can also use flexible copper tubing, which bends in a gentle arc, or you can sweat-solder a 90-degree elbow onto a straight piece of pipe.

To remove faucets, turn off the water and disconnect supply pipes, loosen locknuts on the back of the tub, and lift out the spigot assembly. To install new ones, scrape off any old putty that may remain, put a new bed of plumber's putty beneath the flanges of the spigots, and tighten the locknuts. Remove old faucets and install new ones only after you have installed the overflow-and-drain assembly.

Overflow-and-Drain Assembly

Old drainpipes often need replacing because they rot out or get damaged when the tub is removed from its original residence. A faulty drainpipe assembly is manifestly unsafe and must be upgraded immediately.

The primary difference between the drains of lavs and those on tubs is that the lav overflow is cast inside the lav basin during manufacture. The overflow of the tub is external and must be assembled and installed in a separate operation.

Taking apart the drain-and-overflow assembly is easier if you have already removed spigots. As soon as you remove the tub drain lead (*lēd*) from the branch drainpipe servicing it—assuming that you are disconnecting a tub that is still operable—seal off the branch drain to keep septic smells at bay.

Begin by unscrewing the bolts or screws holding the overflow pipe tight to the back of the tub. Newer assemblies will have a plunger assembly inside the overflow pipe—pull the assembly up and out. Most older hookups lack such a feature, however.

7-31. To remove tub faucets, simply loosen the locknuts from the threaded faucet stems.

7-32. To install new faucets, slide the faucet stems into the tub holes—plumber's putty beneath the faucet bonnets is optional—and tighten locknuts behind.

New faucets courtesy Renovator's Supply

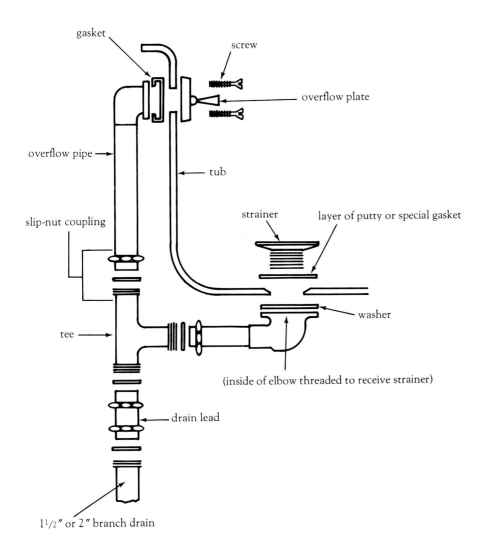

7-33. The overflow-and-drain assembly. Not shown is the plunger assembly that fits down into the overflow pipe.

7-34. To remove an overflow-and-drain assembly, begin by unscrewing the screws that hold the overflow plate; they also hold the top of the overflow pipe in place. Although only one restraining screw is shown here, most newer units have two.

7-35. The lower end of the overflow tube fits into a tee, the drain from the tub fits into the tee's middle leg, and the branch drain feeds into the other leg. Typically, the pipes and tee are badly corroded and must be replaced.

7-37. After removing the drain elbow, remove the strainer stub that is left. If it resists your efforts, saw it off and cut out the remnant with a cold chisel.

Disconnecting the lower end of the assembly (where it hooks up to the drain hole in the tub) is not as easy, for parts are usually corroded together. Since this joint is a slip-nut connection, the tee at the base of the overflow pipe slides off the short section of pipe running from the tub drain hole (fig. 7–35). Often that section will be rotted away and will come off in your hand.

Next remove the elbow beneath the tub hole, into which the strainer screws. A standard pipe wrench alone will not suffice if the elbow is corroded; slide a sturdy length of pipe over the wrench handle to improve your leverage. Be careful not to apply too much pressure, or you will break the jaws of the wrench. Apply Liquid Wrench first and allow it to eat away the corrosion. Then apply moderate pressure to the pipe over the wrench handle. If that attempt does not work, next apply heat and repeat the operation. Striking the fitting with a hammer (wear goggles) may also loosen rusted threads, but be careful not to damage the tub.

Once you have removed that elbow, the threaded stem of the strainer will protrude from the drain hole. To remove the strainer, now held in place by decades-old putty,

7-36. The elbow at the base of the tub is quite often frozen, with a rubber washer also binding the joint. For greater leverage, slide a heavy pipe over the end of the wrench.

don goggles and try tapping up on the strainer with a cold chisel. That failing, saw off the strainer stem and keep working with the chisel; in time, the piece will deform and come out. Carefully—so you do not damage the enamel—scrape out the old putty that was beneath the strainer lip.

The tub should be refinished, if necessary, before installing new hardware. Attaching the new drain-

and-overflow assembly is the reverse of removing it; several kits are available to the salvager.

The parts of the assembly join primarily with slip-nut connections. Slip nuts feature a pliable gasket that, when compressed by the tightening of a nut, expands to firmly embrace the pipe it circles. Feed pipe into the legs of the tee as shown, tighten the couplings by hand, and position the assembly to

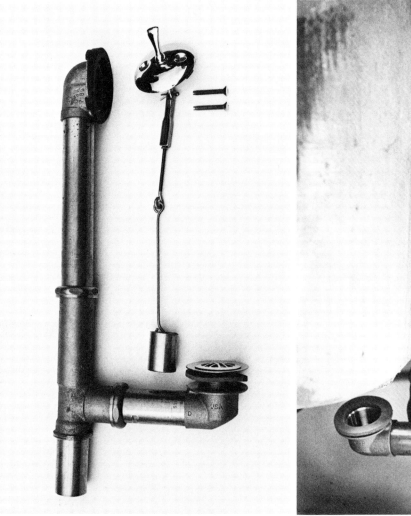

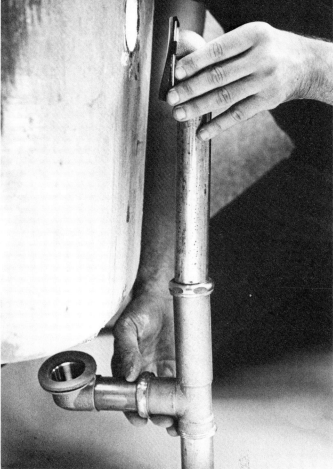

7-38. The parts of an overflow-and-drain assembly. The linked sections with the weight at the end are an adjustable plunger assembly.

7-39. Tighten the slip-nut couplings just by hand and position the pipes; hold the upper end in place with the overflow-plate screws. Note the rubber gasket on the upper end of the overflow pipe.

the outside of the tub. For a watertight seal, there must be gaskets or washers between the openings in the assembly and the holes of the tub.

To draw the assembly fast to the tub, screw the strainer down into the threaded female opening of the assembly. First, however, spread a generous layer of plumber's putty on the underside of that strainer lip (unless a washer is supplied to make the junction watertight). Tighten the strainer as much as you can by hand, using pliers as in figure 7–16 to get leverage for the final few turns.

To draw the top of the assembly to the tub, first feed the plunger

assembly down the overflow pipe. If the plunger is hinged, it can be maneuvered in. Using the cotter pin provided, connect the top of that plunger unit to the toggle sticking out of the overflow plate. Finally, draw the overflow plate to the top of the overflow pipe with the two machine screws provided. Tighten slip-nut fittings with a wrench.

Connect the lead pipe from the tee into the slip-nut coupling on the branch drainpipe. In actual practice the lead from the tee is fitted into the branch-drain coupling *before* the drain-and-overflow assembly is fixed to the tub. For a more conventional tub, which is supported by ledgers

7-40. Complete the attachment by turning the threaded strainer into the elbow of the assembly, the threads of which are just visible inside the drain hole of the tub. The plumber's putty around the lip of the strainer ensures a watertight seal.

Brass overflow assembly courtesy Renovator's Supply

around the tub walls, the overflow assembly may be attached to the tub first, the final connection to the branch drain taking place below the floor. Jiggle the end of the branch drain until its coupling slides over the lead pipe of the tub-drain assembly.

Branch drains for tubs should be at least 1½ inches in diameter; if the fixture includes a shower, a 2-inch drain is recommended.

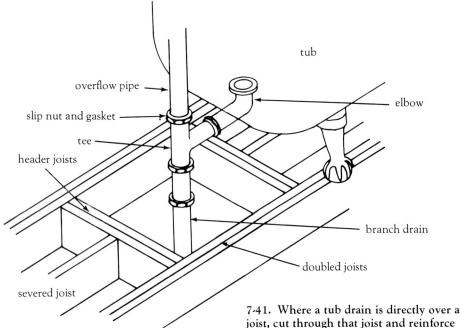

7-41. Where a tub drain is directly over a joist, cut through that joist and reinforce it with headers, which run perpendicular to the grid of joists.

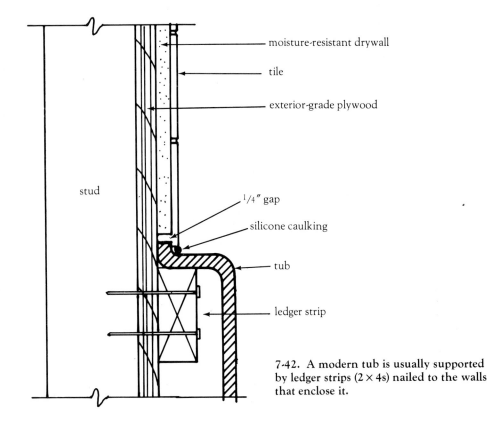

7-42. A modern tub is usually supported by ledger strips (2 × 4s) nailed to the walls that enclose it.

FRAMING DETAILS

Because tubs filled with water weigh quite a bit, overbuild the framing that supports them.

Beneath each of the long sides of a tub, double up joists, nailing additional joists directly to ones already in place; stagger 16d common nails every 10 inches or so. Getting the new joists into place may be something of a chore in the limited space of a basement: remove any blocking between the joists. Then bevel the ends of the new joists slightly so you can fit their ends into place between the bottom of the subfloor and the top of the mudsill or girder. (Several works in the Bibliography explain this procedure at length.)

At the very least, add bridging or blocking between existing joists to stiffen them and to minimize sagging caused by the weight of a filled tub.

Where the drainpipe from the tub exits through the floor, just cut a hole for the exit of the pipe—it is not necessary to frame out the opening. If, however, the drain opening coincides with a joist center, you should "header off" that opening. That is, saw back the offending joist a foot or so on each side of the drain outlet. Nail headers—the same stock as the joists—perpendicular to the joist grid, as shown. The ends of the severed joists are thus nailed into, and supported by, the headers, which run between undisturbed doubled joists.

Legged tubs are, of course, free-standing. Wall-supported tubs, however, need framing in place before finish surfaces go up around the tub. Supports for the shower head and any spigot hardware should be let into (see fig. 7–28) or nailed between studs. Thus, supports will be flush to the edges of the studs and will not interfere with finish wall surfaces to come. Supports for the lips of the tub, however, are leveled and nailed right over the stud edges, thereby creating a ledge on which tub lips rest. In figure 7-42 the finish wall surface overhangs over the tub lips: after being caulked with an elastomeric caulk, the junction will shed water.

TOILETS

Toilets (water closets) are less often recycled than lavatories or tubs, largely because of fear that septic re-

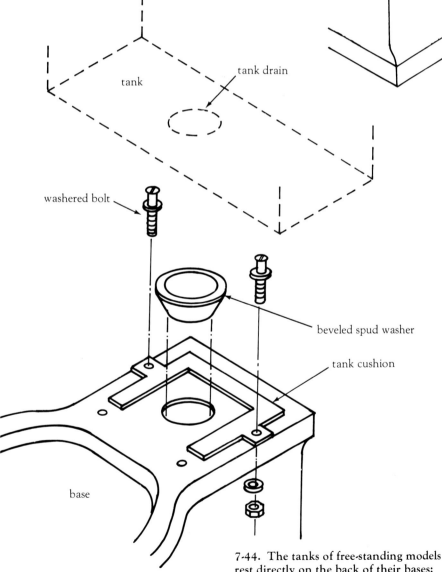

7-43. A wall-hung toilet has its tank bolted into wall studs behind; water flows to the base via a spud pipe.

7-44. The tanks of free-standing models rest directly on the back of their bases; tank cushions accommodate any irregularities.

mains might cause illness. This fear is justified, but properly handled and cleansed, a used toilet is safe.

All in all, a toilet is a simple mechanism. It consists of a single *cold water supply* pipe that runs to a *tank*, which holds the water for flushing; and a *base*, which contains and carries off wastes. Newer toilets feature a "jet-action" to speed wastes along, but mostly falling water and gravity make a toilet work. The tank usually contains a cumbersome *flushing mechanism*, the design of which has been simplified in the last few years. Additionally, *washers*, *gaskets*, and the like fit parts tightly together.

There are primarily two types of toilets: *wall hung* and *free-standing*. These terms describe how a tank is supported, the former being hung by bolts from a wall, the latter resting on the back of the toilet base. The base itself rests on the floor, its foot bolted down. Through

163

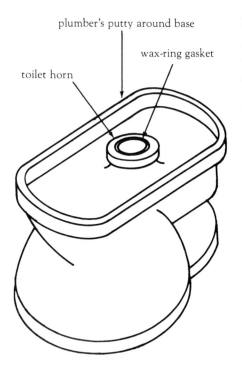

plumber's putty around base

wax-ring gasket

toilet horn

7-45. For a sanitary, airtight joint, a wax ring fits over the horn on the bottom of the toilet base.

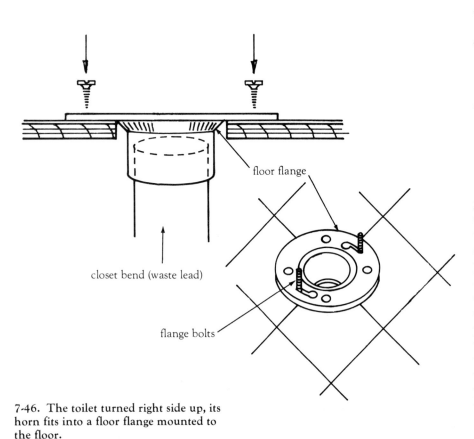

floor flange

closet bend (waste lead)

flange bolts

7-46. The toilet turned right side up, its horn fits into a floor flange mounted to the floor.

an opening in the bottom of the bowl—the *horn*—wastes drop down into a 3-inch waste pipe coming up from below. It is a common misconception that the toilet is permanently fixed to that waste pipe: the pipe is secured to the floor by a special *floor flange*, and the toilet is bolted to that flange (fig. 7–46). To make the whole arrangement sanitary, a *wax ring* (gasket) is placed over the horn of the toilet when that toilet base is inverted. The base is turned right side up: the horn aligned to the floor flange; and the wax ring, pressed by the weight of the base, spreads to seal the perimeter of the flange. The base can be lifted up at any time, although the wax ring should then be replaced.

ASSESSMENT

Your primary concern is that the tank and base are sound, entirely free of cracks. Assume that washers, gaskets, and probably the flushing mechanism should be replaced. Cracks in the porcelain surface should also concern you, because reenameling a toilet is more expensive than refurbishing lavs or tubs and such cracks may be structural.

Don rubber gloves and have a sponge and a pail of warm soapy water handy. Wipe dust off the exterior of the unit so that no cracks are obscured. With a strong flashlight aimed at the surface, look closely for cracks. Critical points are:

- where the base mounts to the floor, overtightened nuts can crack the porcelain
- where wall-hung tanks are bolted to a wall; again, overtightening is the problem
- where free-standing tanks are bolted to the toilet base
- inside the bowl, for it is not uncommon for a wrench or jar to be dropped into a bowl, flawing its surface
- the base, generally, which can crack because it was improperly supported or lacked a layer of putty beneath.

Should you find such cracks, reject the unit unless the cracks are only hairline. If you are unsure, turn the unit so that you can lean on the tank or base, your weight applied down through the crack. Have a friend observe: if there is any discernible movement in the crack, do not buy the piece. (Better get the permission of the seller to make these tests; a seriously cracked piece may fail altogether under moderate pressure, and you might get stuck paying for it, damaged though it was.)

A few parts *must* be present. First, the tank and base should

164

match. Second, the means of joining the two pieces together must be there. If the unit is wall hung, look to see that the *spud pipe* and all parts of the *spud nuts* exist (gaskets or washers can be replaced). The spud pipe itself must be sound along its length, especially where it slips into nuts. If the tank rests on the bowl (free-standing), ascertain that the *washered bolts* are there; they are replaceable but why prolong your search? If you intend to use the original seat, seat bolts should have nuts attached; otherwise you may have to buy a new seat for want of nuts. The *flush-level assembly* should be in good condition, even if the other parts of the flushing mechanism are not.

DISCONNECTING AND MOVING THE PARTS

A salvager rarely removes a water closet still in use, but here is how it is done. Turn off the water supply to the tank, usually controlled by a *shut-off valve* rising from the floor or sticking out of the wall (fig. 7–47). Flush the toilet to empty the tank and then disconnect the coupling nut at the base of the supply riser, where that riser leaves the shut-off valve. A little water will dribble out of the riser, so have a sponge and a bucket handy.

Disconnect the tank next. If the unit is wall hung, first loosen the spud nuts at the top and bottom of the spud pipe. To do this, you will need a *spud wrench*, the jaws of which are wide enough to accommodate the width of the spud nuts. That accomplished, take the top off the tank, loosen and remove the bolts that hold the tank in place, and lift the tank up, off the spud pipe. (There may be an intermediate set of nuts to be loosened, right at the hole in the base of the tank.) If you are working by yourself, support the underside of the tank so that it does not fall and bend the

spud pipe as you remove that last bolt. Set the tank aside.

If yours is a free-standing unit, the tank will be held to the base with two long bolts; remove them with a straight screwdriver; use an adjustable wrench to keep the nuts on the underside of the base from turning. Lift the tank off—you may have to rock it slightly to break any seal to its base—and set it in a safe place.

Clean the inside of the bowl well before removing the base. Scrub the bowl with a bowl-cleaning brush and a commercial product designed for the task. Rinse the bowl well: this task is most easily done with the tank still in place, but a bucket of water poured into a bowl will flush. Afterwards, remove the remaining water in the bowl by plunging or by bailing it out into a pail. A small amount will, of course, run onto the floor when you lift off the base.

Before unbolting the bolts that hold the base down, wad up newspaper and stuff it into two small plastic bags. You will stuff one bag into the drain opening and one into the base of the toilet, to keep septic smells at bay. (You might also wear a cheap respirator mask during the operation; it is not necessary, but suit yourself.) Gently dislodge the porcelain nut caps on either side of the toilet base with a screwdriver; they are held down only with wads of putty. Turn off the nuts with an adjustable crescent wrench and set them aside.

Rock the base slightly to break the seals of the wax ring and the plumber's putty. Lift the base straight up. Immediately stuff the plastic bags into the floor and toilet openings, being careful to leave enough sticking out of the hole so that you can later remove those bags. Wipe off any wastes around the horn of the toilet with a heavy-strength cleaner. Set the unit aside and let it dry.

When you transport the parts of

the toilet, they should be separate, individually wrapped so that they will not strike each other during travel. To prevent damage to any pipe leads, lay the units on their sides. Wash and hose off the base well and allow it to dry outside before hooking it up again in a new location.

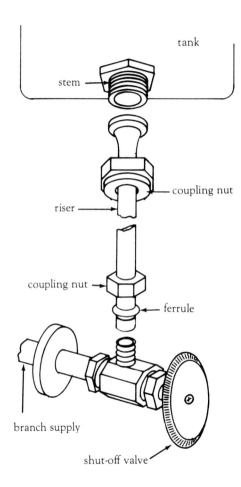

7-47. The supply riser to the toilet tank begins at a shut-off valve sticking out of the floor or wall behind; a ferrule in the valve compresses to ensure a tight fit. Where the riser joins the tank, it couples to the threaded stem of the ballcock assembly. Tank-connection details vary, but most often the head of the supply riser is flared in some manner.

RECONDITIONING TOILETS

Even if the toilet that you get is in good shape, a number of elements may be upgraded to minimize maintenance in the years to come.

Replace Watertight Elements

Any pliable part that ensures a watertight seal should be replaced. Toilet assemblies differ somewhat, but most have gaskets or washers where the supply riser joins the tank; around the drain hole in the bottom of the tank; and where the tank rests on the back of the base or, in the case of wall-hung models, at each slip coupling along the spud pipe.

The wax ring, which seals the base of the toilet to the floor flange, should be replaced each time the base is disturbed for any reason. Plumber's putty beneath the base of a toilet need not be replaced if it is still pliable.

Do not reuse the supply riser of the toilet; buy a new one. Although you may reuse the coupling nut that draws the top of the riser to the underside of the tank, in no event should you reuse the ferrule which tightens around the bottom of the riser where it meets the shut-off valve. Such ferrules are good for one use only, for their metal is compressed when the nut is tightened.

The Flush Mechanism

If the flush mechanism of the toilet looks at all like that shown in figure 7-48 replace it with one that is shown in figure 7-50. The older model is forever getting hung up where lift wires meet, especially if there is any corrosion or mineral

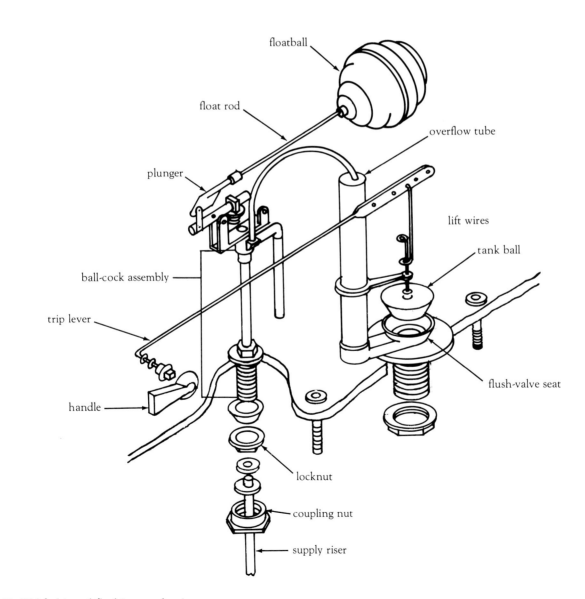

7-48. Old-fashioned flushing mechanism.

166

7-49. A flapper valve simply drops down when the water has flushed out of the tank. Controlled only by a pull chain on the trip lever, it has no parts that can misalign or jam.

Courtesy Fluidmaster, Inc.

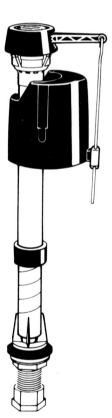

7-50. A Fluidmaster ballcock, being largely plastic, is impervious to mineral buildup; its water level is adjustable for improved water conservation.

Courtesy Fluidmaster, Inc.

build-up. The plastic replacement shown is adjustable for greater water saving. Its connection to the bottom of the tank is almost identical to that of the old parts.

The simple rubber flap of the Flusher Fixer works well, falling over the drain hole when enough water has emptied out; why this device was not used in the first place is a mystery.

REMOUNTING THE UNIT

Very little preparatory work is needed before setting up the toilet. The floor flange, as shown in figure 7–1, should have its center at least 12 inches from the wall behind. The floor does not need any reinforcement beneath the weight of the toilet—unless, that is, the subflooring shows obvious water damage or it is less than ½-inch-thick plywood (or 1-inch boards). If the floor is inadequate, lay a new underlayment over the existing floor and new finish flooring over that.

If your unit is wall hung, you will need to disturb the finish walls and let a board into the edges of the studs, as described earlier. Once the finish wall is replaced, you have a support to which you can bolt the tank.

Otherwise, the procedure is the reverse of removing a unit. Make sure the floor is free from debris and that there is no obstruction in the floor flange. Two special flange bolts should be sticking up out of the flange, ready to receive the base of the toilet. Turn the base of the toilet upside down and spread a layer of plumber's putty around the edge of that base; place a new wax ring over the horn of the toilet. Flip the toilet over, align the holes in its base to the two bolts sticking up from the floor flange, and press the base down to spread the plumber's putty. Tighten the nuts over the threaded bolts—but do not over-tighten—and then cover the tops of those bolts with the porcelain caps provided. A wad of putty in each cap will hold it to the bolt.

If yours is a free-standing unit, attach the tank to the back of the base after spreading out the resilient tank cushion shown in figure 7–44. Two bolts tighten the tank down; again, do not overtighten.

If yours is a wall-hung model, tighten the length of the spud pipe that runs out of the back of the base first, so that its other end sticks up, waiting for the tank to be slipped down over it. Support wall-hung tanks temporarily until you have them bolted to the wall behind. Tighten the slip-nut couplings along the spud pipe. Tighten the supply riser.

Recycled piping makes a euphonious wind chime.
Seen at the JO-EL Shop

Copper slip-fittings (1-in. diameter) as napkin rings.
Seen at Saint Orres inn

A very old brass faucet, possibly late nine-teenth century English.
Gargoyles, Ltd.

A real beauty, this sink has been reenameled and all of its brass parts, including supply risers and shut-off valves, polished with rubbing compound.

Great American Salvage

Marble lavatory with scrolled splashpiece. The sink is floral porcelain, the faucets have a languid, "drooping" quality.

Adolf deRoy Mark

This wall-hung toilet has a round upper piece. Otherwise, its attachments are standard, although the rod of the floatball inside had to be shortened.

Sunrise Salvage

A very unusual base, with diagonally wrapped fluting.

Vigilante Plumbing

Heavy Metal

Safety Tips

- Goggles and gloves are imperative if you must do any drilling when cleaning up or setting heavy metal pieces. If you sandblast a piece to clean it, use a respirator mask.
- When removing and installing heavy pieces, support their weight with diagonal braces attached to a solid support. If, for example, you are bolting a metal bracket into a masonry wall, support the piece until the mortar has completely cured.
- Do not injure yourself when moving heavy pieces: slide or roll pieces whenever possible. Lift minimally; using ramps or levers is much safer. When you bend to lift, bend your knees, not your back. Use a dolly to roll pieces.
- Be sure that the heavy metal objects will be adequately supported after installment. Beneath a wood stove, for example, you may need to reinforce joists. Consult a structural engineer if you have doubts.
- When transporting objects, pack them separately. Metal (especially cast iron) is easily cracked.

Tools

- A wire-brush wheel for an electric drill is useful for removing rust from metal. Sandblasting is excellent if the metal does not have a fine finish that would be damaged by pitting. Wear goggles and gloves for cleaning operations and a respirator mask if you sandblast.
- Spray-painting is preferred if the surfaces of your metal are at all ornate. For that matter, even a flat metal surface can be more uniformly covered if the operator is knowledgeable.
- Dollies, ramps, carrying straps—all will save your back when transporting heavy objects; have friends share the load as well.

A cast-iron furnace door reused as a cleanout trap on an indoor grill in a Brooklyn brownstone. The bricks around the grill came from a demolished chimney.

Anthony Vigilante

Cast iron was the most widely used architectural metal (excluding roofing) in years past. In its molten phase, it can assume any number of forms; once cooled, it can weather high heats without degrading and, because of its chemical qualities, resist rust better than steel. Thus, cast iron is used for stoves and furnaces inside and for a variety of external uses. Its one salient defect is that it is brittle and may crack if dropped or struck with a hammer. The other metals mentioned in this chapter are more or less decorative.

EXTERIOR METALS

Fences, grillwork, crestwork, hinges, brackets, foot scrapers, cornicework, decorative emblems, fountains, and birdbaths are among the many types of exterior metalwork. In some cases the metal is embedded in masonry and can be dislodged only after a lot of chipping with cold chisels or impact hammers and prying with crowbars. Because of the weight and complexity of most pieces, few are salvaged by amateurs. The difficulty of removing and transporting such heavyweights favors using fragments of originals.

Assessing a cast-iron piece involves little more than examining it for cracks. Because a face may be painted, look at its back side as well. If you see anything suspicious, scrape away paint or scale with a putty knife and look closer. If you will be reconditioning the piece, small cracks need not discourage you, but larger ones may open up completely as you transport the object home. Speaking of transportation, a homemade dolly is invaluable for moving big pieces

around. Build an 18- by 24-inch dolly frame out of 2 × 4 scraps, with two ¼-inch bolts at each corner, four sturdy wheels, and nonslip vinyl that is contact-cemented to the top of the 2 × 4s. When conveying pieces of metal, never place one directly atop another, for a pothole may be enough to slam them together. Cushion all pieces with old blankets or the like.

RECONDITIONING

If pieces are intact, you need only clean away surface rust and repaint them. If cracks are to be mended or breaks are to be spliced, clean the piece first so you can see the extent of cracks (unless, of course, you like the patina of the old piece).

Removing Rust

Scraping, sanding, chemical-stripping, and sandblasting are your choices for cleaning up an object.

Unless the cast iron is extremely frail or detailed, I would recommend sandblasting it.

Scrape away loose scale with paint scrapers, stiff putty knives, and wire brushes, the last being best if the piece is contoured. A rotary wire brush in a drill bit also works well.

Sandpaper and rotary sandpaper wheels in a drill bit are gentler than scraping; steel wool, the kindest of all.

If the surface is at all pitted by rust, use naval jelly to root out rust. After scrubbing with steel wool dipped in naval jelly (it can also be brushed on), rinse the piece well with water and allow it to dry totally before priming. Bring the object indoors overnight and put a small heater on it so it will be completely dry by morning.

Sandblasting is a disastrous way to strip wood or brick, but because metal is much harder, it is little affected. Since cast iron is somewhat grainy anyhow, pitting should not

8-1. A cannonball that rolled along since the Civil War is now hanging around, pulling the gate shut.

make much difference. Use the finest sand initially, switching to coarser grades only if finer ones prove ineffectual. Follow manufacturer's suggestions for operating the equipment. In most operations you should wear goggles and a respirator mask; if you construct a plastic tent over the iron, you may be able to reuse some of the abrasive. When the job is complete, remove the tent (if any) and blow off any remaining sand with a compressor hose.

Filling Cracks

After cleaning the piece well, touch up the edges of any cracks so they can be filled. Apply an extra coat of naval jelly to edges and allow it to work twice as long as its label recommends. Rinse well and then scrape edges with a file or wire brush until you see shiny metal.

Epoxy may be used to fill cracks; a variety of types are available: with different setting times and viscosities, with or without reinforcement, with or without color, and so forth. To bridge small cracks—less than ¼ inch across—run a bead of epoxy on each side and allow those applications to harden. Add beads until a gentle mound covers the crack. When the compound is completely dry, you can sand, prime, and paint the whole area.

If the crack is intermediate—about ½ inch across—use plumber's seal (Epoxybond Plumbers' Seal is one such product). A puttylike substance in two parts, knead it by hand (wear gloves) until it is warm and uniformly gray. Although the object should be completely dry, plumber's epoxy will adhere to a moist surface as well—provided you do not jar it before the compound sets.

Finally, large splits can be covered with auto-body epoxy kits, featuring fiberglass sheets that applied in layers, will cover considerable gaps. Overbuild the area

8-2 and 8-3. The onion domes of Saint Orres Inn recall a time when northern California was roamed by Russian traders. The copper covering the roof is salvaged, government-surplus, three-ply circuit boards that were defective on one side. Clever builders shaped the ends with tin snips, turned the defective side down, and overlapped all shingles by about two-thirds.

and then sand it down to achieve the correct contour. Missing parts of a decorative design can be cast with the Monzini compounds mentioned in chapter 5, although those compounds are quite expensive (see chapter 9 for discussion of casting).

Check epoxy labels about compatible primers and paints.

Priming

After removing rust and (as necessary) allowing metal to dry, prime the object as soon as possible. Paint only if the temperature will be 55°F (13°C) or above until the primer is fully dry. Hence, do not start any jobs in the late afternoon, if evenings will be cool. The primer seals the surface of the metal, prevents rust, and ensures adhesion of the finish coat(s).

A number of rust-inhibiting primers are available; Rustoleum brand carries several. A paint store will be able to mix special orders. Primer, like finish paint, consists of

a pigment and a vehicle; both elements are important to the performance of the primer/paint. *Red lead pigment* in an *alkyd* or *oil-based vehicle* is best for metal surfaces that are not rust-free, because the oil soaks into rust scale and helps paint adhere better. *Iron oxide pigment*, which most often has a *vinyl base*, is poor at preventing rust but is a good primer for nonferrous metals such as aluminum, copper, and the like. *Zinc-dust* pigments are effective rust inhibitors in a number of bases, vinyls being most common. *Zinc chromate* inhibits rust if the surface is completely free of rust but is less effective if applied over rusty surfaces. The vehicles for paint determine whether the coating will resist acids and alkalies (fresh mortar or plaster, for example, may be very alkaline). Epoxy, vinyl, phenolic, and neoprene-resin vehicles are resistant.

Apply primers with brushes or spray guns; a thin, even coat is the objective in either case. Brushing it on is perhaps easiest for amateurs,

8-4. Because wrought iron is relatively thin and easily shaped, it takes many forms, such as these industrial brackets on a porch post in Vermont.

Ken McKenzie

because metal paints tend to clog up spray-gun nozzles, requiring periodic cleaning. If you know how to use a spray gun, however, you can uniformly coat even tight spaces. Whatever primer you use, apply finish coats as soon as practicable; primers degrade quickly and admit moisture.

Applying Finish Coats

In general, try for two finish coats with the same vehicle as the primer. If you are unsure of the composition of the primer, use finish coats with oil or alkyd bases. You do not need to sand between coats as when painting drywall or wood, although you must let metal surfaces dry thoroughly.

Finish coats now come in many colors; exterior metal was black so often in the past because the only alternative was a shocking red. Enamel finishes tend to weather better than flat ones.

ATTACHING EXTERIOR METAL

To attach ornamental metal to a wood-frame building, sink lag screws through the mounting tabs of the piece, preferably sinking the bolts into studs behind for greatest support. That failing, toggle bolts or extension bolts will work well; draw the bolt tight to the sheathing.

Exterior metal is commonly attached when masonry materials are being laid. As you lay up the bricks (block, whatever), leave room for the ends of the metal—allow at least $\frac{1}{2}$ inch extra on each side. Set the metal in place and pack in mortar with the point of your trowel. It may be necessary to support the metal until the mortar dries. If you are setting a metal gate, for example, set hinge posts into the mortar joints and align those posts with a plumbed string with two knots tied into it—each knot representing a hinge position.

If the masonry wall is already in place, however, drill into it with a carbide-tipped masonry bit to cut a pocket. Wear goggles. Back the tool out frequently as it cuts, so pulverized masonry will not bind it. Before setting in the ends of the metal object, rinse out any debris and, while the hole is still damp, trowel in an epoxy compound such as Thoro-Grip. Insert the ends of the metal piece, supporting the object as necessary. Allow the compound to dry. Give the ends of metal inserted in masonry an extra coat of an alkaline-resistant paint.

INTERIOR METALWORK: WOOD STOVES

Interior metals are not called upon to resist weather, but often used as part of a heating system, they must withstand extreme fluctuations of temperature. Again, cast iron is king, although cast aluminum and brass are found in later fabrications.

Wood stoves, whether for cooking or heating alone, can be great finds or terrible ones, depending largely upon their condition. If a wood stove is questionable or seems overpriced compared to new models, opt for a new stove, which is probably more airtight. The key to what you get is assessment; be rigorous.

ASSESSMENT

Wood stoves do not transport well: cast iron is brittle and, being so heavy, may get jarred along the way. If a jolt is strong enough, the stove may crack. Look for cracks on the legs of the stove; where legs meet the main body of the stove; where major sections bolt together, such as the main body to the base, the warming oven (if any) to the main body, and so on; and at the

8-5. Famous Beaver cook stove.

stovepipe take-off, where smoke exits and turns upwards. Any stove joints that are reinforced with steel mending plates or the like are suspect. As you examine cracks, observe their direction and think about what might have caused them.

Rust may also be a danger sign. One of the oldest lines in the metal-yard sales pitch is, "It's only surface rust." That may be so, but see for yourself by scraping at rust scale with a penknife. A reasonably maintained cast-iron stove should not have *any* serious rust. Areas where

rust is critical are the bend where a stovepipe connects to the main stove—creosote or condensed moisture running down may hasten rot there—and around a water jacket or pan, where water has collected. Rust anywhere else, such as around legs or the firebox, probably results from the unit being stored in a damp basement or shed or from negligence.

Serious cracks or rust around the stovepipe bend should discourage you from buying a stove. Likewise, if you can see light around the firebox, do not buy, because a stove

that is not airtight will overheat and consume wood too rapidly. Used sheet-metal stoves are therefore rarely worth buying; they are seldom good for more than four or five seasons unless they have been pampered and used infrequently.

If the stove has passed muster thus far, continue your investigation. Are all the parts present and operable? If the stove is presently in pieces, reassemble it; even an expert can miss parts in a pile. Take along two or three dozen 1/4-inch by 1 1/2-inch stovebolts for such temporary connection. Have a friend help lift the heavier pieces and steady sections as you bolt them together. Commonly misplaced parts are:

- shaker grates inside the firebox
- gears that interconnect shaker grates
- firebrick around the sides of the firebox (not all stoves have firebrick—if yours did, you will probably find remnants)
- a water jacket inside the firebox (again, not always present, but nice to have; if your cook stove had one, you will see two holes for water pipes coming out of the back of the firebox)
- miscellaneous lids from the top of the cooking surface, handles, and so forth
- the damper lever and the interior damper of the stove (on cook stoves)

The most important items in this list are the first two and the last one. Wood must sit on grates in a cook stove if air is to get beneath and ashes are to be shaken down; noncooking stoves usually do not have grates. An interior damper— not to be confused with a damper in the stovepipe—is also a must for a cook stove, for it diverts hot air around the oven section. Those items must be present; the rest you can live without.

Is all chrome intact? Does the oven thermometer work? Are there handles for lifting lids and shaking grates? Are all "skirts" and "kickers" (which allow you to open a door with a foot when your arms are full of wood) intact? Are ornamental bolts (plated, for attaching chrome sections) anywhere to be seen? These items are not critical, but replacements must be cast if you want a parlor-quality restoration.

Be wary of any steel-plate repairs around the firebox: steel will lose its temper and eventually distort. It is possible, but difficult, to weld cast iron. Gaps may be filled with refractory cement or, in the firebox, plaster, but movement thereafter may dislodge those repairs. Again, if there are gaps around the firebox, if the doors do not close tightly, or if there are separations around the stovepipe take-off, better buy another stove.

Should the stove be a wood-and-gas combination, be wary about gas elements—have an expert examine them. Such stoves often represent interim technology and do not use gas efficiently. Worse, such stoves could explode. Their ovens are characteristically difficult to maintain at a constant temperature; individual stovetop burners may not light evenly; orifices supplying burners may also leak or need adjustment to burn correctly. Some nice combos do exist, but all should be checked by a gas utility specialist.

Cast-iron wood- or coal-burning furnaces are usually good buys, especially if they are in the basement of the original owner. Hire someone familiar with these furnaces to go out and look at yours to make sure that all parts are there. Wood furnaces converted to coal, or from coal to oil, will often be missing grates and the like.

REMOVING AND TRANSPORTING

Examine the stairs and floors along the route you will transport the wood stove or furnace. Are they sturdy enough to bear the great load? Basement stairs are notoriously ramshackle and could give way: examine them closely, being especially wary of stair treads merely nailed to stringers (the long diagonal supports) or supported by cleats beneath. Check the attachments of the stairs, above and below. If they look sturdy, jump up and down, landing heavily, to make sure stairs are safe.

Be kind to your back. Disassemble stoves as much as is practicable. If there are stairs on either end of the move, at least one person will have to back up, potentially straining his back. Eliminate such bending over by throwing a stout rope (called a "hump strap" in the moving industry) beneath the legs of the stove. Get lots of help. Many hands make work light, but have only one person directing the efforts of the crew.

8-6. A stove in transition.

8-7. This gnome of a stove was fabricated from a butane tank and rests atop a truck brake cylinder. The tank is extremely sturdy, 1/4-in.-thick steel; the door, cut directly from the tank, is backstopped by a 1/4-in. lip welded to the inside of the tank. This demonstrates a very fancy piece of torch work, not a jagged edge or sloppy weld to be seen.

RECONDITIONING AND REUSING

Before reassembling the stove, clean all black metal parts by sandblasting with a fine abrasive; all parts, that is, except gas-burner assemblies. Chrome should also not be sandblasted, nor any glass or brightwork with a reflective surface. If such sections cannot be removed, cover them with masking tape before sandblasting.

Paste stove-polish is best to clean up an old black cast-iron stove; apply paste with a rag as directed by the manufacturer. If the stove is enameled, clean surfaces with a nonabrasive cleanser such as Bon-Ami. Now is a good time to have missing parts recast or scuffed ones re-enameled. Some epoxy compounds patch imperfections on cast iron, but most are not heat–resistant; if you are considering patching with epoxy, check labels for heat resistance.

As you reassemble a stove, note that bolt heads may differ: machine-head or round-head bolts are all-purpose joiners; chrome-headed bolts, or "oval-heads," have low profiles that maintain the sleek look of a trim section. As you reassemble, work from lower sections up.

Before you start reassembly, however, check figure 8–8. Rigidly adhere to recommended distances from combustible surfaces. A bed of paver brick beneath the stove looks nice, reflects heat upward, and will catch any stray ashes or sparks. A bed of bricks will also distribute the weight of the stove to a degree, although you should double joists beneath stove feet. If the subfloor looks old and tired and is less than 5/8 inch thick, it should be upgraded. Place furnaces on a level concrete pad at least 4 inches thick.

Read up on wood heat before you hook up (*Woodburner's Encyclopedia* is a good book; see Bibliography) and attend a course conducted by your local fire department.

Lift pieces as little as possible. If you can rent a dolly on which to roll pieces, do so. Place scrap plywood over finish floors so dolly wheels do no damage. A pickup truck is well suited for moving stoves because, with its tailgate down, you can back up to outside steps, saving some of the carrying.

When transporting heavy items, tie them all the way forward in the truck bed. A stove tied to the front of the truck bed is kinder to the suspension system of the vehicle and less likely to shift during transport. Disassemble stoves as much as is practicable, especially warming ovens above the main body. To prevent cracking, wrap all pieces in blankets.

If you are an amateur mechanic, photograph the stove before disassembly; simple sketches will show the order in which parts should be reassembled.

INTERIOR METALWORK: MISCELLANEOUS PIECES

Clean the following cast-iron items as you would a cast-iron stove. For steel or other metals, apply naval jelly to rusty spots, scrubbing with fine steel wool.

RADIATORS

Old cast-iron radiators are, in my opinion, not worth the trouble to salvage unless they are already in your home and pipe hookups are present. Modern-day convectors are much flimsier and not as exotic looking but, being lower and longer, distribute heat more evenly. They are also much easier to hook up.

Radiators are notorious for leaking once their couplings have been undone, usually requiring new relief valves. Besides, they are beasts to move around.

After sandblasting a radiator, you should not paint it, as paint hinders heat exchange—but few of us find an aging hunk of metal charming. A number of paints will adhere to radiators and can withstand heat, but check labels to be sure. Rustoleum makes one such paint; most aluminum-based or acrylic-based paints are also well suited to the purpose. One thin coat of paint should suffice.

FLOOR GRATES

Sandblasting is suitable for most cast-iron floor grates, especially if they are ornate. You may also dip them in stripper if you remove beforehand the louvered section that fits inside. When reassembling the grate, oil the moving parts of the louver with light oil, but apply the oil moderately or an oily smell will prevail when the heat comes on.

If the grate is nonferrous and has a delicate pattern, it may be plated; do not sandblast it. Get advice from a plating shop about which strippers are acceptable.

METAL MANTELS

Metal mantels have mounting tabs that fit into the mortar behind. Position the mantel and mark where those tabs strike the brick. With a small masonry chisel (any small cold chisel should do), chip out the area of the tabs plus a little for the mortar that will hold the tabs fast. (Note that Thoro-Grip epoxy compound works well instead of mortar.) Wear safety goggles when chipping.

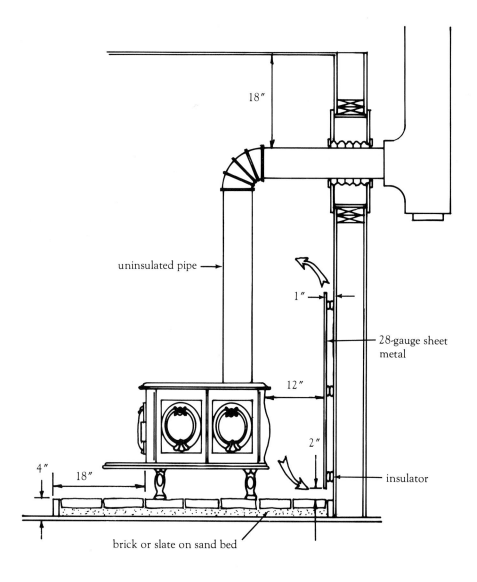

18″

uninsulated pipe →

1″

28-gauge sheet metal

12″

2″

insulator

4″

18″

brick or slate on sand bed

8-8. Wood stove safety. The dimensions given are *minimum* distances. Of particular importance is the sheet of metal behind the stove: that metal must be held out from the wall by mounting it over ceramic fence-post insulators. This 1-in. gap behind the sheet metal—and the 2-in. gap at the bottom—are imperative if air is to circulate.

8-9. Floor registers with louvers.
Great American Salvage.

In some cases the tabs of the mantel turn inward. Apply fist-sized patches of plaster to the brickwork where those tabs align. Prop the mantel in place until the plaster dries. This surface patching method is common for nonbearing mantels.

Finally, you may set stove bolts or small lag screws (which turn into an expandable sleeve) into the masonry mass. To insert such sleeves, drill with a carbide-tipped masonry bit in a heavy-duty drill. Wear goggles.

8-10. Cast-bronze, French mantel and cover; nineteenth century.
Gargoyles, Ltd.

A foot scraper in Philadelphia, wire-brushed and painted glossy black.

A cast-iron furnace door reused as a cleanout trap on an indoor grill in a Brooklyn brownstone. The bricks around the grill came from a demolished chimney.

Anthony Vigilante

Three-panel, cast-iron firebox insert.
Gargoyles, Ltd.

An ornate wall register.
Gargoyles, Ltd.

Recycled scrollwork graces a gate in Albuquerque, New Mexico.
Nat Kaplan

Masonry

Safety Tips

- Rarely are electrical shocks a problem when working with masonry objects. If you must ever cut into finish surfaces, however—say, to free a section of crown molding along a ceiling—turn off electricity to the area and test with a voltage tester to be sure (see figs. 4–1 to 4–3).
- Support masonry pieces adequately during removal and installation. Keep in mind that mortar, plaster, and construction adhesive must be completely cured before they are at full strength.
- If a masonry object is heavy, take care when moving it. Bend your knees, not your back, when lifting and use carrying slings, ramps, and dollies when possible.
- Masonry is relatively brittle; if dropped or struck sharply, the piece may be ruined.
- When cleaning, drilling, cutting, or otherwise altering masonry materials, wear goggles and a respirator mask. If working over your head, wear a hard hat. When using cleaning solutions, wear gloves and long-sleeved clothes to protect your skin. In general, masonry materials such as mortar are hard on skin: avoid handling it. Petroleum jelly and skin creams will reduce skin irritation.

Tools

- Goggles, gloves, and a respirator mask will safeguard your health. If working over your head, wear a hard hat too.
- A trowel and a mason's hammer will see you through most tasks. A cold chisel and a hammer will remove stubborn mortar or unwanted material. Wear goggles when chipping.
- If you must drill, use a carbide-tipped bit in a ½-inch drill; smaller drills will burn out. Wear goggles when drilling.
- For cleaning out mortar joints, use a Carborundum blade in a power saw. A repointing chisel, or tuckpointing chisel, is more difficult to use than the sawblade but is kinder to surrounding brick. Use goggles and a respirator mask for either tool.
- Plaster requires few exotic tools; a metal straightedge and a stiff-bladed scraper should see you through. Lightweight rubber gloves are sufficient protection when mixing and shaping plaster.

Made of old brick and capped with a granite capital, this expressive column holds up a beam in a basement office. The entire structure demonstrates a keen feeling for color and texture—the original stone foundations washed white, the floors of salvaged slate sealed with a semiglossy finish.

Adolf deRoy Mark

Masonry materials vary greatly in composition and appearance, from plaster to brick to marble, but they share certain characteristics that salvagers would do well to note. Such materials are, with the exception of plaster, heavy. Support pieces adequately when attaching or detaching and transport them intelligently so that you avoid injury. For all their hardness, masonry pieces are fragile and may crack or break if struck sharply or dropped. And durable though stone and its relatives are, they will deteriorate when exposed to weather, a particularly important point if the material is porous.

The section on plaster in this chapter emphasizes interior uses, whereas that on bricks and stones is about exterior masonry. The techniques described are not mutually exclusive, however: an artisan who wants to weatherproof plaster may find some of the consolidants in the second section useful; those who want to build up a damaged piece of garden sculpture can learn from the plaster-casting sequence in the beginning. Casting information is also pertinent when using epoxy compounds to replace missing metal elements.

PLASTER

After you remove and repair the original objects that you wish to copy, duplication is essentially a three-part process: creating a *mold* (a negative image of the object), reinforcing that mold with a *shell* (also called a "mother mold"), and after removing the original from the mold, *casting* a new piece.

REMOVING

A plaster object in place must be removed without straining it because it will crack if pried off ineptly. Copying cracked pieces is generally more difficult. You can cast an object in place by applying a mold directly to it, but it is tedious to work over your head (where most ornate plaster pieces are located) and the results will be somewhat inferior. Moreover, damaged plaster usually occurs concurrently with more extensive renovation work, which will make your work tougher. In short, it is easier to cut free the chunk you need to reproduce.

Plaster ornaments are usually applied to wood lath or, in the case of decorative cornices and friezework that run around the top of a room, stuck to the finish coat with an additional bed of bonding plaster. To remove such plaster detail without destroying it, you must get behind the plaster to the wooden lath strips and pry them loose from the joists (or studs) to which they are nailed. If plaster has already separated from its lath, however, slide a flat bar between plaster and lath.

The best way to remove plaster ornaments is to cut them free, using a Carborundum blade in a power

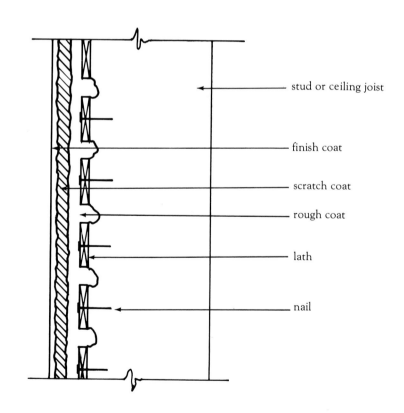

9-1. **Cross section of plaster lath construction.**

stud or ceiling joist

finish coat

scratch coat

rough coat

lath

nail

saw. To do this properly, you will need a few pieces of equipment. To operate the saw safely, wear goggles or safety glasses and a respirator mask. Secure footing, preferably scaffolding or a sturdy ladder, is imperative. Finally, build a tee brace from scrap 2 × 4s to support the piece you cut free, so it does not crash down.

After turning off the electricity running through the affected area, lodge the tee against the section to be cut out. If the tee might damage the surface of the plaster, place a piece of foam rubber atop the tee. Set your saw blade so that it cuts through plaster and wood lath, but stops short of the joist. Cut around the object, allowing an inch or two extra around the perimeter. When the cutting is complete, have a friend slowly pull out the tee as you catch the plaster section. Chances are it will not fall, in which case you must slip your flat bar behind and coax it off. Pry around the entire perimeter of the object evenly to minimize cracks.

CLEANING AND REPAIRING

If an object is painted, steam off that paint. If steam alone does not suffice, brush on methylene chloride, allow it to work, and wipe off dissolved paint with a rag. If the plaster is heavily painted, use methylene chloride *and* steam, holding a wallpaper steamer just above the surface of the object. Work in a well-ventilated area, wear rubber gloves, and wipe paint globs off onto newspaper as you work. If the object is badly obscured with paint, cleaning it without damaging it takes time and effort; wooden clay-sculpting tools may aid you. If you do use paint stripper, rinse the object well when you are done, because chemical residues could interfere with molding materials.

Fill surface blemishes or recreate missing parts so that the new cast-

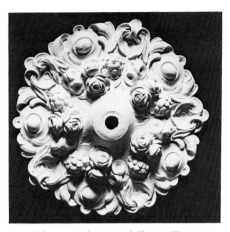

9-2. Plaster ceiling medallion, "Easter Morning" pattern.
San Francisco Victoriana

ing will be as complete as possible. If blemishes are shallow, modeling clay will do; if you need something stiffer, use plaster, patching compound (Polyfilla is one brand), or even epoxy.

If the object is broken, stabilize it before you create the mold and pour the shell. Epoxy compounds are good for a quick fix, as are most white glues; epoxy and fiberglass auto-body kits can be applied to the back side of a severely damaged item, although you should consult the product label to see if it will adhere to plaster. Fresh plaster is also a fair bonding agent, although it must be applied relatively thick (say, ½ inch) if it is to have much holding power.

Repairs done, seal the surface of the object to prevent the molding material from adhering to it. Release agents have been specially created for the task—the consolidants used for stone will work—but the time-honored choice is shellac, cheap and easily obtained.

MOLDING AND CASTING

Once the object is repaired, you are ready to create a mold, into which a new casting can be poured. Molding and casting materials with wide ranges of cost and application are available.

Molding Materials

Liquid rubber latex is a versatile molding material, by far the best for the nonprofessional. It produces a mold that is flexible, sensitive to detail, lightweight, and extremely durable and tear-resistant. It is relatively inexpensive when bought in gallon containers and can be extended and made more rigid by adding filler such as ground latex. The only disadvantage to its use—of small concern to most people—is that it will destroy delicate surface patinas. Latex releases well, but apply a release agent to the more delicate parts of the original, such as those which are undercut. (An undercut profile turns back on itself, for example, a leaf that folds over.)

RTV silicone rubber is a two-part compound, very expensive, that has amazing capabilities. Although it is stiff enough not to need the reinforcement of a shell, RTV can capture the finest detail and will not destroy patina. Its molds can also withstand the heat of low-temperature metals. Use with a release agent. Work in a well-ventilated area.

Polyester resin is an inexpensive but relatively inflexible molding material that is applied in alternating layers of resin and fiberglass. It can be reused many times. Molds are lightweight and yield a fair detail, but any high reliefs or undercuts will require a knockdown mold, a mold in at least two parts. Polyester resin is very good, however, for large, relatively flat sheet castings. Pieces of pipe laid into the layers of fiberglass will produce a strong, rigid mold.

Plasteline is, as its name suggests, a very plastic material that is suitable for small one-time molds. Its plasticity is also its shortcoming to a degree, because it may stick to the object or tear when you try to remove it. If you cool the material by putting it outside on a cold day, however, the plasteline will stiffen

9-3. Mask of Bacchus, in a courtyard in Philadelphia.
"Reflections" Antique Stained Glass

somewhat and can be removed in a coherent form.

Plaster itself is a molding material, although an unwieldly one for molding of any size. Once dry, it is rigid, requiring a knockdown mold for any undercut details. Use a release agent with plaster molds. All in all, plaster is not a great molding material: fair detail, cheap, but heavy and hard to work with.

Casting Materials

Plaster is, however, the preeminent casting material. Poured as a liquid, it assumes the shape of the mold, even a finely detailed one. Because set plaster is so rigid, however, it is imperative that you coat the inside of the mold with a release agent. Release agents can be applied by brushing them on or, even better, by spraying them on with an old pump bottle. You can make an acceptable release agent by boiling a cake of Ivory soap in a quart of water. Let it sit for six hours, then retrieve the gummy residue in the bottom of the pan. Paint a thin coat of this onto the inside of the mold.

The major shortcoming of plaster is that it has little structural integrity. If the casting is too thin, it may be destroyed as you peel off the mold; if too thick, it will be too heavy. You should therefore reinforce plaster, as shown in figure 9–16. Finally, if the casting is at all large, reinforce the mold with a shell.

Casting rubber is similar to liquid rubber latex (the molding material) except that casting rubber has more filler and is thus more rigid. Relatively light and inexpensive, casting rubber can also be trimmed.

Epoxy casting resins are so varied that one could write books about them; the Monzini epoxy compounds that mimic metal are but one example (see chapter 5). Most reproduce detail well, have excellent structural integrity, and after compounds have dried, can be worked with tools. They are, however, very expensive.

Polyurethane foams are commonly used to mimic ornate wood or plaster moldings because lightweight foams attach easily and hold paint well. Most foams are

two-part compounds that set within a half hour of being mixed and poured.

Casting from an Original

Shellac your worktable to prevent materials from adhering to it. Most molds should be lain flat on the table, and any gaps between the table and the object should be filled with molding clay. Crown molding with beveled edges, on the other hand, should be propped up in a molding box, at the angle at which that molding will meet wall and ceiling.

After cleaning, repairing, and shellacking the original, paint on the molding material with a brush. Allow time for layers to dry, as recommended by the manufacturer. In figure 9–4, the artist did not use any reinforcement for the mold, reasoning that latex is strong; moreover, the piece being cast had no undercuts. A less seasoned craftsperson should reinforce the mold, however, alternating strips of cheesecloth or fiberglass with applications of the molding liquid. (Cut strips small, say 2 inches by 5 inches, so that they hug the contour of the piece.) As you paint on the molding material, deliberately brush it an additional 1 inch around the object, onto the tabletop.

The first coat is the most critical to picking up fine detail. Apply molding material generously, working it into any recesses or crevices of the object. Subsequent coats of molding mixture may contain filler, which, being stiffer, impart rigidity to the mold. (The filler shown in our example is finely ground tires—from a retread shop—added to the latex molding material.) Apply the recommended number of coats, usually two or three.

Leave the object being reproduced inside the mold until you have completed the next step, constructing the shell. The shell (also called a "mother mold") sur-

9-4. Brush the molding material (here, liquid rubber latex) generously onto the original object to be reproduced.

9-5. When mixing plaster, always pour plaster into water, never vice-versa. A good mix ratio is ten parts water to seven parts plaster.

9-6. To mix the plaster and water, use your hands to gently sift the materials together, so that no lumps form nor unmixed spots remain. Work from the bottom of the pan up.

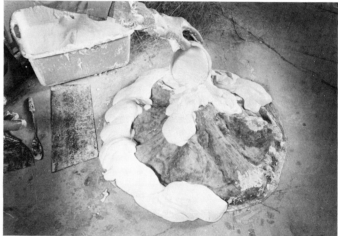

9-7. To build a support shell around the mold, pour the plaster—which is now starting to set—onto the mold and shape it with your hands.

rounds and supports the mold so that it will not distort when casting materials such as plaster are poured in. Before fabricating the shell, however, spray or brush a release agent on the outside surface of the mold.

You can create a shell in two ways. The first and perhaps simplest way is shown in our photo sequence. Apply handfuls of plaster that is just starting to set around the mold (with the original still inside). Pat fiber reinforcement into the damp plaster and shape the plaster so that it has no thin edges. Apply a second layer of plaster, completely covering the fiber and the first layer. Flatten the top of the shell so that, when inverted, the shell will sit flat on the table. When the shell has almost hardened, scoop out three or four poke holes, each an inch or so wide, that go all the way down to the surface of the mold. When you want to remove castings, it will be helpful if you can poke through the shell to jolt the casting loose.

The second way (not shown) to cast a shell is to build a temporary box around the mold and to pour very wet plaster into that box. The sides of the box confine the plaster until it has hardened, at which point you can disassemble the sides of the box. This method, is best suited for those shells that must be cast in two pieces, where the original has undercuttings that would be destroyed if pulled from a one-piece mold.

Once the shell has hardened, break the seal between the shell (and mold with original) and the

189

9-8. Work fast, patting reinforcement (here, fiber) into the plaster while it is still damp. Note that the edge of the shell has been squared off somewhat.

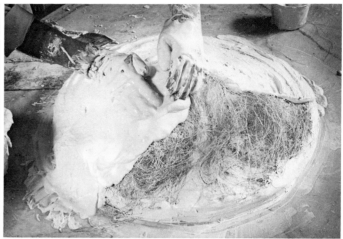

9-9. Apply a second coat of plaster, covering the fiber and the first coat entirely.

9-10. Shape the second coat, squaring its edges and flattening its peak so that, when the shell is inverted, it will sit more or less level.

9-11. When the shell is completely dry, break the surface seal to the table by inserting a wide-bladed knife beneath the edge of the shell.

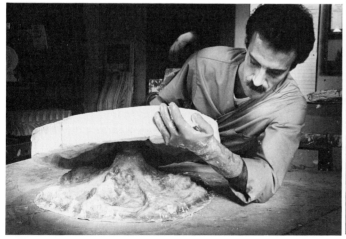

9-12. Lift the shell off the mold as shown—those poke holes will be helpful now—and finally remove the original object from the mold.

9-13. Spray release-agent onto the inside of the mold, which is again inside the level shell, so the casting will not stick.

9-15. Shake the shell so that the plaster settles into all parts of the mold; shaking drives out air bubbles, too.

9-14. Pour in plaster, filling just less than half the mold.

9-16. While the plaster is still damp, pat in reinforcing fiber so that it adheres to the entire surface.

table by inserting a wide-bladed knife beneath the shell edges. Now you are ready to remove the mold from the shell.

If the mold is symmetrical, it may be somewhat tricky to reinsert it into the shell; make a pencil mark on both mold and shell to align the two pieces. Remove the mold, with the original object still inside. To dislodge the mold and its content from the shell, push the piece out through the poke holes you pro-

vided. Because there may be a surface seal around the shell, you might also insert a small knife or spatula between the mold and the shell to get things started. Once the mold is out of the shell, strip it off the original and set that piece aside.

Invert the shell and level it on the table. Reinsert the mold back in the shell, and spray the inside of the mold with release agent. You are ready to make new castings.

Before you pour a new casting

into the supported mold, first coat all sides of the mold completely with the casting material to ensure that no air bubbles will be trapped. Rap the underside of the table with a rubber mallet to help drive bubbles out, or shake the mold. The first pour of casting material should not be too thick; shape it to the sides of the mold for uniform thickness. After spreading around the plaster— but while it still is wet—flatten in reinforcement such as hemp or

9-17. After pouring a second layer of plaster, scrape the edge of the casting so it is more or less flat. Note that the artist has sculpted a cavity in the middle of the casting, to reduce its weight somewhat.

9-18. Use a long straightedge to make the back edge of the casting as flat as you can.

9-19. When the plaster is completely dry, use a flat piece of wood to start the mold away from its shell; use poke holes too.

9-20. Peel the mold away from the casting. Voila!

fiberglass. Apply the second (and last) coat of plaster, spreading it around evenly, by hand. Again, shake the mold to drive out bubbles. Scrape the edge of the casting to make it fairly flat. As the plaster stiffens, build it up around the edges of the mold and then, with a straightedge, again shape the edges flat.

No casting operation is exactly the same, so methods vary. The medallion shown would be too heavy if the artist had merely filled up the mold with plaster; he chose instead to shape the plaster, leaving the center hollow. If the object that

you cast is relatively small and compact, however, you might simply fill the mold with plaster. Let common sense be your guide.

When the plaster has completely set, use a strong flat blade or stick to pry the mold out of its supporting shell. Be very gentle so that you do not chip the edge of the mold; here, the poke holes you sculpted into the shell will allow you to push the mold out. Once the mold is separated from the shell, simply peel the mold off the casting and you have a duplicate of the original object.

ATTACHING

Lighter pieces of plasterwork may be glued in place to drywall or plaster with a construction-grade adhesive that bonds the object to a finish surface. Adhesive is acceptable for larger objects too, but they should be screwed in as well. For greatest ease predrill screw holes with a drill-and-countersink bit in a high-speed drill. Attach drywall screws to a joist or stud if you can, but because the adhesive is doing the actual bonding, screw placement is not critical.

If you are concerned about the

weight of the piece, use toggle bolts through the drywall or plaster lath behind. Cover screw heads, bolts, or gaps with artfully applied dabs of plaster.

BRICKS AND STONES

Those readers who know nothing of basic masonry techniques should consult the Bibliography; our concern here is cleaning surfaces and extending the useful life of individual pieces.

Tools needed are few: a trowel, useful for cutting masonry and applying mortar; a flat bar, for removing old pieces; a hammer and cold chisel, if you must cut or shape; goggles; a ½-inch drill with a carbide bit, as required. Most other items, such as a pail for mixing mortar, are common.

ASSESSMENT

Most salvaged stone is put to incidental use, set in a fireplace wall, or built into a garden wall—so you need not be too concerned about its condition. If you intend to use the piece to support weight, such as a joist or beam, look more closely: the object should be free from major cracks and should be a hard stone such as granite. If there are cracks or spalling (flaking) spots, tap them gently with the sharp point of a mason's hammer or with the edge of a trowel. If the stone breaks down further under such gentle inquiry, use the stone only indoors, in a non-load-bearing situation. Stone that is intact may be used inside or out, although you will extend its life by coating it with a consolidant seal that repels water.

Brick is another story. Although it can be treated with sealants, it is generally not advisable to reuse it outside. Old brick simply

9-21. This alley wall in Frederick, Maryland, was built of old bricks. Because the mason used too strong a mortar mixture, the faces of the bricks spalled and fell away.
Thanks to Dick Kreh

does not weather well, as shown in figure 9-21. Brick is graded according to its durability: SW, severe weathering, for exterior use; MW, moderate; NW, for interior use only. If the brick is old, you have no way of knowing its grade, and if it is really old, it is probably soft. Too strong a mortar can accelerate the crumbling of old brick (see fig. 9-26). Use old brick inside if you think it charming, but only after you have rapped each brick with a trowel to see if it rings true; unsound brick will thud dully. In no event should you use old brick in the exterior part of a chimney; it will certainly spall, could increase the chance of creosote leaks, and in general, is more likely to collapse in the event of a fire. New bricks that look old are available; use them instead.

CLEANING UP

Remove old mortar before reusing stone or brick. Not infrequently, mortar cannot be removed without destroying the brick, in which case,

leave the mortar and simply set the brick in a thicker bed of mortar so that the mortar can accommodate the irregular surface of the old mortar. Obviously, we are talking about cosmetic use, not structural.

One way to remove mortar is to carefully insert the end of a flat bar, where the mortar joins the brick or stone, and rap the other end of the bar with a hammer. Wear goggles. Should a flat bar be too crude a tool, buy a *repointing chisel* (or *tuck-pointing chisel*), which has a relatively sharp, thin blade. An old folk remedy for removing mortar is burying the bricks beneath a pile of oak leaves; supposedly the tannin in the leaves dissolves the mortar in about three months' time.

To clean the surface of brick or stone, try the gentlest methods first. Start with soap and water. Rent a compressor with a spray gun if you have a lot of pieces to clean. Next try a mild mixture of muriatic acid (one part acid to twenty parts water): scrub the mixture on the stone (or brick), allow the acid fifteen minutes to work, and rinse well. Muriatic acid will usually remove mortar or grout stains and whitish efflorescence from residual salts. If the stain is organic, try dilute bleach or a mild solution of oxalic-acid (one part acid to twenty parts water). If all else fails, apply a very dilute solution of hydrochloric acid, to a strength recommended by the supplier; do not use hydrochloric acid on porous or light colored bricks or stones, however. For all of the above, wear rubber gloves and goggles, and rinse off the object well. In no case should you sandblast a finely detailed piece, for sand will obliterate detail and leave you with a pitted surface.

If stained marble is your problem, a marble poultice can be applied to the marble and left on for two days; it need only be kept damp during that period. Poultice is available from Vermont Marble Company. Mequiar's Marble Polish may do the trick too. See Sources of Supply for both products.

CONSOLIDATING AND SEALING TREATMENTS

Consolidants seal stone surfaces and repel water. They are particularly important to use if you live in a cold climate, where absorbed water can freeze and split stone. Several materials, long known to preservationists, will allow you to prolong stone life.

Tegovakon (Conservation Materials, Ltd.) is a silicone consolidant especially designed for sandstones, although it is also appropriate to brick, concrete, plaster, and several kinds of stone (but not marble or slate). After the stone surface has been cleaned, brush on Tegovakon until the stone becomes saturated; thereafter, reapply it once or twice, at two-day intervals. In addition to consolidating, or bonding together surface particles and stopping degradation, this product also waterproofs to a degree. The look of

9-22. "Years ago, a master builder's chimney was his signature," Adolf deRoy Mark told me. Here he has written his name large indeed with this stepped chimney atop a Philadelphia house. Inset into the chimney face are a marble capital and, higher up, a terra-cotta tile.

the stone is unaffected, retaining a natural, dull surface.

Rhodorsil (same source) is a silicone resin that waterproofs carbonate stone such as marble and limestone. It may be brushed or rolled on and has properties similar to Tegovakon.

Liquid polysulfide rubber sealant is another product recommended for porous stones such as parapet caps, which receive a lot of weather.

REPAIRS

Blending patch repairs on stone is difficult because the color and texture of each stone are unique. Epoxy compounds with pulverized stone are perhaps the easiest to use, although they are very expensive; Monzini Company makes a line.

If the masonry piece is a porous stone (such as sandstone or cast concrete) that has seen better days, a simple stucco mix with masonry pigments may be your best bet; they are reasonably priced, too. The mix is always portland cement and sand, but it varies according to the amount of lime, coloring pigments, or other agents added. A basic stucco mix is one part portland cement to one part masonry cement *or* one part portland cement to one-half part lime to three parts sand. Pigments, which should never exceed 5 percent of the total weight of a mixture, should be mixed with other dry ingredients before adding water. Try several test spots before applying the patch to the object in question. For best results clean away any loose fragments and dampen the original slightly. Apply a first coat of stucco; before it hardens entirely, scribe horizontal lines (the "scratch coat") so the final coat will adhere better. In the second coat, try to match the texture of the rest of the piece. Try to achieve the desired results in *one* final coat, but beware of coats that are too thick.

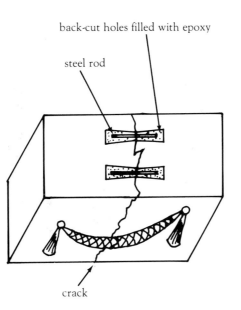

9-23. Repair breaks in masonry pieces by aligning and drilling two sets of holes, filling holes with epoxy compound, and inserting steel rods between the broken sections (top view).

Several thin coats are always better than one thick one. You can also add latex binder additives to a stucco mix to make it adhere better.

If the masonry piece has deep cracks, fill them, preferably with a piece of metal lath or screen stuffed into cracks; undercut cracks so that patches will stay in. If the piece has broken in two or more pieces, key pieces together by drilling with a carbide-tipped bit into each section. As you drill holes for the reinforcing rod, angle the drill bit so that you make each hole wider at its bottom. Fill those holes with an epoxy compound such as Thoro-Grip and insert short sections of rod running from one section to the other (fig. 9-23). It is possible to set broken pieces in position in a wall, without fixing those breaks, but be sure to fill in any surface fissures so that water cannot seep in and, in freezing, deteriorate the stone further. For best results wire together broken sections until the epoxy hardens.

Seal any piece that has been damaged.

MOVING AND MOUNTING MASONRY

When moving heavy masonry pieces, lift with your knees, never with your back. Try not to lift an object directly off the ground, because it is hard to get your knees low enough. Rather, use a stout plank as a ramp, rolling the piece up to a more manageable level.

If you are transporting the piece around your yard, a two-wheeled garden cart is preferable to a wheelbarrow, which can easily tip with an unbalanced, heavy load. If you have a friend who will help, use a portage sling. Tie two heavyweight nylon slings around the piece, then slip a heavy (2-inch) iron pipe through the slings so you can carry the object, supporting its weight on your shoulders.

If the piece is really heavy, say four hundred pounds or more, drill holes in the side of the object as shown in figure 9-25, inserting 1 × 12 bolts into those holes. The bolts themselves feed through stout sections of chain attached to a comealong, a winch, a bucket-loader, or some sort of hoist. Get professional engineering advice when setting so heavy a piece in a masonry wall.

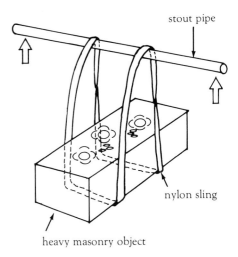

9-24. A stout pipe passed through a nylon sling allows two people to carry a heavy object safari style.

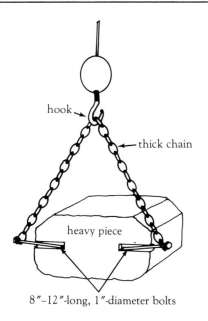

9-25. A bolt-and-chain attachment enables a mechanical hoist to lift without damaging the face of the piece.

Working with Mortar

Masonry objects should be damp before being set into mortar, so that they do not draw moisture from the mix and thus weaken the bond. Hose down bricks or stone at least half an hour before use. Optimal temperatures for masonry work are 40° to 70° F. Below that range, frost is a danger; above 70° or 80°F, mortar may dry out too quickly. A mortar bed ⅜ inch thick is standard for brick and block, although if your piece (or pieces) is non–standard sized, you may have to vary mortar thickness somewhat to bed it. Plumb the face of the masonry piece so its weight is transmitted straight down through the plane of the masonry wall. Whether you are laying a brick wall or a single ornamental stone, point all mortar joints. Pointing compresses and shapes the mortar joint, making it weather better and last longer.

The type of mortar may be important to the masonry unit(s) you set. Old brick, in particular, requires a relatively weak mortar, such as Type O. Types M, S, and N are simply too strong for old brick and would cause it to spall as shown in figure 9–21. Sandstones and other porous stone are best set in Type N or S, but probably not Type M. Very hard stone such as granite may be set in any mortar type, because it is a match for even the most active mortars. Types M, S, and N are suitable for exterior use. Type M is recommended for use below grade or where weathering is severe. Type S has perhaps the best tensile strength of the mortars listed and is most suitable for attaching ceramic veneers. Type N is a good all-around mix, suitable for all above-grade exterior uses, except those exposed to severe weathering. Type O is suitable for interior use only, including moderate load-bearing situations. Type K is very low strength.

Supporting Pieces

If the masonry salvage is relatively light, say, twenty pounds or less, you may use common masonry connectors. If the wall to which you are attaching is solid masonry, drill into it with a carbide-tipped bit and insert a lead shield (also called a lead sleeve). A lag bolt turned into that shield expands it, making a tight friction fit that is tough to dislodge. Where the masonry wall is hollow

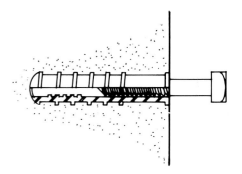

9-27. The most common way to attach to solid masonry surfaces is to drill in with a carbide-tipped drill bit and insert a lead shield (also called a "sleeve") into the hole. The lag bolt that follows forces the sides of the shield apart, making a tight, friction fit.

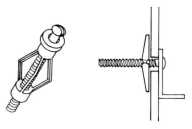

9-28. Where the masonry wall is hollow and the load not too great, use a toggle or molly bolt.

	Parts by Volume			
Mortar type	Portland cement	Masonry cement	Hydrated lime or lime putty	Aggregate measured in a damp, loose condition
M	1	1	—	Not less than 2¼ and not more than 3 times the sum of the combined volumes of cement and lime used
	1	—	¼	
S	½	1	—	
	1	—	over ¼ to ½	
N	—	1	—	
	1	—	over ½ to 1¼	
O	—	1	—	
	1	—	over 1¼ to 2½	
K	1	—	over 2½ to 4	

9-26. Mortar types.

Information from ASTM C–270–8a reprinted with permission of the American Society for Testing and Materials, 1916 Race Street, Philadelphia, PA 19103 (such as concrete block) and the weight of the salvage is not great, use a toggle bolt or a molly bolt.

When setting a large, heavy piece into a masonry wall, center that piece, if possible, over the width of the wall so that the weight of the object is borne straight down. That is not always possible, however, especially when setting, say, an old stone head into a brick wall one wythe thick. If at least half the thickness of the object is supported by brick below, additional support is critical only until the mortar dries completely and thus bonds the object in place. In that event a diagonal 2 × 4 brace to the front of the object should suffice while the mortar dries. For safety, tack or stake the bottom of the brace. If a wall is behind the object, drill small holes through the wall. Run wire around the object and through those holes. When the mortar is dry, snip the wire and pull it out.

If more than half the thickness of the object will be unsupported by the masonry wall beneath—or if you are generally apprehensive about the weight of the piece—you can tie in the object. Perhaps the easiest way to tie in is to drill, with a carbide-tipped drill, two ¾-inch holes into the back of the piece. Go in at least 2 inches deep. Do not hurry the drilling: the slower you go, the less likely the stone is to crack or break. Back out the drill bit occasionally to clear the hole of pulverized stone. Do not jab or jolt the bit; it should cut without your leaning on it. Do not drill too close to the edges of the stone.

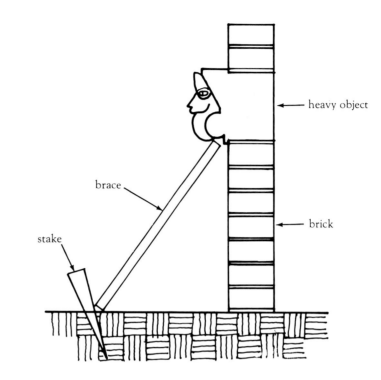

9-29. Prop a heavy object in place with a diagonal brace until mortar dries.

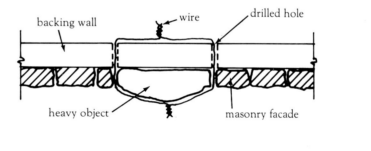

9-30. If there is a wall behind, drill holes through it and run wire around the object and the backing wall.

9-31. Connect a masonry piece to a masonry wall by aligning and drilling holes running between the two. Fill holes with epoxy compound and insert steel rod, which should penetrate at least 2 in. into both the wall and the piece being hung.

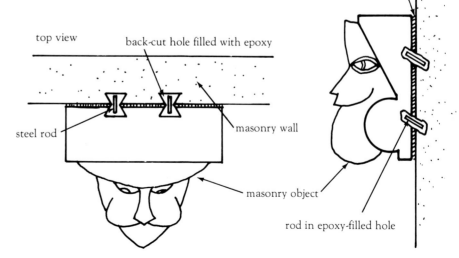

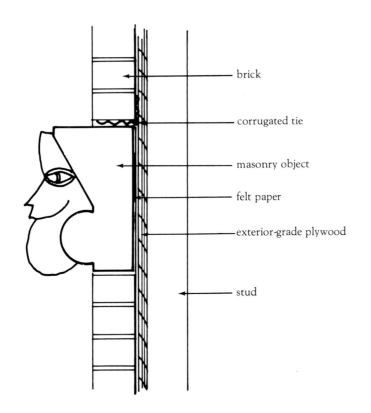

brick

corrugated tie

masonry object

felt paper

exterior-grade plywood

stud

9-32. Corrugated metal ties are commonly used to tie brick facades to wood-frame walls behind. The tie, nailed to the wood, is set right into the mortar.

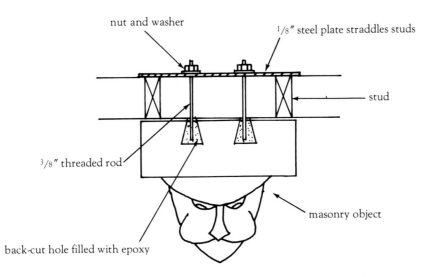

nut and washer

1/8″ steel plate straddles studs

stud

3/8″ threaded rod

masonry object

back-cut hole filled with epoxy

9-33. For maximum holding, epoxy threaded rod into the masonry object and then drill all the way through the wall behind. Pass the rods through the wall and apply nuts.

Clean out the holes you drilled, dampen them slightly, and set a ½-inch threaded galvanized rod into each, using an epoxy compound such as Thoro-Grip to hold the rods fast. For best results angle the rod slightly upward toward the piece being supported. Once the epoxy has set, drill similar holes into the wall behind. Epoxy the free end of the rods into that wall. Brace the object until the epoxy sets.

Should the wall behind be wood-frame construction, drill holes through the sheathing, feed the bolts through and hold them fast with washered nuts on the other side. For maximum holding and the best distribution of loads, run a predrilled ⅛-inch-thick steel plate perpendicular to and behind the studs, feed the threaded rods through that plate, and tighten the assembly. Although the epoxy compound is quite difficult to pull out, it is impossible to know the exact strength of an old stone. Therefore, tighten nuts securely, but never overtighten them or you could pull the epoxy out of the stone.

As noted above, point all joints for greater strength and better weathering; mortar is ready to point when it will retain a thumbprint.

A doleful lion fountain beneath an exterior stairway to a basement office.
Adolf deRoy Mark

A highly ornamented red terra-cotta block caps a column beneath a barrel arch.
Adolf deRoy Mark

A recycled masonry bracket and a short section of ornamental cast iron top a brick courtyard wall. The back side of the bracket was drilled to receive the ends of the iron, the holes filled with mortar, the iron slid into the holes, the bracket set in mortar above the brick.
Adolf deRoy Mark

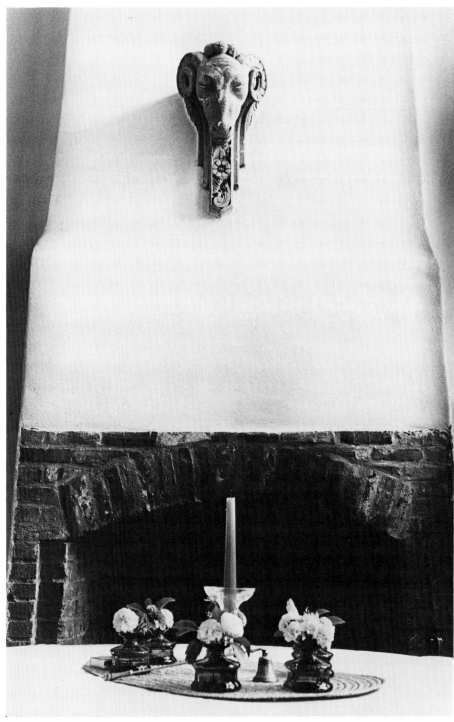

The good luck of finding two ornamental ram's-head brackets is coupled with the talent to use them well. Inside a Philadelphia town house, one head, set into the chimney mass, oversees the dining area. Outside, the other ram is reflective, spouting water by the side of a cobblestone pond.

Adolf deRoy Mark

Structural Elements

Safety Tips

Salvaging structural materials is definitely *not* for people unfamiliar with buildings. Lumber, individually and assembled, is heavy, and the stresses upon joints can be great. Assessment and removal are further compounded by rot and insect damage. The whole chapter that follows, in fact, states and restates the dangers inherent in the work.

- Have the utility company shut off service to the building about to be disassembled, including removing their meter and service leads. If you need power for tools, rent a portable generator.
- Tetanus shots, hard hats, goggles, gloves, and hard-toe shoes are imperative; this is no place for tennis shoes.
- Brace all structures adequately so that individual pieces will not shift as you remove elements.
- Use a metal detector before cutting into any salvaged wood: hitting only one nail can injure you and damage your tool.
- As you remove lumber, take out all nails; a demolition site is no place to land on a nail. Plan in advance what you will do with the debris that accumulates.
- Sound footing is imperative; many salvagers therefore erect scaffolding for any work above the first floor.
- Check your insurance and that of the property on which you are working. Proper coverage is one of the main reasons why nonprofessionals do not scavenge buildings: insurance companies are unwilling to underwrite the risks.

A house on a cliff overlooking the Pacific, with seals sunning on the rocks below and whales blowing in the distance—a house built by Harold Brayton (see also figs. 10-1 to 10-3).

Tools

Several pages of tool descriptions are included in this chapter. Some of the more common tools are wrecking and utility bars, sledge hammers, and nail-pullers.

- A metal detector is imperative to prevent damage to tools and to your person.
- For your safety, use goggles, heavy work gloves, long pants and long-sleeved shirts, and heavy-soled shoes.
- A respirator mask is advisable, especially when demolishing finish surfaces such as plaster.
- Have a first-aid kit on-site and a clear idea of the location of the nearest hospital, should an emergency strike.

Hearing of a single barn that yields a quarter-million board feet of wood or seeing one timber eighty feet long that was dragged from a virgin forest of redwood, the imagination reels and the modern age falls away. Even the big-armed bunch who dismantle and move buildings for a living are impressed with it all. Here, a timber twenty yards long and three feet across, with nary a knot; there, an old barn skeleton, its sheathing off, post upon beam upon post of rich-hued, highly figured chestnut fine enough for furniture—there are whole counties of such barns! Giants seem to have been at work, and not all have gone. Watching a seasoned worker with a pulley manhandle a half-ton "stick" (as he calls it), I laugh incredulously and think of a comic-book god scooping up an errant locomotive. The world is wondrous after all.

Heady stuff, all of this, but dangerous beyond telling. As Harold Brayton, who wrestled with redwood for decades, puts it, "If you're stupid with this stuff, it'll kill ya." So in this chapter I am merely reporting, not advocating, work methods. Dismantling and moving buildings is knowledge obtained only through experience, modified by the oddities of each situation. "No two buildings are ever alike," I heard over and over again. To quote Alex Grabenstein of Frederick, Maryland, "After a while you listen to the structure, to learn what's groaning and creaking under stress."

Differing building methods are only part of the story, some big timber being joined with spikes, some with bolts and metal plates, some without any metal at all. Wood-frame construction of this century, nailed 2-inch dimensional

10-1. The materials on this house, from dismantled bridges and dry docks, are immense: the ridge beam is 18 in. × 36 in. × 72 ft; the post beneath it, 20 in. × 36 in., the rafters, merely 8 × 18s.

10-2. The wooden plugs you see are as big as cantaloupes.

10-3. Everything about the house is massive, yet it seems to hover like a seagull over the ocean, and the always blowing air along the Mendocino coast adds to the illusion.

lumber, is something else altogether, with its own set of quirks and pratfalls for the salvager. Nor are salvaged materials necessarily cheaper, although they may be. When considering select redwood, for example, there are no modern equivalents to compare to. What salvaging may save in cash, it usually expends in sweat: "It's a very labor-intensive way to build," notes big-timber specialist Trey Loy of Littleriver, California. "And it seems that you spend half your time just pulling nails." Finally, most salvagers spend months and years accumulating enough materials to rebuild with, which means some heavy equipment, room to store everything and, as important as all the rest, patience.

SHOULD YOU BUY IT?

Assessing a building for purchase depends upon a number of variables. Are you buying the whole building or just part of it? Are you dismantling the building or moving it more or less intact? In what condition is the building? How much will it cost you?

If you are buying *all* of the building, the seller may include a penalty clause if you take only part of the structure or if you fail to remove the structure by the time specified. Do not underestimate the time factor—it may take a crew about twice as long to tear down a frame structure than it does to erect

one, discounting finish aspects. Occasionally contracts are sold allowing the salvager to take out only the choice parts of the structure, but open bidding for such rights will be keen among salvaging firms in the area. Since the owner of the building is ultimately the liable party for injuries on the premises, most sellers prefer to deal with as few parties as possible; thus, whole house rights are the most common arrangements.

If you intend to have the building moved to another site, there are a host of questions about the route along which the house is to be moved, permits to be obtained from various authorities, and so on—most of which will be handled by the house-moving contractor (see chapter 11). Your own lawyer

10-4. Farther up the Pacific coast, another creation of Harold Brayton, with the same fusion of Northwest and Far East.

should review that contract. Who, for example, oversees the foundation on the new site? Who will check the code compliance of that new site? A very important question is accessibility to the original site—can heavy equipment get in there to do the job? Talk to several house-moving contractors before settling on one or, for that matter, before buying a house in the first place.

If you want to dismantle the house, the overriding question is how much usable material is there? Does the contract include mechanical systems? If lumber is your concern, make a careful survey of the property, noting the dimensions of the place generally and then exploring specifically to determine the size and condition of studs, joists, rafters, flooring, and so on. Make extensive lists. It is difficult to guess how much structure will be lost in dismantling, but 10 percent is an often quoted number: loss either in outright breakage or in the amount of shattered ends that you must cut off. With care it is possible to remove posts and beams of heavy timber structures without breaking ends or having to shorten pieces, but if the house is built with a lot of eight-foot 2 × 4s, you may end up with a lot of seven-footers. How you intend to reuse the wood is all telling. If you want it for sheds and outbuildings, short lengths may not be a problem. If you want to build a residence, keep in mind that framing with lumber from several sources is very frustrating. Joists from different places, for example, may have to be ripped down or shimmed up if you want a level floor. So, as you calculate quantity, think in groups of joist stock, rafter stock, and so on.

The condition of the structure is critical because a rotten building yields less and it is unsafe to work in. Look first at the roof. If it is shot, chances are that most of the rafters and top plates (the top of the walls) will be gone too. The framing in the first floor is also telling: sills are often gone on older houses, but the joists and carrying timbers may not be. You can dismantle a post-and-beam structure with rotten sills, but not a stick-frame house so afflicted. All other things being equal, look next to the top-plate area, where rafters rest on the tops of the walls: if you find much rot there, do not dismantle the building. Rafters with rotted ends are very dangerous to take down; anything can happen.

To really scrutinize a building, you should crawl around inside with a flashlight and a pocketknife, probing the ends of joists, rafters, the tops of studs and posts, and so on. If the blade sinks in a half-inch or more with moderate pressure, the wood is no good. Be very careful in old buildings; never go scouting in one without a tetanus shot and a friend to keep you company. Proceed very cautiously and test all floors carefully before walking on them. Stairs are particularly prone to failure. The outsides of floors and stair treads—rather than the middles—are more likely to support your weight.

As you probe, look for insects too. A seemingly sound beam may actually be riddled with insect borings, which a penknife will disclose. The major pests are termites, powder-post beetles and carpenter ants. Wood with any traces of such infestation must be fumigated before you transport it, preferably after disassembly so workers do not have to handle wood too soon after it has been treated. Better yet, avoid buying a house with such pests.

How much you pay for the building should thus include all aspects of disassembling and transporting it to another site. Other cost considerations vary greatly. Is a house historically significant? If the house is in an urban area, could materials be stolen at night? Is there electricity on-site? Can a crane get close to pluck up heavier members? A lot of factors must be considered; it is worth paying an experienced house dismantler/mover a consultant's fee once you begin serious negotiations for an old building.

10-5. Tools of a heavy-timber man. From left: utility bar, crowbar, an old railroad bar of some kind, a railroad spike puller, hand-fashioned pry bars (recovered from an old blacksmith's shop).
These tools and those following courtesy of Trey Loy

10-6. As you jolt down the sliding handle of this nail puller, its teeth dig in and clench the head of a nail; the foot of the tool adds leverage.

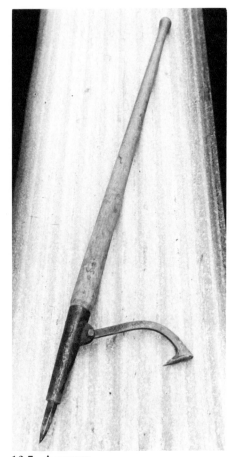

10-7. A peavey.

TOOLS AND EQUIPMENT

As with salvaging methods, tools are nonstandard, often homemade, found or modified to fit the need of the user. Common to all salvage operations, however, are nail removers. Where practicable, remove nails as soon as possible: handling and stacking lumber will be much easier and your workplace will be much safer. Even an experienced salvager must sometimes move quickly, coming down scaffolding, for example, and that is no time to land on a nail sticking up from a board.

A *metal detector* is the first tool of many salvagers. You should eyeball a timber first and quickly circle (with chalk) any metal that you see sticking out—but you may not see it all. Rather than risk injury or tool damage, scan pieces with a metal detector too. Small stud finders work pretty well, but serious salvagers use old army surplus rigs with a separate battery pack.

Flat bars, crowbars, and *wrecking bars* are the mainstays of removing nails and prying pieces apart. They are much sturdier than the claws of a hammer, which will actually shear off if the stress is too great. Spend money for good-quality bars; tempered ones will be springier and last longer.

Nail pullers are specially made for pulling out nails—they can go after nails whose heads have broken off. Most pullers have a pair of pincer jaws that dig into the wood as the worker jolts the metal sleeve on the handle of the tool (fig. 10–6). The jaws of the nail puller will blemish the wood but will not harm it structurally.

Locking pliers, such as Vise-Grips, are generally useful and should be in your tool kit.

Homemade and found tools include a *nail jimmy* shaped from a truck leaf spring—sharpen one end and you have a tool that can lift off even delicate siding without breaking it—and *long bars* such as those shown in figure 10–5, which give you leverage to separate or maneuver very large timber.

Hand sledges and full *sledge hammers* are often necessary to persuade long-nailed boards to part.

Several tools originally designed for logging are useful to salvagers. A *peavey* is a long-handled tool with a fixed point at its end and a swinging point next to it, for turning and rolling big pieces. A similar tool, with two swinging hooks like ice tongs in the middle of the handle, is the *sweet william*, which enables two workers to lift or drag heavy timber. A *comealong* or *hand winch* increases the mechanical advantage of its user, enabling you to remove stubborn pieces or to stabilize a structure as you remove parts. A *chain saw,* preferably one with an old blade (should you come upon any unanticipated nails) is the mainstay of cutting tools; it may be used for cleaning up lumber ends or for cutting them free; it is, however, a very dangerous tool—never use it when you are on-site alone. Finally, *hatchets* and *axes* are useful utility tools, good for cutting stakes, knocking pieces apart, whatever.

Hoisting apparatuses, such as *pulley blocks, ropes, wire cable,* lengths of *heavy chain, hooks,* and the like, are not essential for all jobs, but they make loading and unloading larger amounts of wood much easier.

House jacks, or *contractors' screw jacks,* are handy at both disassembly and reassembly, enabling the worker to take stresses off pieces so they can be removed, replaced, shimmed up, and so on. When used in tandem with cribbing or posts, such jacks must always be plumbed so that they are not "kicked" out of place by the tremendous loads involved.

10-8. A contractor's screw jack.

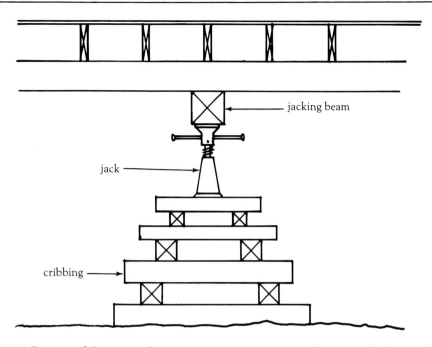

10-9. Because of the tremendous pressures upon a contractor's screw jack, be sure that its base of cribbing is solid and level, and that the jack itself is plumbed.

A *pickup* or *flatbed truck* comes in handy, whether for hauling or pulling pieces free, as a winch might.

Safety equipment includes *hard hats, steel-toed shoes, goggles* (if you are working over your head or with cutting or striking tools), *heavy leather gloves, sound protectors* if power equipment is running, and *stout but nonbinding work clothes*. Take a *first-aid kit* onto the site—and get a *tetanus shot*.

Marking and layout tools are necessary to keep disassembled parts straight, especially if you will reassemble a frame on a new site. *Crayons* or *chalk* work well enough but can rub off; better are pieces of *plastic name-embossing tape* tacked to the ends of timber. A *chalkline* and *framing square* will tell you if pieces are bowed or out of square. To keep track of nuts, washers, and bolts that you want to reuse, tie them together with *wire*.

Scaffolding is almost always necessary when salvaging, whether to support a ridge beam as you remove rafters (one approach), to strip sheathing, or to move safely when you are not sure of floor strength. Many types are available, from tubular to homemade from 2 × 4s; all must be plumbed, leveled and, if possible, tied or nailed to a nearby sturdy structure. Mason's scaffolding has spread base-legs through which you can run a wheelbarrow, making cleaning up

much easier. Sound *planking,* at least 2 inches thick, is always useful whether for scaffold catwalks, on ramps for wheelbarrows, as inclined planes for lowering timber, whatever.

Cleanup tools are important to a dismantling because so much debris can accumulate that it becomes difficult to move. *Wheelbarrows* have been mentioned. *Square-nosed shovels* are the best for moving debris, round-nosed ones do not hold as much. Heavy rubber *trash barrels* are more sturdy than cheap plastic or even metal ones. *Dumping containers* can be rented.

Cribbing, short sections of 4 × 4s or 6 × 6s, provide a sturdy base for jacking, for portable power generators, for planks that might sag under great weights.

Portable generators are relatively nonessential unless you need power for, say, a reciprocating saw, a sprayer to apply preservative, a heavy-duty drill needed to bore out wooden pegs.

From here, the list goes in many directions: larger salvage outfits keep massive steel I beams around for

supporting house sections; tanks fabricated from old barrels, for soaking timber in preservative; old metal roofing or plastic to cover lumber piles, and so on.

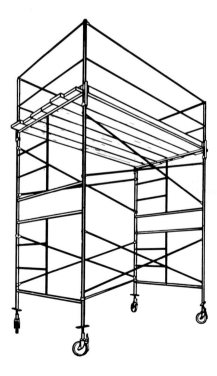

10-10. Tubular scaffolding.

DISASSEMBLING A STRUCTURE

Most of the comments below describe heavy-timber buildings; very few crews (I came across none) disassemble wood-frame houses constructed of 2-inch lumber. More often, such "stick-built" houses are moved on a flatbed or simply razed; rarely are they dismantled piece by piece by a professional crew. Nails are again the culprits, labor costs being too high to have several people pulling nails. Moreover, as noted above, the ends of the lumber are often shattered or splintered as sections are knocked apart, making the venture even less economically feasible.

When first assessing the structure, make a floor map of any serious structural defects or spots where the flooring seems weak. Those spots should be in the back of your mind until the job is over. Bolster weak sections by running braces (2 × 4s, 4 × 4s) diagonally to surfaces that are sound and stable. Inside the structure, this means nailing diagonal braces to joists or beams, not merely nailing them to the floor surfaces (fig. 10–15). Use 16d or 20d common nails. If the structural element in question is a wall or a post, brace outside the structure as well, running a brace to the ground and securing its lower end with a stake driven at least 2 feet into the ground.

As you remove sheathing to get at the frame of the building, stresses may shift, because sheathing itself acts as a bolster for the frame. Work slowly and judiciously, noting the squeaks and groans of lumber under stress and adding braces whenever in doubt. *Nail all braces to solid support*, even if this means ripping up flooring or prying off sheathing first.

If you are at all unsure about the floors, bolster them with planking laid over existing floors; for maximum strength, such planking

10-11. Several small barns in Vermont were dismantled and transported to Weston, Connecticut by The Barn People, a small outfit in South Woodstock, Vermont.

Photo, Mike Greenberg

10-12. As the barn parts were reassembled, builders used comealongs to draw sections together, bracing corners as they went.

Photo, Mike Greenberg

10-13. The new structure is greater than its parts, combining the rustic quality of the wood with very nice finish touches. Here, the steps are 2-in. hardwood, highly polished, with the outer edge of the treads left rough, as they were in the log.

Mike Greenberg, designer and builder

10-14. Modern fixed-pane windows and salvaged diamond-pane sash dress up the rough cut siding.

Mike Greenberg, designer and builder

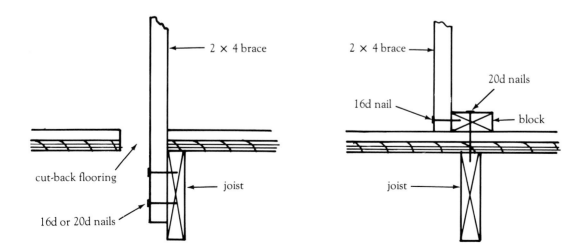

10-15. As you dismantle an old building, it is imperative that you firmly brace its frame so that it will be sturdy as you remove other structural elements and sheathing. Bracing itself must be nailed to framing members; otherwise, the brace could dislodge.

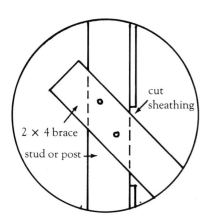

cut
sheathing

2 × 4 brace

stud or post

should run perpendicular to joists. In extreme cases first set carrying timbers beneath the floors, to pick up the weight of the deficient joists above; those timbers, in turn, must be supported underneath by sturdy posts. Posts must be supported all the way down to the basement floor. Adding such bolsters is a lot of work, but there is really no safe alternative.

As you set up scaffolding, make sure that all legs are resting on solid surfaces. Additional planks beneath legs will help spread loads.

Start at the top and work down.

Once you have set up scaffolding that lets you work at a comfortable height beneath the roof, start prying roofing boards off by inserting a wrecking bar between the top of the rafter and the bottom of the roof sheathing. You can work from the outside, atop the roof, but only if the sheathing is absolutely solid. In that case, however, you will have to buy or rent roofing jacks, which nail into rafter centers, to do the work safely.

All in all, it is best to remove roofing from inside. Your footing is much more secure when you stand

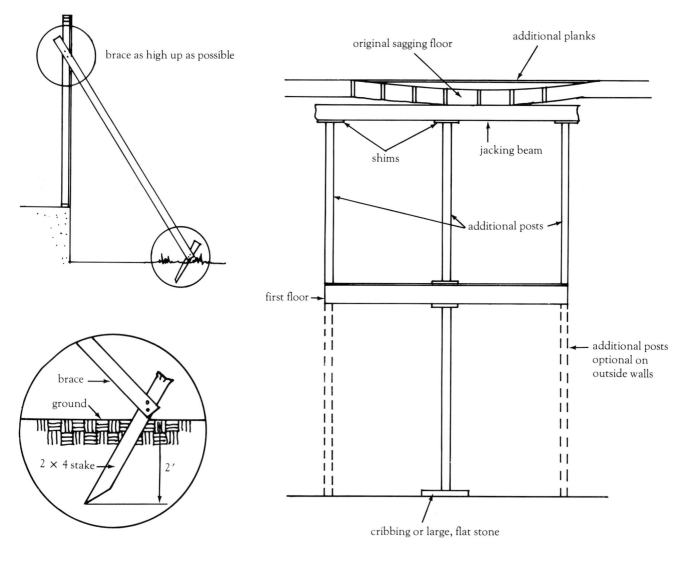

brace as high up as possible

original sagging floor

additional planks

shims

jacking beam

additional posts

first floor

additional posts optional on outside walls

brace

ground

2 × 4 stake

2′

cribbing or large, flat stone

10-16. When bracing side walls, break through the sheathing and nail directly to the studs or posts. Stake the lower end of the brace so it cannot kick out.

10-17. Internal bracing must be soundly footed, which may mean going all the way down to the basement floor.

on a scaffolding platform: you can move around easier and can apply greater pressure to pry off stubborn boards. Boards are also less likely to suddenly fly off. The only advantage to working on the roof, in fact, is if you decide to strip roofing and cut through sections of roof to expose the rafters. *Wear goggles and a hard hat.* Pull up all nails and then set your power saw just to the thickness of the sheathing; use a carbide-tipped blade to take care of any nails left behind.

Strip off the sheathing about half the way down the roof, one side at a time, and then brace the rafters with 2 × 4s running diagonally across; nail braces into at least five or six rafters at a time. Although you should leave nail heads sticking up for easier removal of the bracing, do knock them well into the structure beneath. For greater rigidity, add a few braces from the ridge down to the floor joists as well. You should not be atop the lower half of the roof as you unsheath it; your weight might cause the rafter grid to shift and topple. Besides, you should be able to stand on the attic floor itself to reach the roofing by this time.

To be cautious, run guy wires to the outside of each gable end, attaching the wires with eyelet bolts. (Nail rafter tops together with braces where there is no ridge member.) With the ridgepole or ridgeboard held in place with guy wires, there is little chance that the rafter assembly will fall over—unless, that is, it has rot. If rafters, ridge, or top plates have deteriorated, almost anything can happen. Danger lurks in unsound wood, a strong reason not to buy a building in the first place.

Once the sheathing is stripped off the rafters and rafters are braced, start removing individual rafters. The most common technique is to remove them an opposite pair at a time, first unpegging or unnailing them at the bottom and then at the

top. There are as many opinions about this step as there are salvagers: some prefer to cut most of the top connections while the lower half of the roof sheathing is still nailed on. But, in general, it is better to strip all sheathing and then loosen the bottom of the rafter first. Finally, dislodge the top of each rafter and, with the aid of a helper or two, lower rafters to the roof deck.

The best tool to use at the rafter top is a nailpuller or a flat bar; either is light to handle and much less concussive than, say, a hammer or a hand sledge. Scaffolding is really worth the trouble at this point, even if it is only a relatively narrow walkway beneath the ridge; the unanticipated weight of a freed rafter could knock you off a stepladder. Remove rafters at the end of the building last; if the ridge is made up of several boards, leave all rafters supporting ridgeboard ends until last.

The last pairs of rafters to be removed are usually slowly lowered or, bracing knocked away, allowed to fall. If you are careful and have enough help, you can lower the ridge at one end and then slowly lower the last pair of rafters at the other end. This is often not possible with a heavy ridgepole, however, so some salvagers clear the roof deck of people and slowly turn down come-alongs on the guy wires, tightening one wire while slackening the other. You can use many methods for this final, critical step: building cribbing up to the ridgepole is another possibility. But when time is more critical than a few broken rafter tenons, most salvagers prefer to ease down the last pair of rafters or just drop them over. In fact, if the building is small, many salvagers just pull them over without bothering to strip off sheathing first.

What to do with the rubble soon becomes a problem. To dispose of debris from within, pull up strips of flooring on several floors, creating

a sort of drop chute straight down to the basement. All stuff not worth saving goes down into the foundation hole, to be filled over later with dirt.

It is important that you remove debris as it accumulates, scooping it out of the way with square-nosed shovels (coal shovels are lightweight and have good capacity). Clean the entire floor at least daily. Remove nails from lumber as soon as possible, preferably at once. Several contractors I spoke with said that they dismantle buildings until they had enough wood for a truckload, at which point they remove all nails not previously drawn out, load the stuff, take it home, stack and sticker it. The work site is thus always safe and clear, wood does not have a chance to get rained on and warp, and on-site theft is minimized.

Getting the wood down from upper stories is rarely a problem. Slide rafters over the end of the building and let them lean against the side of the building until you take them to the truck. Slide more delicate boards, such as roof sheathing or siding, down in a jury-rigged chute of sheet-metal roofing scrap and 2 × 4s, or simply drop them straight down. Because wood is strongest in compression, boards dropped straight down, on end, are less likely to break than those dropped on their faces.

Should the building be held together with steel plates, bolts, and the like, save pieces by tying them together with wire, making a sort of garland.

Treat subsequent floors and walls much as you did the roof, stripping off sheathing and the like about halfway and then bracing to prevent toppling. Actually, since walls join at corners, they are relatively stable, but you must brace them after lowering the first wall section. Lower walls in the reverse manner that you would raise them in new construction: strip it of sheathing, brace it, lower it, then

10-18. This barn was quite a dandy in its day, painted bright red, with windows trimmed with white around green shutters.

Vintage Lumber and Construction Company

10-19. Although these workers seem to be doing a softshoe and cane dance, they are actually holding boards in place as they pry them loose with crowbars.

Vintage Lumber and Construction Company

10-20. A board is less likely to break if dropped straight down, on edge.

Vintage Lumber and Construction Company

disassemble it. Nail several long braces near the top plate, stationing a worker or two at each brace. Holding the lower ends of braces, workers walk back slowly so that the wall eases down. Once the wall is flat on the deck, hammer off top and bottom plates and remove all nails.

If you want to remove paneling, trim, flooring, or other relatively light pieces, always slide your flat bar right next to the structural member—even if it means bashing holes in the old plaster to do it. The best way to remove old wide-board flooring is to get beneath joists and pry up.

HANDLING HEAVYWEIGHTS

Once you have disassembled an old building, you must then move it, load and unload it onto trucks, and handle it again at a new site. The basics of handling are known to most people, in fact, are parts of most junior-high science curricula: levers and fulcrums, inclined planes, and other simple machines enhance the force that you apply.

With a peavey, one worker can move heavy timber. Though not an easy task, this is possible by digging the swinging hook of the peavey

into the wood and flipping the beam over and over. If the piece is small enough, you can use the peavey on the end of the wood to lift and carry it one end at a time. The long handle of the peavey allows you to get far enough away from the timber so that you are out of danger; the tool obviates any need to stoop over and risk a hernia.

The sweet william, which has two free-swinging tongs in the middle of the handle, enables two workers (one on each side) to move a heavy log. If you cannot locate a william, use a peavey to roll the timber onto a nylon sling or length of chain, which can then be slipped

10-21. Stone and half-log house in northern Virginia.

10-22. At exterior corners, the chestnut logs are notched—a detail of the original building.

10-23. In addition to its beauty, the house is energy-efficient. Once, the spaces between logs were filled with plaster; in this reincarnation those spaces are covered with wire mesh. The mesh is faced with Structolite, and the resultant cavities were shot full of treated cellulose. To cut infiltration, any gaps were caulked with dark silicone.

10-24. Where timbers meet the fireplace face inside, the builder hand-crafted joinery.

over a stout handle that two people can carry.

To get timber up onto truck beds and the like, use the length of the timber itself as a lever, either by lifting only one end at a time or by putting a block beneath the middle and rocking the timber like a seesaw. By alternately adding higher supports beneath each end of the timber, you can raise it without ever having to lift its entire weight. Using stout planks as inclined planes saves effort too, especially if you have some short lengths of galvanized pipe (or anything that will not crush) to use as rollers on the incline. Make sure, however, that your plank will not slip; stake or tack-nail each end. If the plank looks too light for the load, either use a heavier plank or support the underside of the plank with cribbing.

A comealong is particularly effective for pulling a load up an incline: because the tool will hold a load in place, it leaves your hands free to add rollers or to make other adjustments as the timber ascends.

PULLEY SETUPS

Pulley setups are also called block-and-tackle. The blocks, as shown in figure 10–27, are individual sheaves in a frame; a tackle is any arrangement of blocks, lines, hooks, whatnot. Whether attached to a truck frame, a sturdy tree near the building site, a tripod—wherever it is used—a pulley gives its operator a

10-25. The master bedroom before finish details were completed. The faces of all logs were power-planed and coated with tung oil.

Building in figures 10-21 to 10-25 designed and constructed by Morton Riddle, IV; half-log construction from Vintage Lumber and Construction Company

10-26. A pulley setup with a movable boom, used here to load and unload truckloads of salvaged materials.

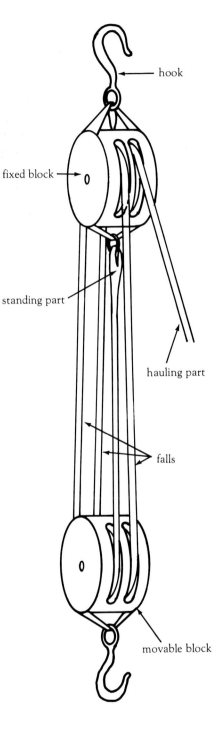

10-27. Block-and-tackle parts.

217

great mechanical advantage in lifting or lowering heavy objects.

A pulley is only as strong as its weakest element, which could be the tree to which it is attached, the length of chain around the object being hoisted, or the rope or wire cable you use as your line. Most often the line is the weakest element because it is simply not strong or new enough. Below are rules of thumb for assessing the strength of *fiber line* (such as manila line or hemp) and *wire cable* (also called steel cable or wire rope). *Note:* The manufacturer of a rope is the final authority on how much it can hold; the formulas below are generalizations only.

Start by examining your blocks—should they be used with fiber rope or wire cable? Blocks designed for wire cable are generally heavier, with a large sheave that is deeply grooved. The sheaves of blocks intended for fiber line are smaller in diameter, somewhat wider, with shallower grooves. The sheaves of wire-cable blocks are larger so that the wire will not bend sharply and pinch; the grooves narrow because wire cable, being stronger, tends to be smaller. Were you to use fiber line in a wire-cable block, the fiber line would likely abrade and wear prematurely. Finally, the size of rope or wire cable to use in the block should be stamped on its casing somewhere; if not, seek advice from a supplier of hauling equipment or use the rules of thumb below.

Measure the *circumference* of fiber line and multiply that number by three to determine the dimension of the block you need. This answer is acceptable, give or take an inch. If you are matching wire cable to a pulley block, the rule of thumb is twenty times the *diameter* of the cable to obtain the diameter of the block sheave.

To determine the safe working load (*SWL*) of fiber line (rope), measure the circumference at three points along the line and determine the average circumference, which is represented by C in the equation

$$SWL = C^2 \times 150 \text{ lbs.}$$

If the rope is brand new and in excellent condition, *add* 30 percent to the answer derived from the equation. If the line is used but has been carefully maintained and looks in good condition, use the value obtained from the equation. If the rope looks like it should be replaced, *subtract* 30 percent from the answer the equation yields.

To determine the *SWL* for wire cable, measure the *diameter* (D) of the cable at three points, preferably using a caliper; in a pinch, use a pair of locking pliers, which can be calibrated to the cable and then "read" by holding their jaws against a ruler. It is important to note, however, that such cable is not round but more nearly hexagonal. Take the largest reading, that is, measure from two opposite points of the "hexagon." Plug that number into the following equation:

$$SWL \text{ (in tons)} = D^2 \times 4.$$

If the diameter is 1¼ inches, the equation looks like this:

$$
\begin{aligned}
SWL &= (5/4)^2 \times 4 \\
&= {}^{25}/_{16} \times 4 \\
&= 6\tfrac{1}{4} \text{ tons.}
\end{aligned}
$$

It is especially important to remember that the above equation is but a rule of thumb. If the wire cable is at all pinched, frayed, rusty, or otherwise in less than prime condition, reduce the *SWL* by as much as 50 percent.*

---

*These equations were originally developed by the U.S. Navy as a training manual and are now available from Dover Press, New York, in *Basic Construction Techniques for Houses and Small Buildings*. This publication also offers a fuller discussion of block-and-tackle than is possible here.

ORGANIZING MATERIALS

If you intend to reassemble a building much as it was originally, use coordinates, such as E3, E4, etc., or 5F1, 5F2, etc., to indicate exactly which pieces go together. Draw extensive maps on graph paper before you start dismantling. The most durable way to mark timber ends is with plastic embossing tapes (the kind you can dial and punch out letters and numbers with) carpet-tacked to timber ends. Chalk and crayon smudge and become unreadable; carpet tacks hold better than staples.

At the new site, stack lumber so that the wood you need first is closest to the spot you will build on. This may take some doing, because those pieces that should be stacked near the new foundation were probably the last pieces removed from the old site. Leave lots of room to maneuver between piles. When you stack wood, take pains to level the bottom of the pile as best you can; thereafter, sticker the pile with uniformly sized sticks. Cover the pile with old metal roofing weighted down with large stones or bricks. Plastic will also keep rain off, but do

10-28. If you intend to reassemble building parts as they were originally, carefully number each end.

10-29. To allow air circulation, sticker each row of lumber; this pile is capped with old sheet-metal roofing.

not completely cover the pile or you could hasten rot by trapping moisture. Keep the grass around such piles cut short.

Consult the Bibliography for additional sources about dismantling and heavy-timber moving.

RECONDITIONING AND REUSING LUMBER

The first step of reconditioning is taking out all nails; that accomplished, cut away sections of unsound wood and treat for insect infestation. Applying pest poisons can be hazardous work, so get advice from the supplier of the chemicals you use and follow safety precautions to the letter. Perhaps the easiest chemical to use is hydrogen bromide, which can be applied with a spray gun; wear goggles, a respirator mask, and cover all skin with long sleeves and the like. For some chemicals you should build a plastic tent over the wood, wrapping it tightly around the woodpile, once treated.

USING PRESERVATIVES

After the pesticide has done its work, apply preservative to the wood to preserve it from moisture and rot. Some of the bigger salvage yards, using block and tackle, lower timber into long vats of preservative, effective but impractical for the small-scale operator. Perhaps best for small quantities of wood is spraying or brushing the substance on, especially treating end grain, which is most likely to absorb water. Apply preservatives (or any chemical) well in advance of reusing the wood, to let the solvent dry and to minimize the amount that rubs off onto workers.

You can choose from a number of preservatives. *Creosote* is perhaps the most effective and durable but by far the nastiest to work with; many people have a strong allergic reaction to it. Being very oily, creosote sinks into wood well. Almost as effective is *penta concentrate*, although it is not quite as effective in high-moisture areas. It is, however, slightly less noxious. Because of their toxicity and strong vapors, creosote and penta should be used only on lumber that will be

outside or away from the living space of a house. That is, you may treat the mudsills of a house with creosote but not the beams or joists in the basement. *Cuprinol* and other metal-based preservatives, although less durable than creosote and penta, is more benign to humans; wood so treated may be used on decks, joists, and the like, although these structural members should be allowed to dry after application. Cuprinol will even accept paint, unlike creosote and penta, which are too oily to do so.

RESURFACING

Because old lumber will have been knocked about somewhat, it is commonly resurfaced, if not to a smooth surface, at least to a uniform one. Quite often, wood will have been covered with a layer of grime or, in the case of lumber salvaged from industrial buildings, grease.

A chain saw held at angle to the timber will give a clean, if somewhat rough, surface. Hold the chain saw as if you were going to cut off a section and then tilt the axis of the saw and the face of its blade slightly, about ten degrees each way. With the saw running full throttle, walk down the length of the timber, lightly shaving off just the top surface of the wood. Try not to gouge or round the wood, nor to be too fastidious; a few uncleaned spots will not hurt. Because a chain saw is a very powerful tool—and a heavy one—use the lightest saw that will do the job; a 12-inch blade should suffice for all but the biggest timber. Because you might have missed a nail or two when cleaning, use an old chain for this operation, and by all means, wear goggles. Do not lean over the blade as you work; it could kick back.

All wood gets scuffed during handling. Some builders therefore prefer to resurface timber after it is in final position. Morton Riddle,

10-30 and 10-31. Even short pieces of old wood can be put to use, such as this entrance-panel chalet by Trey Loy.

whose work is shown in figures 10–21 to 10–25, preferred to erect the half-timber house and then power-plane the logs in place, after which he added the masonry between logs. Trey Loy, who erected a frame completely before closing it in (sheathing) and adding stud walls, was able to sandblast the timber and let the wind carry away much of the abrasive sand (see the photos at the end of chapter 1).

Perhaps the easiest way to resurface timber is to let nature do it. The crafty builders who constructed Saint Orres Inn trekked down to the ocean and ported back logs that had swept downstream during spring rains. These logs, which had been live trees standing too close to a river bank, were completely slick and debarked by the time they got to the Pacific. After trimming ragged ends, the builders set the posts in place.

STRATEGIES OF REUSE

As the time to rebuild approaches, most salvagers have piles of timber, many of which are odd sized and often from different sources. Since the point of salvaging is saving money—or trading labor for money saved—it will not do to run off to the lumberyard when starting a project as most new builders do. The salvager often plans in reverse: instead of drawing up a dream house and then buying lumber to accomplish those plans, start by looking at the pieces already assembled and asking what you can build with the stuff at hand.

This reverse-order planning means that the lumber available may determine the size of some rooms and, not infrequently, the size of the house itself. Start, then, by making careful lists of what you

have collected. Because it is difficult to frame from disparately sized lumber, try to keep different lots together, by using, for example, all the wood from one source as joists in one room. You can then fill the gaps in your materials list by salvaging more or by going to the lumberyard.

USING SHORT LENGTHS

Salvaged lumber will occasionally be too short because its ends shattered and were trimmed back or, simply, they never were long enough. You can build with short or smaller-dimension lumber in a number of ways, but be advised that such methods take longer.

If you wish to use undersized stock for floor joists, shorten the distance of clear spans. The easiest way to do this is by supporting the joists beneath with a carrying timber or girder—or two (or more) carrying timbers running parallel if need requires. If you have a few monster timbers that can carry your joists for the length or width of the structure, fine, but a timber or girder is more commonly supported at equal intervals by posts. Top these posts with ¼-inch steel plate to spread the load. If your girder must be fabricated from several short pieces, join those pieces over posts. Girders are often fabricated from several lengths of 2-inch stock, with all joints offset by at least 4 feet, and all joints on the outside of the girder package supported by posts spaced at one-third intervals beneath (fig. 10–34).

Do not laminate studs or posts from short stock. Their strength derives from loads being transferred downward through wood grain; interruptions to the grain mean unequal load distribution and, in extreme cases, wall failure.

Rafter grids can be built up from pieces that would be under-

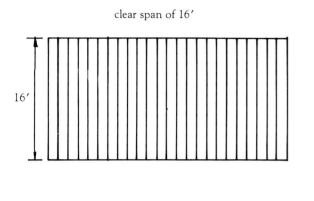

clear span of 16'

16'

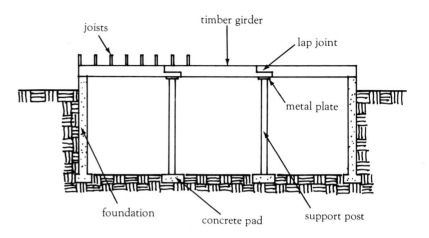

joists

timber girder

lap joint

metal plate

foundation

concrete pad

support post

10-33. Where your girders are fabricated from sections of heavy timber, support timber joints with a post beneath. To spread the load, top the post with a 1/4-in. steel plate.

carrying timber or girder

clear span of 8'

8'

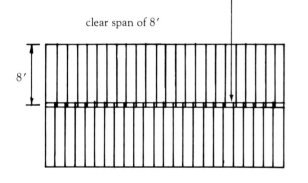

2 girders

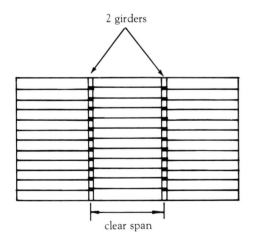

clear span

10-32. By using carrying timbers or girders beneath, you shorten the distance that joists must span. By adding just one girder down the length of a 16-ft.-wide building, for example, you create a clear span of 8 ft., which a 9-ft. joist could handle nicely.

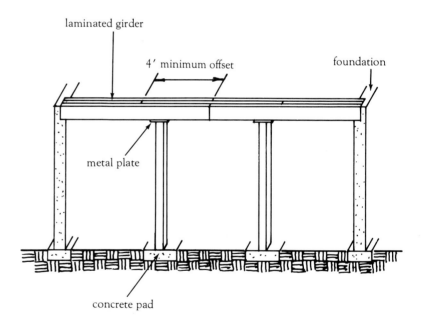

laminated girder

4' minimum offset

foundation

metal plate

concrete pad

10-34. Laminated 2-in. stock may also comprise a girder, but be sure to overlap any butt joint by at least 4 ft. and support the girder with lally columns (steel posts filled with concrete) spaced at one-third intervals—or closer, as need be.

sized were they used alone. But, by using purlins, which run perpendicular to rafter lengths, you can decrease the clear spans of the rafters. Purlins, in turn, may be supported by posts. Collar ties and king posts further reinforce rafters, as shown in figure 10–36.

USING STEEL REINFORCEMENT

Steel plates, angle iron, bolts, washers, and nuts are indispensible adjuncts to heavy-timber building and should be squirreled away for future use.

Flat plates can splice lumber sections together, though never in midspan. Center such splices over posts when possible. For the best-looking or least obvious joinings, let in the plates; that is, trace around the plate and chisel out a recess so that the plate face is flush to the surrounding wood. Two or three ½–inch lag bolts (or lengths of steel reinforcing rod) sunk into each of the sections will hold the plate-assembly fast. Have the holes in the steel plate predrilled by a scrap yard, or by a friend with an acetylene torch.

A continuous piece of steel plate may be sandwiched between two wood members to impart great strength and thus increase the spanning distance of the wood. The usual way to join this predrilled steel plate (called a flitch plate in such an assembly) is to lay it out on one piece of lumber, trace and drill bolt holes, feed bolts through and mark (for drilling) the second piece of lumber with the bolt ends. Tighten the entire package using washered nuts; bolts should be staggered about 12 inches apart.

Steel angle iron is used quite often by restorationists to bolster heavy timber pieces that may be

10-35. Purlins run perpendicular to rafters, supporting rafters from beneath and thus allowing the builder to use slightly smaller rafters. The king-post trusses support the purlins and the ridge beam. Detail shown is in a cabin at Saint Orres Inn.

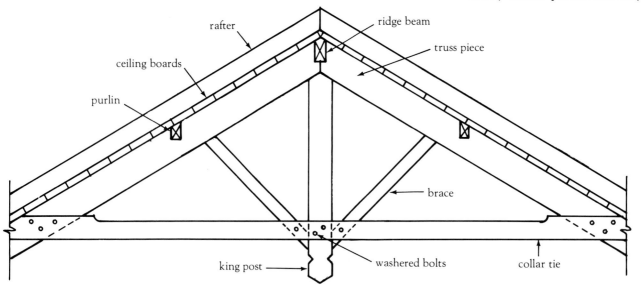

10-36. A king-post-and-purlin assembly is a time-consuming detail, which saves no lumber in the long run, but it looks good and, theoretically, allows you to use smaller rafters.

222

somehow deficient. Placed beneath the end of a joist, angle iron reinforces joints especially subject to splitting (fig. 10–38). Placed on the underside of a sagging joist and jacked up to a desired position, angle iron bolted to the joist will eliminate sagging when screw-jacks are removed (fig. 10–39). Finally, an exposed beam may be bolstered in a cosmetically acceptable way by letting in tee steel, as shown in figure 10–40. Use a circular saw and a chisel and wear goggles for the job.

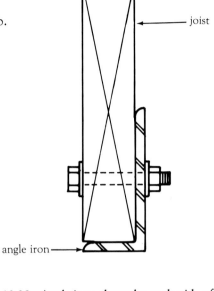

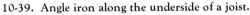

10-39. Angle iron along the underside of a joist.

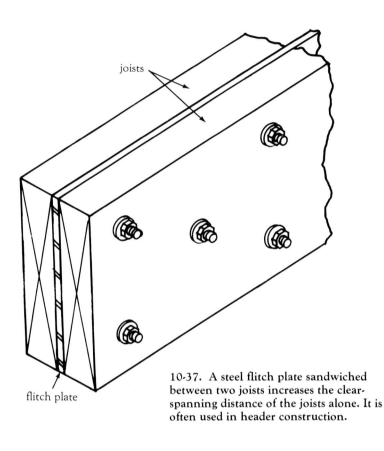

10-37. A steel flitch plate sandwiched between two joists increases the clear-spanning distance of the joists alone. It is often used in header construction.

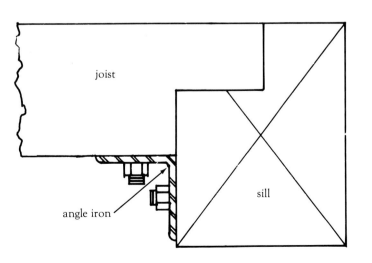

10-38. Angle iron beneath the end of a joist.

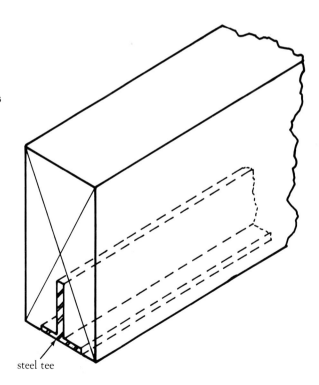

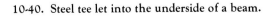

10-40. Steel tee let into the underside of a beam.

The boarding house in Gualala, California, that became Saint Orres Inn (shown in all photos on this and the facing page). It might have been easier just to raze the old place, but the Coastal Commission would have inundated the new owners with regulations. It would be hard to imagine a more drastic renovation, but virtually all the materials on-site—and many more trucked in—were salvaged.

View from the northwest. The turret at right houses the great dining hall, the trellis (bottom left) was fashioned from logs that washed down to the Pacific.

Photo, Nicholas Wilson

224

The great dining room, the size of which was dictated by the lumber piles thus far assembled from a lumber mill in Philo, a barn in Manchester, a school in Napa. All beams were sized on site with an Alaskan sawmill.

Looking up, you see steel plates reinforcing beams in the dining hall.

A cupboard niche.

Of the many builders who work with saved lumber, none do it with greater reverence than Nat Kaplan of Albuquerque, New Mexico. In this interior he has left the adobe bricks less plastered than is usual, so that they retain their individual shapes, thus echoing the soft contours of old wooden beams and a decorative bracket. A most graceful, serene composition.

In another interior by Nat Kaplan, a transom window serves as a display area for ceramics.

A two-hundred-dollar house nestled in a redwood forest. The windows, originally on a gas station in Oakland, California, cost ten dollars. A most ingenious man, the builder directed gravity-fed water downhill into his wood stove and thence down to a shower head in a burnt-out redwood stump.

Ted Thoman

Houses on the Move

Safety Tips

In the preceding chapters, I have drawn information from several sources; in this one, mainly from one house-moving company, Nicholas Brothers of Hopewell Junction, New York. This decision was made for several reasons. The outfit is, for one thing, now in its fourth generation, the company having begun at the turn of the century, when horses provided the muscle; the DeNicholas family has moved homes all along the East Coast. Because the trade is so specialized and requires an incredible collection of heavy and expensive equipment, there are very few companies of this nature, and each tends to dominate a broad geographic area. Then too, the skills required take a lifetime (or several lifetimes) to acquire.

For all of the above reasons, there is no such thing as an amateur house mover; the risks and expenses are colossal (insurance is astronomical even for established concerns). The best that a prospective client can do is to contact an established house-moving firm, have a very specific contract drawn up, take lots of photos of the house before it is moved, and stay out of the way.

A full entourage, including police, cherry pickers, and fascinated observers, accompanies house movers on their journeys.

Photo, David Dickson

Few things are as impressive or as disconcerting as a whole house being wheeled up a street. Invariably, passersby and motorists stop dead in their tracks and gawk. It is definitely not an everyday experience, despite the fact that eighty thousand structures are moved each year. We marvel not that the job is done well or ill, but that it is done at all. A friend's small son reckons time according to a house he saw moved. Instead of, "That happened when I was in the first grade," he begins, "You remember . . . that was a couple of months after the house came up the street."

Of the many houses moved each year, most are slated for demolition because they stand in the path of a proposed highway, airport, public housing project, or some such large-scale renewal. Houses are also moved to new sites because of recurrent floodplain damage, neighborhood rezoning, and commercial development—especially large estates being turned into condominiums. Historically important houses are moved from time to time, to forestall demolition, to create a historical district elsewhere, or simply to set them on a more desirable site. Almost any structure that can be had cheap, whether for back taxes or for a low bid in a condemnation auction, is probably worth buying and moving. Nationwide, moved houses average one-half to two-thirds the replacement cost of comparable new houses.

Most house moves are less than ten miles, more often, less than a mile, because of the expense of redirecting traffic and removing obstacles en route. Not uncommonly, an owner has a house moved a very short distance on the same property to get farther away from a busy street, to have it set onto a foundation when none existed before, or to permit extensive structural work such as replacing rotted sills.

PLANNING

Most of the planning for such a specialized project is best done by the mover, because an amateur simply cannot envision many of the problems. The mover will map out the route, checking the heights of bridges, underpasses, trees, utility wires and the like; and contact the appropriate utility companies, police, highway personnel, and municipal authorities. There are some things that the would-be homeowner should do, however.

With the help of a lawyer, negotiate for the purchase of the house, whether by bid, through a realtor, or however. Because a municipality has a reason for selling the building (or for having possession of it at all), it may set stipulations on the sale, most notably a time limit by which you must have it moved. Have a lawyer check particulars. And, looking ahead, you must own property to which you can move the house; confer with zoning officials and the like on the new site.

Arrange for the foundation on the new site, as well as water and electricity, sewerage connections, and so forth. An experienced contractor or architect can help you here. The house mover will work closely with your contractor, as the site may need to be specially prepared so that equipment can get in and out with a minimum of conflict. It would be counterproductive, to say the least, for the housemover to need an access ramp where the underground electrical cables are located. The house mover can perform the contracting function, but to ensure that your interests are represented, hire your own contractor and let the professionals work out the details.

If you plan to renovate the house, add a deck, upgrade mechanical systems (such as a new water heater), replace a rotted sill—now is a good time to do so. If you intend to add onto the house soon, it may be much cheaper to have the foundation enlarged now.

Discuss thoroughly your contract with the house mover, so that you know exactly what services you are getting. If excavation and grading must be done, who pays? If repairs must be made to the exterior of the house—perhaps the siding must be cut into—who will pay? (Minor expenses are usually assumed by the client.) What damages shall be assumed by each party? Major damages are usually the responsibility of the house mover, but small repairs may not be—spell them out.

Finally, deal only with a house-moving concern that has a good track record. Such a firm will have the experience and the considerable amount of specialized equipment needed to do the job. They will also be insured against all manner of liability; in fact, about half of a mover's expenses are insurance premiums. Once you pay for the house, it is your property; should an inept house mover drop the load in the middle of a freeway and then skip town, you could be in a terrible mess. Go with experience. To prepare yourself psychologically for the venture, talk with previous clients of the mover.

11-2. Preliminaries are all-important to such neighborhood events: ropes and theories must be tested, stragglers impressed into service, and, of course, one's pipe must be properly lit.

11-3. Because the ground is so rocky and uneven, straight poles are used as trestles and rollers. As the gentleman at left scurries to his post (or perhaps oversees matters), the pulley lines are tugged in earnest.

11-1. The windswept town of Salvage, Newfoundland, has few trees to speak of, most of the vegetation being scrub pine and the like. Because Salvage is a poor fishing village, the inhabitants would not think of tearing down a still-sturdy building, no sir! Here, at the start of house moving, the lead pully chain is secured to a cleft in a rock.

11-4. On the other end of the building, the rest of the crew puts backs, legs, and a lever or two to work.

11-5. The building is in final position, the crew gone to observe their victory from a distance, perhaps to share a round or two.

PREPARING THE BUILDING

Although the house mover attends to most details of preparation, you should photograph the house extensively beforehand, especially if it is masonry, so that you can check for cracks or major settling after the house has been moved. At the same time, have your contractor "read" the old house with a transit level—before the house is disturbed—to gather data for the new foundation. Because an old house will have settled, a new foundation must be custom-tailored to fit the oddities of the old structure. Putting an old house on a new, perfectly level foundation could be disastrous to finish surfaces.

The house mover decides how the structure will be moved—whether in pieces, without its roof, or completely intact. This decision depends upon the size of the house and the obstructions en route. Although it may seem easier to move a few wires than to cut up a building, in fact, it may cost a thousand dollars per busy intersection to handle such matters. Keep in mind that the house sits atop a grid of steel I beams and dollies, which may add 10 feet to the height of the house. Because most wires are 18 feet high, the difficulty becomes apparent.

To prepare the house for the move, shut off power and then disconnect water, electricity, and heating lines. No pipe or duct should extend below the bottom of the joists, or those lines could become damaged. Neither should pipes be cut too short, for that makes reconnection difficult on the other end. Should the structure need reinforcement in any way, try to have it done now. Houses usually do not need extra bolstering unless they are cut into sections, although the masonry portico shown in chapter 12 did require bracing.

Chimneys are left intact when they are sound, but when mortar is questionable, house movers prefer to tear them down. Even the incidental shocks of transportation could topple a weak chimney; besides, so heavy a load requires additional bolstering.

With this preliminary work accomplished, the mover now punches holes in the foundation, so that he can glide steel in and begin jacking. On concrete foundations a pneumatic hammer is used; on concrete block, a sledgehammer; an acetylene torch cuts through reinforcing bars. Holes are punched every 2 to 3 feet around the foundation, but enough foundation must remain to support the house until the steel is jacked. If a foundation is failing at any point, the house mover must be cautious indeed.

JACKING THE STRUCTURE

Two layers of steel lie beneath a house being moved: at least two massive I beams called *track steel*; and smaller *needle steel* beams that rest atop (more or less perpendicular to) the track steel. The track steel, also called "main steel," or just "steel," can be huge: some of the I beams that I saw lying around the Nicholas Brothers' yard were at least seventy feet long, with a depth of three feet or more. Track steel is the main support, so it usually runs parallel (more or less) to the length of the house. The needle steel, also called "cradle steel," runs perpendicular to the joist grid in the house.

After the holes have been punched in the foundation walls, the steel is slid in on rollers, track steel first. Once the track steel is roughly in position, the mover builds up cribbing (short sections of 6 × 6 or 8 × 8) beneath. In the

11-6. In this 1949 move, the remnants of the foundation stick up, toothlike, after the steel has been inserted.

Figures 11-1 to 11-6, Nicholas Brothers archive

middle of each cribbing platform is a hydraulic jack, which raises (and lowers) the steel until it is perfectly level. This operation sounds easier than it is, for it is necessary to fine-tune and adjust the cribbing, to tamp the floor where necessary, to add and adjust the hardwood shims that ensure solid support.

Once the track steel has been leveled, needle steel is slid in, over the track steel. The shimming that follows is incredibly exacting, because every point that needle steel crosses beneath a joist or beam must be fully supported. By being so fastidious, however, the mover minimizes the chances of shifting en route; in fact, a house so bolstered will be much better supported than it was on its original foundation. Where the joist grid changes direction, additional needles, sometimes perpendicular to the first course of needle steel, must be added. As adjustments are required, hydraulic jacks are raised (by remote control) small amounts, shims are added, other points are reshimmed, and so on. Finally, when all needle steel is shimmed tight to the underside of the joists, jacks raise the house up off its foundation.

Before seeing how the house is moved from the old foundation, consider the jacks themselves. In the old days, screw jacks similar to that shown in figure 10–9 were used. Because the capacity of screw jacks is much less than that of hydraulic ones, hundreds and hundreds of screw jacks, each on a platform of cribbing, were needed to raise a house. The feats performed with such rudimentary equipment seem all the more amazing: in 1917, for example, John DeNicholas's grandfather moved a twenty-four-family, five-story apartment house—using horse power, of course, and wooden beams instead of steel. Today each hydraulic jack under the track steel has its own gauge so that it is possible to calculate the exact weight of a building. Screw jacks are still used,

11-7. This two-story brick house in New Haven was in good condition, but its site was wrong. Note too that its chimneys were ragged, so they were torn down before the move began.
Photo, David Dickson

but mostly for safety, to support a jacked point should a hydraulic jack fail unexpectedly. Hydraulic jacks vary in size from 25- to 100-ton capacities (or more). Although an average residence requires only four or five 100-ton jacks, one five-story brick building moved for the Board of Education in Toronto required four lines of jacks, roughly forty or fifty 100-ton jacks in all. That building was estimated at five or six thousand tons, or ten or twelve million pounds, yet it was moved on a weekend without moving a stick of furniture inside.

UP AND OUT

Once the building has been severed from its foundation, it must be placed upon dollies so that it can be wheeled away. Getting the dollies in place, another tricky part of the operation, is usually accomplished in one of three ways.

The way most favored by the Nicholas Brothers is to knock out one wall of the foundation (once the house is raised up) and grade the site to provide a gentle ramp into the basement. The earth ramp is built up with cross-ties and planking so the dollies have a wooden roadway to roll on to prevent them from sinking into the earth. The house is elevated several more feet, and dollies are wheeled into the basement. Being able to roll the dollies into place beneath the track steel presupposes that the house mover carefully placed jacks and cribbing, of course. When the dollies are in position, the house is lowered, the track steel now resting on the dollies.

Although the ramp is as gradual as practicable (a 10-degree slope is optimal), the truck pulling the load has quite a struggle to pull the dollies up the ramp. It is often necessary to supplement the truck's efforts with a power winch, as shown in figure 11–17. Where a slope is too steep, it may be necessary to set the house at an angle on the steel, pull it up the ramp, and then reset the house so that its base is parallel to the steel.

11-8. To minimize the number of serious obstructions en route, the owner, an architect, decided to tear down the gable ends and take down the rafters.

Photo, David Dickson

11-9. To get the building on and off dollies, it was necessary to build ramps down into the foundation, allowing dolly wheels to roll freely.

Photo, David Dickson

needle steel

track steel

original grade

11-10. To move the house off its foundation, an earth ramp is excavated down to the bottom of the basement. A foundation wall is knocked out after the building has been jacked and dollies are rolled underneath.

foundation wall removed

cribbing

A second technique for getting the house up and out is to raise the house 10 feet on cribbing and fill in the foundation with stone and gravel. After the fill has been thoroughly tamped, the cribbing and plank roadway are laid, the dollies rolled under, and the house lowered. The dollies thus proceed from relatively level ground. This technique is well suited to historical structures that could be wrenched by the straining of the truck pulling up a ramp.

A third technique is to slide the house off the foundation, onto solid ground, and then jack it up so dollies can be maneuvered underneath. This technique features yet another layer of steel, called *sliding steel*, beneath the track steel. Once all steel is in place, the track steel (and all above) slides away from the foundation on the sliding steel. This method works acceptably and seems a direct descendent of the old way of moving houses, in which horse-powered winches pulled houses on soaped wooden beams. Once off the foundation, the house was jacked so that wagon dollies could be rolled under.

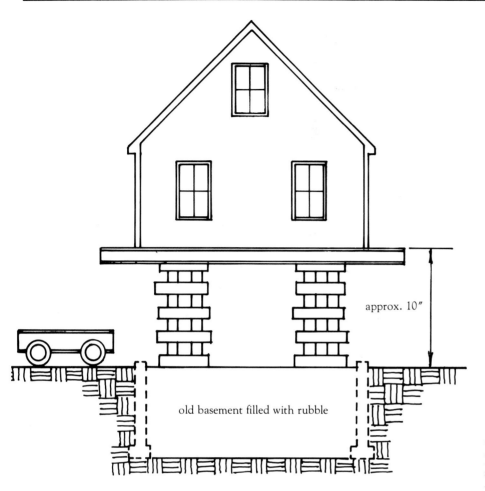

approx. 10"

old basement filled with rubble

11-11. A second method of removing the house from its foundation involves filling the foundation with stones and gravel and raising the house about 10 ft. on cribbing.

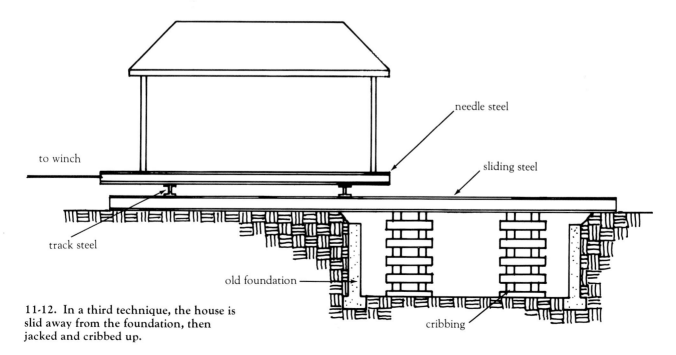

needle steel

sliding steel

to winch

track steel

old foundation

cribbing

11-12. In a third technique, the house is slid away from the foundation, then jacked and cribbed up.

11-13. A single, intermediate-size dolly, about 6 ft. long.

Dollies vary in size and bearing capacity, some steer, some have jacks built in, and so on. Setting dollies varies according to the house mover, but Nicholas Brothers favors a three-point system, with dollies (and track steel) converging in a point towards the front of the load, as in figures 11–14 and 11–15. The average capacity of each dolly is 100 or 150 tons, depending upon the weight of the structure being moved; dolly tires are 36-ply, rated at 18,000 pounds pressure. Yet even such monsters have their limits: when one mover underestimated the weight of a masonry house at 250 tons (he assumed that its walls were hollow block), the actual weight of 500 tons blew every tire in the setup and twisted all the wheels beyond recognition.

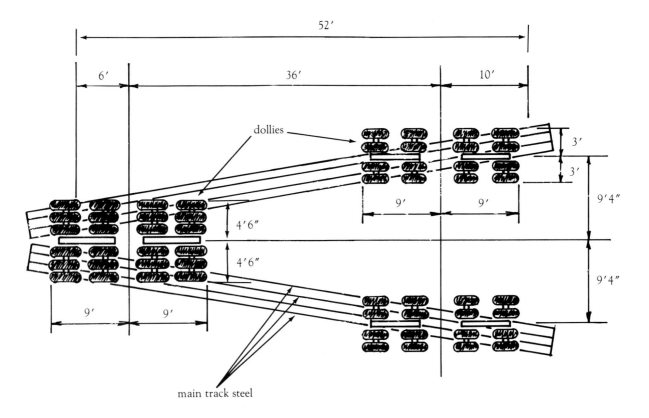

11-14. The number of dollies and the size of each is determined by the weight of the house, but Nicholas Brothers favors a three-point system, in which the main steel converges towards the front of the building. The schematic shown was a particularly large job, a masonry building requiring twelve dollies and six sections of main steel.

Adapted from *Heavy Construction News*, May, 1972.

11-15. This shot, a closer look at the house shown in figure 11-6, illustrates the three-point system in practice. Note that the ends of the main steel converge over the front set of dollies.

Nicholas Brothers archives

11-16. Every intersection along a journey brings police cars, workers in cherry pickers to get wires out of the way, and bystanders.

MOVING

House moving itself is rather uneventful, accidents rare indeed. The move is attended by a lead car with flashing lights and by police, as needed, to control traffic and the like. Utility lines must be picked up out of harm's way as the building proceeds. Moving a house does not tie up streets for weeks as it used to in the old days, but coordination of services en route is crucial. During the recent move of a 52-foot high historical house in Canada, it was necessary to involve the Toronto Transport Commission, Ontario Hydro, Bell Canada, Metro Toronto and Traffic Departments, Department of Public Works, Fire Department, Metro Parks, and Metro Police. Along the urban journey of that building, it was necessary to remove 3/4 mile of trolley wire, two utility poles, eighty-two street lights, several traffic lights, telephone poles, and a burglar alarm system. In addition, sixty-five manhole covers had to be shored up so they would not collapse as a dolly wheel passed over.*

* As reported in *Heavy Construction News*, May, 1972.

11-17. At the new location, the house is painstakingly backed down the wooden rampway onto the new foundation. An auxiliary winch truck was required to aid the main hauling truck.

THE NEW SITE

At the new site, the procedure is more or less reversed, with the building carefully wheeled into place and lowered onto its new foundation. After that, dollies, ramps, cribbing, and jacks are removed and repairs are made as needed. Electrical, water, and heating lines are hooked up; the site is graded. As impressive as the whole feat is, a professional house mover makes it seem like an everyday occurrence, which, for him, it is. "There isn't a building I can't move," John DeNicholas replied to one skeptic. "The Empire State? You kidding? Just let me know when they want to move it and I'll move it."

11-18. The roof resurrected, a new porch.

Photos and building restoration in figures 11-16 to 11-18, David Dickson

Moving a full-scale model of the Santa Maria. The top of the truck is just visible above the knot of onlookers.

Nicholas Brothers archive

When John DeNicholas says he will move anything, take him at his word. This example was a twelve-apartment tenement moved out of the path of the Cross-Bronx Expressway in New York. Although original plans left all furniture in place, people were to evacuate until the move was completed. But first the kids kept running back in, then it was housewives who needed "one last thing." Because housing was so short in 1947, following World War II, most of the tenants had no other place to go. A compromise was effected: temporary electrical and water hookups were attached, make-shift walkways erected, and everybody moved back in for the duration of the move. It must have been a particularly festive occasion, with people at the windows waving handkerchiefs and halloo-ing to their neighbors as the building crept along.

Nicholas Brothers archives

239

CHAPTER TWELVE

A Case History

There is money and beauty in salvaging—they are what draw most of us. But now and then somebody gets bitten by the bug of conviction and gets bitten good, so that he or she hangs on and saves some doomed object, hangs on despite the long odds, the low (or no) pay, and the tiring hours.

Scott Witter does not seem like a zealot. A building contractor since being graduated from Pratt School of Architecture in Brooklyn, New York, he drives a motorcycle, laughs a lot, and resuscitates buildings that have been, in several cases, slated for demolition. It may be that he is so mechanically ingenious that he sees solutions where the rest of us see only punky wood and headaches. But when he heard that Pratt was planning to demolish a Norman portico—a faithful sandstone copy of a twelfth-century entrance to the Canterbury Cathedral King's School—Witter saw red.

I asked Scott how he got into "the business." "When I was still in school," he told me, "I found an old firehouse—Engine No. 209—on Bedford Avenue. It was beautiful, with red sandstone and brick, an arched entrance, a brass pole that the firemen used to slide down, and a skylit gallery. So, I found out who controlled it and went through miles of red tape to see if I could

rent it. The deal was finally set, and I was ready to start working on it. That evening I went down to check it out, and they'd torn it down."

A group of about a dozen neighbors got together to save the portico, Scott agreeing to undertake the contracting if the others would handle the paperwork and raise money for the cause. They approached Pratt, which wanted the old portico out of the way so a new addition could be attached to the library. Pratt's administrators were reluctant at first but finally agreed that, if the job could be done for the three thousand dollars slated for demolition, they would go along. "They figured we'd give up," Scott chuckled, "But they had to go through the motions of offering it to the community. Three thousand dollars was a ridiculously small budget for moving a building—and they were not fronting any of the money. But at least we had our foot in the door."

So, while Scott began to prepare the portico section for the move, the neighborhood group frantically sought money to finance a crew of professional movers.

Actually, Witter's first task was to figure how much the structure weighed. His method was ingenious. He carefully measured the portico from all conceivable points and made measured drawings. Then, us-

The Pratt portico, intact.

ing a scale of 1/4 inch to 1 foot, he fashioned a model out of clay. That accomplished, he put the model on a set of weighing scales, and to the opposite scale-pan added rough clay until the two sides balanced. He next mashed the rough clay into a compact cube. By carefully measuring the cube, he was thus able to extrapolate—working backward from his 1/4-inch to 1-foot scale—how many cubic feet were in the original portico. He went to an architectural reference work and looked up the weight, per cubic foot, of stone and thus finally determined that the portico weighed 150 tons. As it turned out, he was off by 10 tons (the portico weighed 140 tons) because the foundation of the structure was hollow, which Witter could not have known before the building was jacked up. Not a bad estimate at all.

The early days of the project were a shoestring affair indeed, subsisting on what personal credits Scott could wrangle from friends, the proceeds of T-shirt and baked-goods sales, and volunteer labor, mostly friends and Pratt students. In addition to a borrowed truck and a loaned torch with which to cut reinforcing bars and grates, the group

had miscellaneous hand tools and one broken jackhammer, which cost Scott money to fix.

The tile roof was dismantled first. It was actually rather easy to take apart because the original builder had scrimped, using undersized nails. Of the 90 percent of tiles that were intact, about 85 percent were saved. Then began the arduous work of separating the portico from the main building. Working on borrowed scaffolding, Scott and the others used mallets and stone chisels, jackhammers and cutting torches to punch and cut through

12-2. The clay model, 1/4 in. to 1 ft. scale.

masonry and steel. It went slowly, but it went, until an unexpected catch stopped the work and threatened to shut down the project altogether.

One of the early stipulations of the agreement with Pratt was that the salvaging crew take out insurance. With the chronic shortage of money, this never was done. Thus, when Pratt found out that the crew still had no insurance, administrators were understandably horrified. No more work until the crew had taken out a million-dollar insurance policy. Things looked bleak. Scott had personally gone in the hole several thousand dollars' worth, expecting to get it back when the job was funded. Now, not only would he lose the time and money invested, but the portico seemed doomed.

But this story has a happy ending and an eleventh-hour angel in the person of Lucy Bitzer, a neighbor who contacted the National Endowment for the Humanities, the federal agency responsible for the funding of the library renovation. She advised them that they were actually funding the destruction of an architecturally and historically significant site, which was eligible

12-1. Tile roofing removed and sheathing being stripped.

12-3. After the portico sections had been detached from the main building and preliminary backhoe work was complete, the house movers began. Here, a worker resets a hydraulic jack capable of raising 100 tons.

12-4. As jacks raised the structure incrementally, new cribbing was added.

12-5. The portico, raised 3 or 4 ft.

12-6. After the portico had been raised about 10 ft., steel beams and dollies were set beneath and wooden rampways were constructed.

for listing on the National Register of Historic Places. NEH realized that they were therefore violating the National Historic Preservation Act of 1966. A telegram, with assurances of funding and directions to cooperate fully with the neighborhood group, was dispatched to Pratt. The crew, having secured the required insurance, feverishly completed the preparation for the move. (The insurance policy was never needed, the only injury being a cut finger.) With the grant now in hand, Pratt became the contractor and provided the foundation for the new location of the portico.

The preparation took almost as long as the move itself. Once the section was detached from the main library, Scott, finding only loose rubble fill at the top of the portico, strengthened the structure by adding a reinforced concrete tie and by welding on bracing (salvaged steam pipe). By the time the backhoe operator had exposed the foundation, the contract had been signed with the house movers. Six frantic weeks had passed.

12-7. A power winch pulls the portico up the initial incline.

Having given so generously of his time, Scott now had to return to work as a contractor to recoup the income he had lost during the project. (He received the contract sum, which covered about half of out-of-pocket expenses.) But he returned to document the progress of the beloved portico as it moved across campus. The portico, as you can see, found a new location and is now awaiting the return of its roof. Scott, incorrigible doer, was back in action before the year was out, salvaging a two-story meat market with a spectacular limestone facade complete with animal-head capitals which he is now trying to sell. But that is another story....

12-8. Wooden roadways, assembled from thousands of 6 × 6s and 2 × 12s, were laid and relaid along the route of the move. Note the diagonal bracing welded to the top of the structure: without such bolstering, the masonry might have crumbled.

12-9. Approaching the new site.

12-12. But one capital of Scott's romanesque meat market.

12-10. After the portico was lowered down a ramp excavated next to the school's gymnasium, dollies and cribbing were gradually removed until the structure rested fully on the new foundation.

12-11. The portico in repose, awaiting its roof.

Sources of Supply

Adhesive Products Corporation
1660 Boone Avenue
Bronx, NY 10460
casting and molding materials

American Society of Testing and
    Materials
1916 Race Street
Philadelphia, PA 19103

Architectural Antiques Exchange
715 North Second Street
Philadelphia, PA 19123

Architectural Antiques, Ltd.
812 Canyon Road
Santa Fe, NM 87501

"The Barn People"
Box 4
South Woodstock, VT 05071
dismantling barns

Eric Bauer
Fayston, VT 05674
custom forging

Frederick Bissinger, architect
"Camp Discharge"
Spring Mill Road
Gladwyne, PA 19035

Black and Decker
Towson, MD 21204
power tools

Brookstone Company
127 Vose Farm Road
Peterborough, NH 03458
hard-to-find tools

Allen Brown
Box 240
Prospect Avenue
Mount Airy, MD 21771
design and refinishing

Conservation Materials Ltd.
340 Freeport Boulevard
Box 2884
Sparks, NV 89431
preservationist supplies

DiBartolomeo Woodworking
986 Pratt Street
Philadelphia, PA 19124
restoration, custom cabinetry

David Dickson, architect
Red Star Construction
52 Lyon Street
New Haven, CT 06511

Epoxybond
Atlas Minerals & Chemicals
Farmington Road
Mertztown, PA 19539

Etcon Corporation
12243 South 71 Avenue
Palos Heights, IL 60463
electrical equipment, tools

Fluidmaster, Inc.
1800 Via Burton
Anaheim, CA 92806

Gargoyles, Ltd.
512 South Third Street
Philadelphia, PA 19147
architectural antiques

Goldblatt Tools
511 Osage Avenue
Kansas City, KS 66105
masonry tools

Great American Salvage
3 Main Street
Montpelier, VT 05602

Michael Greenberg
9 Sachem Road
Weston, CT 06883
builder and designer

Irreplaceable Artifacts
526 East 80th Street
New York, NY 10021

JO-EL Shop
7120 Hawkins Creamery Road
Laytonsville, MD 20760
lighting fixtures

Nat Kaplan, architect
8300 Rio Grande Boulevard NW
Albuquerque, NM 87114

Kindt-Collins Company
12651 Elmwood Avenue
Cleveland, OH 44111
low-melt metals

Klein Tools, Inc.
7200 McCormick Boulevard
Chicago, IL 60645
electrical tools

R. Lear Design
30 Main Street
Southhampton, NY 11968

Leviton
59–25 Little Neck Parkway
Little Neck, NY 11362
electrical switches, supplies

Trey Loy
Box 381
Littleriver, CA 95456
builder, heavy-timber specialist

Adolf deRoy Mark, architect
218A Spruce Street
Philadelphia, PA 19106
or
Box 1052
Carefree, AZ 85377

Ken McKenzie, architect
Woodstock, VT 05091

Medeco Security Locks, Inc.
P.O. Box 1075
Salem, VA 24153

Mequiar's Marble Polish
Mirror Bright Polish Company
Box 17177
Irvine, CA 92713

John Midyette III, architect
834 Canyon Road
Sante Fe, NM 87501

C. Neri
313 South Street
Philadelphia, PA 19147
antiques, interiors

Nevr-Dull Magic Wadding
The George Basch Company
Freeport, NY 11520
polishing delicate metals

Nicholas Brothers, Inc.
Route 82 and Ryan Road
Hopewell Junction, NY 12533
building movers, shoring and rigging

Nowell's, Inc.
490 Gate 5 Road
Sausalito, CA 94965
lighting fixtures, antiques

Pamran Company, Inc.
1101 Cedar Creek Drive
Racine, WI 53402

Petersen Manufacturing Company
De Witt, NB 68341
Vise-Grip pliers

Pootatuck Corporation
R.R. 2, Box 18
Windsor, VT 05089
Lion miter-trimmer

RACO Inc
P.O. Box 4002
South Bend, IN 46634
electrical boxes

Reflections Antique Stained Glass
300 Kater Street
Philadelphia, PA 19147

Rejuvenation House Parts
4543 North Albina Avenue
Portland, OR 97217

Renovator's Supply
Millers Falls, MA 01349

Morton Riddle, IV
Route 2, Box 853
Purcellville, VA 22132
designer and builder

Ridgid Tools
The Ridge Tool Company
400 Clark Street
P.O. Box 4023
Elyria, OH 44035

Saint Orres Inn
P.O. Box 523
Gualala, CA 95445

San Francisco Victoriana
2245 Palou Avenue
San Francisco, CA 94124

Gregory Schipa
R.D. #2
Randolph, VT 05060
*disassembles, moves, and restores
   historical structures*

Schlage Lock Company
P.O. Box 3324
San Francisco, CA 94119

Silk Degrees
P.O. Box 5253
Santa Cruz, CA 95063
exotic lampshades

Silvo Hardware Company
2205 Richmond Street
Philadelphia, PA 19125
all hardware conceivable

Stanley Tools
P.O. Box 1800
New Britain, CT 06050

Sunrise Salvage
2210 San Pablo Avenue
Berkeley, CA 94702

Thoro-System Products
7899 Northwest 38th Street
Miami, FL 33166
epoxy masonry materials

United Housewrecking
328 Selleck Street
Stamford, CT 06902

Urban Archaeology
137 Spring Street
New York, NY 10012

Vermont Marble Company
61 Main Street
Proctor, VT 05765

Vigilante Plumbing
576 Union Street
Brooklyn, NY 11215

Vintage Lumber and Construction
   Company
Rt 1, Box 194
Frederick, MD 21701
*post-and-beam structures, hardwood
   flooring*

Whink Products Company
Eldora, IA 50627
stain removers

H. Weber Wilson
9701 Liberty Road
Frederick, MD 21701
antiquarian

Window-Fixer
Quaker City Manufacturing
Sharon Hill, PA 19079

Scott Witter, architect
117 Hall Street
Brooklyn, NY 11205
large building dismantling, restoration

ARRANGED BY CHAPTER

(For addresses, see the larger Sources of Supply list)

Chapter 2
Epoxy stabilizers: Conservation Materials, Ltd., Brookstone Company
Glazier's pliers: Brookstone Company
Replacement channels: Window-Fixer

Chapter 3
Doweling jigs, butt gauges, butt markers: Stanley Tools

Chapter 4
Reciprocating saw with offset blade: Black and Decker
Miter trimmer: Lion miter trimmer, Pootatuck Corporation
Slate hook: Brookstone Company
Shave hooks, profile gauge: Brookstone Company
Flameless stripper: He-Jet, Pamran Company Inc.

Chapter 5
Solvol Autosol Metal Polish: Conservation Materials, Ltd.
Monzini casting materials, RTV rubber molds: Adhesive Products
    Corporation
Cerro Alloys: Kindt-Collins
Deadbolts, strike reinforcers: Schlage, Medeco

Chapter 6
National Electrical Code: see Bibliography
Electrical fixture parts: Angelo Brothers Company
Replacement shades: Renovator's Supply, San Francisco Victoriana
Continuity tester: Etcon Corp.
Voltage tester: Etcon Corp., Klein Tools
Vice-Grip Pliers: Petersen Manufacturing Corporation
Electrical boxes: RACO
Rheostats, specialty switches: Leviton

Chapter 7
Basin wrench, other plumbing tools: Ridgid Tools
Overflow assembly: Renovator's Supply
Stain remover: Whink Products
Marble polish: Mequiar's/Mirror Bright
Fluidmaster ballcock assembly, overflow flap: Fluidmaster Corporation

Chapter 8
Large-scale epoxy Repair: Epoxybond
Epoxy cement: Thoro-Grip/Thoro-System Products

Chapter 9
Pollyfilla patching compound: Conservation Materials Ltd
Liquid rubber latex, RTV rubber, polyester resin: Adhesive Products
    Corporation
Tuckpointing chisel, other specialty masonry tools: Goldblatt Tools
Marble polish: Vermont Marble Company; Mequiar's/Mirror Bright
Stone consolidants, Tegovakon, Rhodasil: Conservation Materials Ltd.
Monzini epoxy compounds: Adhesive Products Corp.
Thoro-Grip epoxy consolidants: Thoro-Systems Products
ASTM: American Society of Testing and Materials

Chapter 10
Nail-pullers, wrecking bars, comealongs: Silvo Hardware Company

Metric Conversions

1 inch = 2.5 centimeters
1 foot = 30.5 centimeters
1 ounce = 30 milliliters
1 quart = 1 liter
1 pound = .5 kilograms
1 ton = 907.2 kilograms

Annotated Bibliography

PERIODICALS

Magazines and newsletters are invaluable sources of information, which, unlike books, are updated each month or so, bringing you fresh ideas on tools, materials, and applications.

Architectural Antiques and Artifacts Advertiser, P.O. Box 31, 459 Rockland Road, Merion, PA 19066. Sources of supply, who's who of salvage, tidbits about upcoming sales and the like. Published erratically.

Demolition Age, National Association of Demolition Contractors, 940 Pine Street, Glenview, IL 60025. Mostly for those in the trade, much info on manufacturers of demolition equipment, which can be hard to find. Monthly.

Fine Homebuilding, Box 355, Newtown, CT 06470. A design and how-to hybrid; occasionally runs articles on reused materials, especially design tidbits and methods of work. Bimonthly.

Fine Woodworking, Box 355, Newtown, CT 06470. The preeminent journal of woodworking. Bimonthly.

New Shelter, 33 East Minor Street, Emmaus, PA 18049. Articles on energy conservation, occasional articles about recycled materials. Eight times a year.

Technology and Conservation, The Technology Organization, One Emerson Place, Boston, MA 02114. Very technical magazine for historic preservationists, but great for services and sources of supply. Quarterly.

BOOKS

Bullock, Orin M., Jr. *The Restoration Manual*. Norwalk, CT: Silvermine Press, 1966. A rather wordy little book, but with some specifics about masonry preservation.

Callender, John Hancock, ed. *Time-Saver Standards for Architectural Design Data*. New York: McGraw-Hill, 5th ed. 1974. A thick, expensive professional builder's book, but surprisingly readable; buy it if your building plans are extensive.

Canadian Mortgage and Housing Corporation. *Canadian Wood-Frame House Construction*. Reprint of U.S. Agriculture Handbook No. 73, Ottawa, Canada: CMHC, 1979. General building techniques, spans, materials—clearly written.

Feirer, John L. *Cabinet-making and Millwork*. Peoria, Illinois: Chas. A. Bennett Co., Inc., 1977. The best book on cabinetmaking and installation.

Kreh, Richard T., Sr. *Simplified Masonry Skills*. New York: Van Nostrand Reinhold Company, 2nd ed., 1982. The most useful of masonry texts, specific and concise.

Litchfield, Michael W. *Renovation: A Complete Guide*. New York: John Wiley & Sons, 1982. A compendium of all the major building skills (especially mechanical systems) and most of the minor ones; extensive illustrations.

National Electrical Code. Quincy, MA: National Fire Protection Association, 1981. *The* authority on safe electrical procedure; revised every three years.

Shelton, Jay. *The Woodburner's Encyclopedia*. Waitsfield, VT: Vermont Crossroads Press, 1976. All about wood stove safety.

Time-Life Books. *Basic Wiring.* Alexandria, VA: Time-Life Books, 1977.

Time-Life Books. *Floors and Stairways.* Alexandria, VA: Time-Life Books, 1978. Nice section on altering structure beneath floors.

Time-Life Books. *The Old House.* Alexandria, VA: Time-Life Books, 1979. A slight book with some excellent tips on restoring old house parts.

U.S. Navy Bureau of Naval Personnel. *Basic Construction Techniques for Houses and Small Buildings.* New York: Dover Publications, 1972 (unabridged reprint of 6th edition of Builder 3&2, as published in 1970 by the Training Publications Division of Naval Personnel Support Activity). As the above credit may suggest, a product of the bureaucracy, but reasonably priced and full of information about masonry, moving heavy materials, and the like.

Wilson, H. Weber. *Your Residential Stained Glass.* Frederick, MD: Self-published, 1979. Mr. Wilson is shown in this book's section on stained glass repair. (To obtain a copy of this book, write to H. Weber Wilson, 5701 Liberty Road, Frederick, MD 21701.)

Wilson, J. Douglas. *Practical House Carpentry.* New York: McGraw-Hill Book Co., 1972. Nice details of finish carpentry and trim installation.

Index